THOMAS AQUINAS AND THE PHILOSOPHY OF PUNISHMENT

Thomas Aquinas
AND THE PHILOSOPHY OF PUNISHMENT

Peter Karl Koritansky

The Catholic University of America Press
Washington, D.C.

The paper used in this publication meets the minimum requirements of American National Standards for Information Science—Permanence of Paper for Printed Library Materials, ANSI Z39.48-1984.
∞

Library of Congress Cataloging-in-Publication Data
Koritansky, Peter Karl, 1974–
Thomas Aquinas and the philosophy of punishment /
Peter Karl Koritansky.
p. cm.
Includes bibliographical references (p.) and index.
ISBN 978-0-8132-1883-0 (pbk. : alk. paper) 1. Thomas, Aquinas, Saint, 1225?–1274. 2. Punishment—Religious aspects—Christianity. 3. Retribution—Religious aspects—Christianity.
I. Title.
B765.T54K63 2012
364.601—dc23 2011033836

To my wife, Pam

Contents

Acknowledgments

Because I have been thinking about the question of punishment nearly from the time I have been studying philosophy, there are a great many people who have contributed to what has gone into this book. I would especially like to thank those who guided me and helped me articulate the ideas for my doctoral thesis (on the same topic) at the University of Toronto: Clifford Orwin, David Novak, and Joseph Boyle. Although Joe Boyle will not agree with important parts of the argument of this book, I have to say without qualification that he is one of the best supervisors that any graduate student could hope to find. I also wish to thank my father, John C. Koritansky, professor of political science at Hiram College, who gave me invaluable advice and stretched my thinking on these issues both at the time of the dissertation and in the composition of this book, as well as Peter Erb of Wilfred Laurier University, Mary Keys of the University of Notre Dame, and Robert Kraynak of Colgate University, all of whom read the entire manuscript prior to its submission and offered immensely helpful comments. I also wish to thank the University of Prince Edward Island's Office of Research and Development, which awarded me a small grant for the project. Most of all, I thank my wife, Pam, whose love and encouragement provided confidence and clarity during this project's best and most difficult moments.

Some sections of this book have been adapted from my previously published works and permission to use this material here is gratefully acknowledged. In particular, pages 30–38, 108–13, 139–43, and 157–69 are adapted from my own essays in *The Philosophy of Punishment and the History of Political Thought,* edited by Peter Karl Koritansky (Columbia, Mo.: The University of Missouri Press, 2011), and appear here by permission of the University of Missouri Press. Copyright © 2011 by the Curators of the University of Missouri. Pages 76–91 and 99–102 are adapted from "Thomas Aquinas: Political Philosophy" and appear by permission of Peter Koritansky and the *Internet Encyclopedia of Philosophy* (the original article can be found at http://www.iep.utm.edu.a.aqui-pol.htm). Lastly, pages 122–32 are adapted from "Two Theories of Retributive Punishment: Immanuel Kant and Thomas Aquinas," *History of Philosophy Quarterly* 22, no. 4 (October 2005): 319–38, and appear here by permission of the *History of Philosophy Quarterly.*

THOMAS AQUINAS AND THE PHILOSOPHY OF PUNISHMENT

Introduction

MODERN PHILOSOPHIES OF PUNISHMENT AND THE RETURN TO AQUINAS

This book presents the moral, political, and legal thought of Thomas Aquinas as capable of providing a justification for the institution of punishment. It does so, in particular, by presenting Aquinas's theory as a legitimate alternative to the prevailing justifications for legal punishment in the modern era, namely, utilitarianism and modern retributivism.[1] As I will argue in the first two chapters, utilitarianism and modern retributivism have ultimately failed to provide a compelling basis for punishment. Whereas utilitarians fail to establish any meaningful link between punishment and justice, modern retributivists have never convincingly explained why punishment must be understood primarily in terms of retribution. As we will see in the ensuing chapters, utilitarianism and retributivism (of the kind we shall examine here) are both modern phenomena, the former originating in the thought of Jeremy Bentham and the latter in the thought of Immanuel Kant, and each stems directly from distinctively modern understandings of the common good and the role of political society. It is hardly surprising, therefore, that the great critics of modern thought have

1. I use the qualifier "modern" to describe retributivism because, as we shall see, Aquinas is also a kind of retributivist, though a retributivist with very different philosophical commitments.

focused their criticisms in particular upon modernity's treatment of punitive matters.

Two examples briefly deserve mention. The first is Friedrich Nietzsche's claim that the modern debate over punishment is ultimately irresolvable because punishment itself has no inherent meaning. Punishment may not be rationally justified, therefore, but only described, and Nietzsche's own description is chilling. Rather than having anything to do with justice or the welfare of society, punishment is ultimately a legitimization of cruelty. The fact that we punish is only explainable by the fact that we have a deep, even natural, desire to inflict suffering upon our fellow human beings, a desire even more fundamental than that of revenge. Whether people say they are punishing to deter potential criminals or to reestablish the equality of justice, therefore, their true motives are historically traceable to this one fundamental desire. The upshot of Nietzsche's analysis is that the crime is ultimately only a pretext for the pleasure we take in inflicting suffering through punishment: "To see others suffer does one good, to make others suffer even more."[2]

The other contemporary voice is the great French postmodernist Michel Foucault. Like Nietzsche, Foucault denies that there is any moral basis for punishment and his evaluation also leads to the conclusion that punishment may only be described (historically or genealogically) rather than justified. Particularly sharp is Foucault's criticism of modern society, which understands itself as having sanitized punishment and thus having improved upon an institution characterized by nothing but bloodlust and vengefulness in ages past (Foucault's *Discipline and Punish* begins with a grisly account of one such punishment). Rather than having made punishment more rational or moral, however, we moderns have done nothing more than to turn it into a powerful means of social control. Particularly poignant is Foucault's analysis of utili-

2. *Genealogy of Morals,* trans. Walter Kaufmann and R. J. Hollingdale (New York: Vintage Books, 1989), Second Essay, sec. 6.

tarian motives such as rehabilitation and deterrence. By elevating these new "humanitarian" goals as punishment's justifying principles, the powerful are able to remove punishment from the bloodthirsty mob and place it into the hands of experts whose alleged knowledge of society and the criminal psyche enable them to wield much more control, not just over criminals, but over the rest of society as well. For Foucault modern society itself is like a kind of prison and citizens are automatically considered as either criminals or potential criminals. In the final analysis, because rehabilitation and deterrence are merely the means for maintaining control, punishment's alleged moral justification by modern standards are no more rational or moral than the vengeful punishments of old. Hence, Foucault would be no more accepting of modern attempts to justify the institution of punishment than Nietzsche.

Nietzsche's and Foucault's accounts of punishment are, of course, far too complex to be captured here.[3] The crucial point is simply that both thinkers have flatly denied the central premise upon which the great modern debate between utilitarianism and retributivism is based, namely, that punishment may be justified at all. Contemporary thinkers are left, therefore, with three options. If the prevailing modern schools of thought are indeed untenable (as I hope to show in the first two chapters), one may either follow Nietzsche and Foucault in holding that no justification of punishment is possible. Alternatively, one may discover a new theory of punishment not subject to the problems inherent in utilitarianism and retributivism. Finally, one may *rediscover* a theory of punishment long forgotten. The present study follows the third path by examining the punitive theory of Thomas Aquinas.

3. The brief comments made here are largely inspired by two essays treating each thinker's analysis of punishment in great detail: Jeffrey Metzger's "Nietzsche's New Naturalized Conception of Justice and Punishment," and Jeffrey Polet's "Punishing Some, Disciplining All: Foucault and the Techniques of Political Violence," both in *The Philosophy of Punishment and the History of Political Thought,* edited by Peter Karl Koritansky (Columbia, Mo.: University of Missouri Press, 2011).

To be sure, it will strike some readers as odd that the ideas of a medieval theologian can be inserted into this long and complicated contemporary discussion. After all, Aquinas comes from a time renowned for a brutality in punishing that, if contemporary thinkers can agree on anything, all will agree should be locked away in the past never to return. What could someone from the age of "the rack," the "water wheel," and the "iron maiden" possibly have to contribute to a discussion of punishment in the twenty-first century? Punishment in the Middle Ages, moreover, seems to have had a theoretical component that citizens of the modern world can hardly take seriously. Continuously derided for their inability to distinguish between the proper roles of secular and ecclesiastical authority, the medievals are seen to have missed the concomitant (and equally crucial) distinction between crime and sin. Thomas Aquinas himself made arguments for the physical punishment of heretics, even with the infliction of the death penalty, and his own Order of Preachers was instrumental in the execution of the Spanish Inquisition, one of the darkest moments in the history of Christianity. In addition to these obstacles for seriously considering the philosophical (as opposed to the merely historical) aspects of Aquinas's theory of punishment, one must also confront the pervasive belief that Aquinas's thought is inextricably linked to presuppositions of divine revelation and Christian theology. Even granting that arguments emerging from this type of discourse are internally coherent and persuasive to the audience to which they were addressed, many would wonder how they can have any merit in a secular and pluralistic age such as our own.

My hope, of course, is that all of these questions will be sufficiently answered by the end of the book. It is necessary, however, to address them at least briefly here at the outset in order to defend the claim that bringing Aquinas into the philosophical debate on punishment is not as hopeless as it may seem. Regarding the fact that Aquinas comes from the medieval period about which there is much to be ashamed, one can hardly say that he is merely a man of his time. We simply have no idea as to what Aquinas thought about the various means of torture commonly used in the Middle Ages, and it may very well be that he was altogether disapproving. Regarding his argument for the punishment of heresy, the issue is more complex. In a well-known statement in the *Summa Theologiae,* Aquinas advances an argument that seems to typify what modern political thought (perhaps even modernity itself) originally set out to eradicate. To paraphrase Aquinas, heretics present the worst possible threat to the common good because they jeopardize the spiritual welfare of others. If the death penalty may be used to punish murderers and thieves, therefore, it is all the more justified in the case of those "stubborn" heretics who persist in defying the Church's teaching even "after the first and second admonition."[4]

To be sure, one hardly needs to accept every aspect of modern thought to see the folly in this argument. Aquinas's understanding of heresy depends on the distinction between those outside the Church who simply do not believe (and who are "by no means to be compelled to the faith") and those baptized Catholics who have renounced their faith in the manner of breaking an agreement.[5] Aquinas does not elaborate upon the alleged analogy between heretics and those who stand in breech of contract, but simple reflection yields that any such comparison is far from justifying his conclusion. Most Catholics in the thirteenth century were baptized as infants, and any commitment made at the time of baptism was done by a parent or guardian, and so any

4. *Summa Theologiae,* II-II, 11.3. The term "heretic," of course, does not encompass any lack of assent to the Catholic faith. Heretics are, strictly speaking, those within the Church who renounce some aspect, or even the totality, of that faith. Jews and Muslims are not heretics, therefore, and Aquinas nowhere implies that such non-Christians should be compelled to accept a faith to which they do not assent. For a helpful discussion of Aquinas treatment of heresy in its historical context, see Michael Novak's "Aquinas and the Heretics," *First Things* 58 (December 1995): 33–38.

5. *ST,* II-II, 10.8.

lack of assent to the Catholic faith would seem to be much more analogous to an ordinary infidel than to a conscious breaking of a promise. Even granting that a certain heretic was baptized as an adult, moreover, it is no less appalling to the modern reader that a temporal punishment could be issued for holding (even promulgating) a religious belief, however false that belief may be.[6] The modern refusal to accept Aquinas's position on heresy comes not from any bogus distinction he may have made while making his argument, but from the entire relationship between spiritual and temporal authority that his argument presupposes. To punish heresy as a crime involves the mistaken assumption (made by Aquinas and many others of his time) that political authority should be used to enforce the laws of the Church. One certainly need not accept the view that Church and State be separated entirely to understand that the "power of the sword" is never something that ecclesiastical authority can wield in order to settle in internal conflict. As many would argue, Aquinas's view of politics and law is so entangled with the "category mistake" described above (of which his position on heresy is merely a symptom) that none of his teachings, and least of all his theory of punishment, can be taken seriously today. Often implicated is his theory of law itself, according to which all laws are derived from the "eternal law," or that by which God providently rules over all of creation. If both the moral law and the civil law depend upon and derive their legitimacy from the law of God, how can any of Aquinas's arguments in the areas of law, politics, or morality be persuasive to those who do not share his faith?

Whereas rationally persuading the nonbeliever may not have been as important to the patristic sources from whom Aquinas derives the doctrine of eternal law,[7] Aquinas himself is very interested in developing arguments that do not depend upon religious

6. For evidence that the modern Church has rejected Aquinas's teaching on heresy, see the Vatican II Declaration on Religious Liberty, *Dignitatis Humanae,* sec. 10.

7. See Augustine's *On Free Choice of the Will,* 1.15.

belief. If the eternal law were synonymous with divine law (the law expressly given in divine revelation), Aquinas's arguments would, of course, only be persuasive to his fellow Catholic Christians. In point of fact, however, the doctrine of eternal law is derived, according to Aquinas, from what can be demonstrated about God through the natural powers of the human intellect, among which is the knowledge that God exists as a being who consciously and providently governs the created universe.[8] To be sure, one may object to Aquinas's philosophical reasoning as to the existence of the eternal law and of the God from whom it originates, but it would be a misunderstanding of Aquinas to dismiss his entire political, legal, and moral doctrine on the grounds that they only make sense within a Christian context. To be sure, faith and reason are ultimately harmonious in Aquinas's view, but this does not mean that certain truths cannot be understood on the basis of natural reason alone. The existence of God is not the only example of this. As we shall observe in chapter four, Aquinas's account of morality in terms of natural law (which is nothing other than the eternal law as it applies to human beings) rests on the premise that certain core truths of the moral life are attainable by reflective men and women without any assistance from divine revelation. In this spirit, Aquinas is fond of citing St. Paul's Letter to the Romans in which he asserts that the Gentiles who are without the law are still culpable for violating its requirements since the law is "written on their hearts."[9] As I hope will become clear in the following pages, Aquinas's general theory of punishment is also something that may be grappled with as independent of Christian revelation, and also therefore as something that stands to persuade a modern audience without Christian commitments.

8. See *ST,* Ia., 22.1. The argument that God is provident does not depend upon an appeal to divine revelation any more than the arguments that God exists, which Aquinas famously says need not be articles of faith, but are, rather, for those who understand the arguments' persuasiveness, "preambles" to faith demonstrated by reason (*ST,* Ia., 2.2 ad 1).

9. E.g., see *ST,* I-II, 91.2 (sed contra) and *ST,* I-II, 100.1 (sed contra).

In order to demonstrate that Aquinas's contribution to the contemporary discussion of punishment is necessary, the first two chapters of this book include analyses and criticisms of modernity's two leading punitive theories, utilitarianism and retributivism. The third chapter focuses not specifically upon Aquinas's theory of punishment, but upon his general approach to moral and political questions in order to identify the different starting point that he uses and which ultimately is the reason that his theory of punishment is not subject to the same devastating criticisms that utilitarianism and retributivism level against one another. In the fourth chapter I turn specifically to Aquinas's treatment of punitive matters, and especially to the moral basis of punishment rooted in his theory of natural law. Finally, in chapters five and six, I examine Aquinas's understanding of punishment in political society, the genuine alternative that it presents to the philosophy of punishment today, and the relationship between Aquinas's teaching on the death penalty and that of the contemporary Catholic Church. Throughout my discussion of Aquinas, I have found it necessary to distinguish my interpretation of the thirteenth-century thinker from that of other scholars, in particular that of John Finnis. In some cases, the question of interpretation is vital for presenting Aquinas as a legitimate alternative, but I have made every effort to limit all interpretive disputes to those areas directly affected by the central goal of the study: a presentation of Aquinas's theory of punishment as superior to that of utilitarianism and modern retributivism.

One final disclaimer: as I hope to show in the following pages, Aquinas's theory of punishment derives from a much broader understanding of morality, law, and the common good that are mostly foreign to modern theories of punishment. Aside from presenting Aquinas's metaethical views, I cannot possibly hope to demonstrate the superiority of Aquinas's entire moral and political worldview on these broader issues in the following pages.[10]

10. For a recent study that does present Aquinas's moral and political teaching as a compelling alternative to contemporary philosophers, see Mary Keys's *Aqui-*

What I *will* argue is that Aquinas's theory of punishment does not fall prey to the same inconsistencies and absurdities found in the modern theories under examination. For those who already accept the principles underlying Aquinas's moral and political teaching, this conclusion may reaffirm that acceptance. For those who already reject Aquinas's principles, even a compelling theory of punishment deriving from those principles is unlikely to persuade them of much. For those unsure of Aquinas's principles, perhaps the argument of this book will prompt them to take a closer look at what underlies his impressive contribution to punishment theory.

---

nas, Aristotle and the Promise of the Common Good (Cambridge: Cambridge University Press, 2006).

1

THE PROBLEM WITH THE UTILITARIAN THEORY OF PUNISHMENT

The most fundamental and enduring criticism of the utilitarian theory of punishment (hereafter, the UTP) is the claim that utilitarianism necessitates a disjunction between punishment and justice.[1] The basis for this criticism is the fact that utilitarians insist that the moral and political justification of punishment is exclusively derived from the beneficial consequences that punishment can promote, such as rehabilitation, deterrence, and the protection of society from a dangerous criminal. Conspicuously absent from the list of good consequences, however, is the reestablishment of the equality of justice, the rendering to the criminal of his just deserts, or, in a word, retribution. To punish from a retributive motive is, according to the UTP, to look back needlessly upon the crime committed rather than upon some good that punishment can bring about. To see the UTP for what it truly is, of course, it will be necessary to understand its place within the broader claims of utilitarianism itself. For this there is no more

1. E.g., see Armstrong's "The Retributivist Hits Back," in *The Philosophy of Punishment,* ed. H. B. Acton (London: Macmillan, 1969), 138–58; H. J. McCloskey's "A Non-Utilitarian Approach to Punishment," *Inquiry* 8 (1965): 249–63; and C. S. Lewis's "The Humanitarian Theory of Punishment" in *God in the Dock,* ed. Walter Hooper (Grand Rapids, Mich.: William B. Eerdman, 1970), 287–94.

reliable source than Jeremy Bentham, who continues to represent the UTP in its most detailed, consistent, and powerful form. Only by seeing the problems with Bentham's approach to punishment, therefore, can we understand its most critical weaknesses and the need to seek out an alternative.

Jeremy Bentham's Principle of Utility: An Overview

The disjunction between punishment and justice is evident in Bentham's thought, in which punitive matters, moreover, occupy a central place. We may even surmise that Bentham's reflection on the issue of punishment and its rationale was a vital source for his whole developed system. It is certainly a subject to which he thought his utilitarian approach could make a considerable contribution. To gauge precisely how Bentham's thought regarding punishment informs his more general moral understanding of things would, of course, require carefully tracing his remarks on the issue throughout his extended corpus. For present purposes, however, we may concentrate on his celebrated *Introduction to the Principles of Morals and Legislation,* which presents the clearest and most systematic account of his utilitarian understanding of ethics and political science.

The first chapter of Bentham's *Introduction* is devoted to explaining what he calls "the principle of utility." But before the principle of utility is introduced in explicit terms, Bentham expresses, in the opening lines of the work, what he considers the psychological foundation of this principle.

> Nature has placed mankind under the governance of two sovereign masters, *pain* and *pleasure.* It is for them alone to point out what we ought to do, as well as to determine what we shall do. On the one hand the standard of right and wrong, on the other the chain of causes and effects, are fastened to their throne. They govern us in all we do, in all we say, in all we think: every effort we can make to throw off our subjugation, will serve but to demonstrate and confirm it. In words a man may pretend to abjure their empire: but in reality he will remain subject

to it all the while. The principle of utility recognises this subjugation, and assumes it for the foundation of that system, the object of which is to rear the fabric of felicity by the hands of reason and of law. Systems which attempt to question it, deal in sounds instead of sense, in caprice instead of reason, in darkness instead of light.[2]

As Bentham sees it, human life is reducible to two primary motivations, the pursuit of pleasure and the avoidance of pain. This fundamental fact about human nature lies not only at the core of what human beings actually do, but also serves as the basis of what they *ought* to do. Whereas it is unqualifiedly good to maximize pleasure, it is likewise unqualifiedly bad not to minimize pain.

An obvious question arises at this point. If the same principle explains not only human action, but also right human action, why is there any need for ethics at all? Why not simply leave it to human beings to act as they are naturally programed to act, namely, to pursue pleasure and avoid pain? If pursuing pleasure is what we naturally want and also what we naturally ought to want, why should one need to write a treatise on morals and legislation? Bentham attempts to answer this question in a twofold way. First, although human beings naturally desire to pursue pleasure and avoid pain, not all recognize this as the primary motivation of their lives. Some people have actually attempted to shun pleasure while pretending to value what they consider to be higher goods, when all the while they have only been pursuing pleasure under a different name. Furthermore, even if one is honest enough with oneself to recognize one's subjugation to pleasure, one does not always know how to obtain the pleasure that one seeks. Second, Bentham's moral outlook includes not only the natural human tendency to maximize one's own pleasure, but the need to maximize the pleasure of other human beings. In other words, Bentham's understanding of morality necessitates that humans recognize the pursuit of pleasure and the avoidance of pain not only

2. Jeremy Bentham, *Introduction to the Principles of Morals and Legislation* (hereafter *IPML;* London: Athlone Press, 1970), chap. 1, sec. 1.

as the fundamental fact of their own lives, but as the fundamental fact of human life in general. A morally right action is defined as that which maximizes the pleasure or (what amounts to the same thing) the happiness of the entire political community. Although ultimately rooted in human nature, Bentham recognizes that the altruistic tendency of human beings comes much less naturally than the hedonistic egoism that underlies it.[3] Whereas morality is rooted in the maximization of pleasure as its psychological basis, Bentham certainly cannot be said to reduce morality to psychological phenomena. Because the happiness of the entire community is at stake, morality must involve not only rational reflection as to how that happiness ought to be maximized, but also a willingness to compromise one's own happiness so that the greatest possible happiness for all might be achieved.

One must not conclude from this that Bentham is a communitarian, since his understanding of the "happiness of the community" is based upon a radical individualism. As he puts it, the interest of the community is nothing more than the "sum of the interests of the several members who compose it."[4] The reason for Bentham's reduction of the political community to individuals comes back again to the centrality of pleasure. Since communities do not, strictly speaking, feel pleasure and pain, they do not have any real interests. Only individuals feel pleasure and so any discussion of the common good must constantly refer to what Bentham consid-

3. This seeming conflict between Bentham's psychological hedonism and the altruism that his moral philosophy requires has made for considerable difficulty in the history of utilitarian thought. The answer to the problem is not altogether clear from the *IPML*. Some have attempted to argue that there is no conflict between egoism and altruism because, in the long run, reason will discover that these two principles (both based on the pursuit of pleasure) end up prescribing the same course of action. Others have dealt with the problem by attributing to Bentham two sorts of ethical norms, one that prescribes actions necessary to maximize one's own pleasure, another that prescribes actions necessary to maximize the pleasure of human beings in general. Because it does not bear directly on his theory of punishment, this controversy cannot be discussed here. One particularly thoughtful treatment of the problem, however, has been given by J. Brenton Stearns, "Bentham on Private and Public Ethics," *Canadian Journal of Philosophy* 5 (1975): 583–94.

4. Bentham, *IPML,* 1.4.

ers its basic elements. Political society is, for Bentham, primarily a collection of individuals who cooperatively pursue their individual interests. Bentham does not depart, therefore, from the tradition of Hobbes and Locke insofar as he considers political society as an instrumental good, that is, a good for individuals. By gathering in society, individuals are more prosperous, safer, and have more reliable access to the means by which they experience a greater amount and a greater intensity of pleasure.

The centrality of pleasure in Bentham's thought provides the basis for his fundamental moral principle which, as he says in the *Introduction,* "is the foundation of the present work." He calls this principle, of course, the "principle of utility" and defines it as follows.

> By the principle of utility is meant that principle which approves or disapproves of every action whatsoever, according to the tendency which it appears to have to augment or diminish the happiness of the party whose interest is in question: or, what is the same thing in other words, to promote or oppose that happiness. I say of every action whatsoever; and therefore not only of every action of a private individual, but of every measure of government.[5]

The morality of every action, Bentham argues, can be judged only by reference to the principle of utility, or by the degree to which that action increases or decreases the overall happiness of the person or group of people in question. In his own words, "an action may be said to be conformable to the principle of utility . . . when the tendency it has to augment the happiness of the community is greater than any it has to diminish it."[6] With this one principle Bentham provides the basis for his ethics, his legal theory, his political philosophy, as well as what will become his theory of punishment.

By saying that the happiness of individuals is the only significant reference point for morality, Bentham rules out the possibility of regarding certain kinds of pleasures as intrinsically superior

5. Ibid., 1.22.
6. Ibid., 1.6.

to others. To do so would be to qualify the principle of utility and thereby to admit some other principle of greater or equal importance. It is only the quantity, and not the quality, of happiness experienced by individuals that provides a standard for good and evil, right and wrong, or justice and injustice. This is at least in part what Bentham has in mind when he explains that the principle of utility is the only possible basis for the use of the terms "ought" and "right."

> Of an action that is conformable to the principle of utility, one may always say either that it is one that ought to be done, or at least that it is not one that ought not to be done. One may say also, that it is right it should be done: that it is a right action; at least that it is not a wrong action. When thus interpreted, the words *ought* and *right,* and *wrong,* and others of that stamp, have a meaning: when otherwise, they have none.[7]

The Application of Utilitarianism to Punishment

Bentham's theory of punishment is directly rooted in the principle of utility. Explicitly taking up the question of punitive matters late in his *Introduction,* he renders a tentative definition of punishment to which he refers throughout the work.

> We now come to speak of *punishment:* which, in the sense in which it is here considered, is an *artificial* consequence, annexed by political authority to an offensive act, in one instance; in the view of putting a stop to the production of events similar to the obnoxious part of its natural consequences, in other instances.[8]

As an "artificial" consequence of an offense, punishment can only come as a result of some act of a governing body, and is therefore subject to the same principle of utility as all other acts of government. Punishment is only justified if it tends to promote the greatest happiness of the greatest number. In Bentham's words, "the general object which all laws have, or ought to have, in com-

7. Ibid., 1.10.
8. Ibid., 12.36.

mon, is to augment total happiness of the community; and therefore, in the first place, to exclude, as far as may be, every thing that tends to subtract from that happiness: in other words, to exclude mischief."[9] The next remark Bentham makes introduces perhaps the most essential concept for his theory of punishment: "But *all* punishment is mischief: all punishment is itself evil. Upon the principle of utility, if it ought at all to be admitted, it ought only to be admitted in as far as it promises to exclude some greater evil."[10]

Punishment is essentially evil, Bentham recognizes, because it directly and intentionally inflicts suffering, harm, and unhappiness upon some person or persons. It is, then, directly contrary to the interests of at least someone whose interests are entrusted to the very institution responsible for punishing. How, then, can punishment be justified? According to Bentham, the suffering of the criminal must be *outweighed* by the happiness experienced in the community (or the unhappiness that is prevented) resulting from the criminal's punishment. Indeed, there is nothing *intrinsically* good about the suffering of the criminal in itself. The only goods of punishment are those that come as a consequence. This is ultimately the reason why Bentham insists that punishment must look forward:

> The immediate principal end of punishment is to control action. This action is either that of the offender, or of others: that of the offender it controls by its influence, either on his will, in which case it is said to operate in the way of *reformation;* or on his physical power, in which case it is said to operate by *disablement;* that of others it can influence no otherwise than by its influence over their wills; in which case it is said to operate in the way of *example.*[11]

9. Ibid., 13.1.

10. Ibid., 13.2 (my emphasis).

11. Ibid. It is noteworthy here to mention that Bentham does not ignore the possible utilitarian advantages to simple retribution. That is to say, he does not ignore the possible benefit that comes from the pleasure enjoyed by victims in seeing their criminal assailants suffer at the hands of the state. However irrational it may be, it may be advantageous to indulge somewhat the indignation of society.

The most important effect of punishment, says Bentham, and the one which demands the greatest attention from the legislator, is "example" (or deterrence). This is so because, by deterring potential criminals from future offenses, a single act of punishment is potentially able to have a positive influence on the happiness of the greatest number of people. To prevent a certain criminal from harming society by incarcerating or reforming him is good. But to make an example of him is potentially to protect society from a limitless number of criminals now and in the future.

After Bentham emphasizes that punishment is only justified if it produces an amount of happiness sufficient to outweigh the suffering it causes, he proceeds to derive the various circumstances under which punishment is unjustified. Taking deterrence as the chief motive for punishing, Bentham asserts that punishment may be "groundless," "inefficacious," "unprofitable," or "needless." Although these are distinct ways in which punishment may be rendered illegitimate, they all exemplify how Bentham's penology is brought under the principle of utility.

According to Bentham, a punishment is groundless "where there is no mischief for it to prevent; the act not being mischievous upon the whole."[12] Certainly, if the main purpose of punishment is to deter crime, it makes little sense to punish actions that are not criminal. Bentham has in mind, here, actions that would otherwise be considered crimes, only they are committed with the consent of the would-be victim. "Provided it be free and fairly obtained,"[13] such consent is proof that the act contains no mischief since to harm someone is essentially to commit an offense against that person's will. Furthermore, punishment cannot reasonably be

---

Still, Bentham is quick to add that the possible utility of mere retribution must not be overestimated, and that the primary motivation for punishment must still be reformation, disablement, or, above all, deterrence. The pain of punishment is always greater than the pleasure an offended party enjoys in seeing it. As Bentham says, "no such pleasure is ever produced by punishment as can be equivalent to the pain."

12. Ibid., 13.3.

13. Ibid., 13.4.

inflicted for an act when the mischief caused by that act is outweighed by a greater benefit that it brought about or a greater evil that it prevented. Indeed, assaulting a man is normally a criminal and punishable offense, but not when assaulting him, for example, is necessary to prevent him from murdering an innocent person.

Second, punishment may be inefficacious, says Bentham, "where it cannot act so as to prevent the mischief."[14] Here, Bentham is thinking of punishing acts that simply could not have been prevented by the threat of punishment. Such is the unreasonableness of punishing offenders by an *ex post facto* law. Punishment will only deter a criminal if he knows beforehand that such an act is forbidden, as well as the severity of the punishment attached to it. For the same reason, it is unreasonable to punish infants, madmen, and those acting under extreme intoxication. If punishment is primarily a deterrent, this means it functions chiefly as a threat, but a threat presupposes some degree of rational calculation to discern that the pleasure of the crime is not worth the pain of the punishment. Upon those incapable of such calculation punishment can have no deterrent effect and is therefore inefficacious.[15] This is also the case when crimes are avoided so as to avoid such a great evil that no possible punishment could seem greater. For instance, if a man commits a grievous act of treason so as to avoid being subjected to extreme torture than which no greater punishment could be imagined, the threat of punishment will obviously be inefficacious as a deterrent. Neither he, nor any possible future criminals in the same position, could possibly be deterred by the fear of punishment.[16]

14. Ibid., 13.3.

15. Childhood and intoxication, Bentham thinks, "cannot be looked upon in practice as affording sufficient grounds for absolute impunity" (*IPML,* 13.9). This is so presumably because such criminals do possess some degree of rational ability, not to mention the advantage of protecting society from them if they are considered dangerous.

16. One wonders whether, under Bentham's own principles, such a man could be effectively punished for treason if the specifics of his situation, which forced him to commit the act, were kept hidden from the public.

Third, Bentham explains that punishment is unprofitable (and hence unjustified) "where the mischief it would produce would be greater than what it prevented."[17] This, of course, is measured in terms of the overall happiness of the community, and Bentham seems to have in mind the irrational infliction of severe punishment for relatively small offenses. For instance, the pain involved in permanently incarcerating a man for a parking ticket far outweighs the happiness which might come from such grievous suffering, for example, stricter adherence to parking laws. Again, the goal of the punishing authority is to promote the overall happiness of the community, and when the suffering caused by the punishment is greater than the happiness that results, he has failed in his primary function and has cost the community an overall net loss of happiness. Such is often the case, Bentham adds, when large multitudes are punished, when punishment is violently opposed by public opinion, or when met with the strong disapprobation of "foreign powers."

Fourth, and finally, Bentham asserts that punishment is needless "where the mischief may be prevented, or cease of itself, without it: that is, at a cheaper rate."[18] Some crimes are most easily handled without recourse to punishment at all. Bentham's examples of this are "all those offences which consist in the disseminating pernicious principles in matters of *duty* . . . whether political, moral, or religious."[19] To punish a man for promoting harmful ideas is often less effective, and often causes more overall unhappiness, than merely ignoring the problem or publicly refuting the offender in question. In such cases, says Bentham, "the pen is the proper weapon to combat error with, not the sword."

Bentham's articulation of groundless, inefficacious, unprofitable, and needless punishments, each in their own way, show how a certain act of punishment might violate the principle of utility and end up causing more suffering and unhappiness than it prevents. In the next chapter, Bentham approaches the same concept

17. Ibid., 13.3.

18. Ibid.

19. Ibid., 13.17.

from a different angle. He begins by enumerating the four objects, or goals, of punishment following upon the principle of utility and serving as the basis for specific rules a legislator must follow. The four objects, which are again designed to keep the institution of punishment within the embrace of the principle of utility, are explained thus:

> (1) His first, most extensive, and most eligible object, is to prevent, in as far as it is possible, and worth while, all sorts of offences whatsoever: in other words, so to manage, that no offence whatsoever may be committed. (2) But if a man must needs commit an offence of some kind or other, the next object is to induce him to commit an offence *less* mischievous, *rather* than one *more* mischievous: in other words, to choose always the *least* mischievous, of two offences that will either of them suit his purpose. (3) When a man has resolved upon a particular offence, the next object is to dispose him to do *no more* mischief than is *necessary* to his purpose: in other words, to do as little mischief as is consistent with the benefit he has in view. (4) The last object is, whatever the mischief be, which it is proposed to prevent, to prevent it at as *cheap* a rate as possible.[20]

No institution of punishment can eradicate all crime. Therefore, the punishing authority must be satisfied with limiting criminality as much as possible within its power. As Bentham warns, just as one must be careful not to punish too severely, thus causing more unhappiness than is necessary, one must also be careful not to treat crime with too much leniency. To achieve the four objects of punishment mentioned above, authorities must adhere to the following rules that are designed to maximize the institution of punishment's overall output. The first rule is that "the value of the punishment must not be less in any case than what is sufficient to outweigh that of the profit of the offence."[21] This rule is derived from the chief end of punishment, which is deterrence. It is only reasonable to threaten criminals with a punishment severe enough to outweigh the pleasure they might receive

20. Ibid., 14.3–6.
21. Ibid., 14.8.

from the crime itself. To punish rape or theft with a small fine, or murder with only a short jail sentence is not nearly enough to prevent most criminals from such offenses.[22] "The offence," Bentham says, "will be sure to be committed notwithstanding," and "the whole lot of punishment will be thrown away: it will be altogether *inefficacious.*" As Bentham continues, such leniency is often considered to be merciful. In reality, however, it is cruelty. Most importantly, it displays cruelty to the public by failing to deter criminals from harming their neighbors, "suffering them, for want of adequate protection, to be exposed to the mischief of the offence."[23] Ironically, such leniency is even cruel to the criminal himself, since even a small amount of inefficacious punishment is more than the principle of utility permits him to suffer. Punishing him, Bentham thinks, with an excessively severe yet efficacious punishment is far more preferable to "punishing him to no purpose, and without the chance of compassing that beneficial end, by which alone the introduction of the evil of punishment is to be justified."[24]

22. It is noteworthy to mention here rules seven, eight, and nine, which Bentham adds to his first rule later in this chapter. As he observes, punishment must be enough to outweigh the pleasure of the offense for which it is inflicted, not from the point of view of the legislator, but from that of a criminal about to commit the crime itself. In light of this, three factors must be considered: first, as Bentham says, "the profit of the offence is commonly more certain than the punishment, or, what comes to the same thing, *appears* so at least to the offender. It is at any rate commonly more *immediate.*" In other words, the threat of punishment to a criminal about to commit an offense is far more distant that the pleasure of the offense itself. This is so either because the criminal thinks he may commit his crime undetected, or because he has not thought sufficiently about the unpleasantness of the punishment. Therefore, punishment must be increased in order to make up for the criminal's lack of foresight. In Bentham's words, "the punishment must be increased in point of magnitude, in proportion as it falls short of proximity or certainty."

Similarly, some crimes are commonly habitual, which means that the legislator must punish such criminals assuming they have committed similar crimes in the past. This seems harsh, Bentham admits, but the consequences of failing to take this into consideration is that the pleasure involved in the collection of related crimes, of which the detected crime is only a part, will outweigh the pain of the punishment, ultimately rendering that punishment inefficacious.

23. Ibid., 14.9.

24. Ibid.

This first rule, and the next three that follow upon it, serve Bentham's principle of utility by ensuring that punishments are severe enough to be efficacious, that is, that they are severe enough to deter the crime for which they are inflicted. In this way, one might say these rules establish the "floor" for punishment on the scale of severity. If rules one through four, however, establish the floor, rule five establishes the "ceiling." That is to say, it ensures that punishments are no more severe, or that they cause no more unhappiness, than necessary to have the desired effect. In Bentham's words, "the punishment ought in no case to be more than what is necessary to bring it into conformity with the rules here given."[25] If a penalty is greater than what is necessary to prevent the crime for which it is inflicted, even if it still produces more happiness than if it were not inflicted at all, that penalty nonetheless produces needless suffering upon the criminal and must therefore be reduced to a level just beyond what will effectively deter.

In summary, Bentham argues that an act of punishment, like any act, must conform to the principle of utility by not causing more unhappiness than it prevents. Since punishment inherently causes at least some unhappiness for the criminal and those close to him, it must prevent a still greater amount of unhappiness through its felicitous consequences. Therefore, punishment must be severe enough to have its desired effect, though not so severe as to inflict needless suffering upon the criminal once that desired effect has been achieved. For Bentham, it is nonsense to think that criminals have less of a claim to happiness than anyone else. That is to say, the fact that one has committed a crime makes that person's happiness no less constitutive of the net happiness of the community the legislator is obliged to promote. This tenacious and exclusive attention to the consequences of punishment gives Bentham a decisively forward-looking perspective upon the question of punishment. He emphatically distinguishes himself from those who believe that punishment is somehow necessary

25. Ibid., 14.13.

for the atonement of past offenses or the reestablishment of the equilibrium of justice. All such concerns, he thinks, are nonsense and usually amount to nothing more than examples of a spurious justification for the irrational tendency of retributive vengeance. Such is his attitude toward any penology that fails to recognize the absolute supremacy of utility.

Retrieving Justice and Desert: H. L. A. Hart's Alternative to Strict Utilitarianism

Although the UTP has been restated since Bentham, philosophers' reasons for rejecting it continue to be the disjunction it creates between punishment and justice. To be sure, Bentham would deny this. He has not disassociated punishment and justice, but has rather redefined justice in a way that gives punishment an entirely new focus. Punishments are just, he might say, only when they conform to the principle of utility by maximizing the amount of happiness in the community and minimizing pain. What Bentham has actually done is to disassociate punishment from the concept, not of justice, but of desert. The standard against which he holds punishments is that of effectiveness; that is, whether punishments effectively rehabilitate, protect society from the dangerous criminal, or deter.

It is precisely on this point that many legal theorists have found the UTP so unsatisfactory. By separating punishment from the concept of desert, they argue, the UTP actually *has* separated it from justice, since it is only as deserved or undeserved that punishments can be just or unjust. What is lost is any commitment to ensuring that the punishment fits the crime, or that criminals are punished in proportion to the severity of the crime they committed. If deterrence happens to be achieved by the severe punishment of a less severe crime, or the less severe punishment of a more severe crime, the principle of utility requires it. Bentham's assertions to the contrary notwithstanding, it may sometimes be profitable to punish those who are not responsible for their crimes at all, such as the mentally handicapped. Worst of all, the UTP may in some cases justify the punishment of someone entirely innocent. So long as utilitarian goals are served and pleasure and pain are maximized and minimized accordingly, the punishment of an innocent scapegoat (whom everyone believes to be guilty) would be permitted, or even required, by utilitarian principles. A classic formulation of this objection is presented by H. J. McCloskey, who provides an example that he believes illustrates its alarming and morally unacceptable implications. He asks us to consider a situation in which the sheriff of a small town in the American South is confronted with a serious crime believed to have been committed by a black man. In this case, the criminal has not been apprehended, and the outrage among the townspeople has resulted in several lynchings of innocent black citizens. The only way to bring an end to these lynchings, the sheriff reasons, is for someone to take responsibility for the crime so as to assuage the indignation of the angry mob and restore relative peace to the community. Because there is no forthcoming guilty person, the sheriff concludes he has no choice but to frame an innocent man, punishing him as though he were guilty and thus putting an end to the random killings of other innocents. As McCloskey argues, such a gravely immoral course of action could very easily be endorsed by the utilitarian position on the grounds that it would "save more lives," and result in the net gain of happiness that the principle of utility requires. Granted, the sheriff is choosing to inflict a grievous amount of suffering upon one member of the community, but that man's suffering is outweighed by the suffering that is sure to follow otherwise.[26]

26. For McCloskey's argument, see his "A Non-Utilitarian Approach to Punishment," *Inquiry* 8 (1965), 249–263. For a utilitarian response, see T. L. S. Sprigge, "A Utilitarian Reply to Dr. McCloskey's 'A Non-Utilitarian Approach to Punishment,'" *Inquiry* 8 (1965), 264–291. See also McCloskey's "Utilitarian and Retributive Punishment," *Journal of Philosophy* 64, no. 3 (1967).

Although he does not explicitly address the case of punishing an innocent person as a scapegoat, Bentham does discuss a similar case that illustrates the utilitarian difficulty with ruling out punishments that seem to be grievously unjust. Under most traditional understandings of desert, a necessary condition for punishing a criminal is the determination that he acted voluntarily. Hence, those who commit crimes without the full exercise of their rational faculties are invariably considered less culpable and deserving of less punishment. At first, this may seem consistent with Bentham's refusal to allow the punishment of children, the insane, and the severely intoxicated. As we have seen, however, Bentham does not argue that punishing such people is unjust or undeserved, but rather that it is "inefficacious." Bentham himself highlights that his reasons for opposing such punishments are different from the reasons traditionally provided. It is not because these three kinds of agents lack the exercise of their free choice that they do not deserve to be punished. Bentham is too consistent a thinker to make appeals to desert. It is rather because the *threat* of punishment in these kinds of cases could have no effect upon the agent, "with respect to the preventing him from engaging in any act of the *sort* in question."[27] It would seem, therefore, that Bentham has reached the same conclusion as traditional jurisprudence (based on desert) without adopting any of its principles. Even those who might disagree with Bentham's premises will be consoled by the fact that his principle of utility does not punish those who cannot be considered culpable for their actions. Since punishing such persons is not useful anyway, Bentham avoids the scandalous conclusion that children and the mentally incompetent may be punished as though they were rational adults.

Based on Bentham's elimination of inefficacious punishment, one might argue that he would rule out the punishment of the innocent as scapegoats under that same rationale. After all, if the threat of punishment cannot succeed in deterring those without

27. *IPML,* 13.9.

the use of their reason from committing crimes, even less can it prevent a crime where there is no crime to be prevented. In other words, it would seem equally (if not more) unreasonable to punish someone who never intended to commit a crime as it would be to punish someone mentally incapable of being dissuaded by a punishment's threat. If the reason for not punishing the insane is that the threat of punishment could not have influenced their behavior, how much more irrational would it be to punish someone who did not need to be deterred in the first place. It may seem, therefore, that the punishment of the innocent would thus constitute the perfect example of an inefficacious punishment, since even children, the criminally insane, and the intoxicated are sometimes and to some degree capable of being influenced by punitive threats.

As it has been pointed by the profoundly influential legal philosopher (and Bentham scholar) H. L. A. Hart, Bentham's grounds for rejecting the punishment of those not responsible for their actions (children, the insane, and the intoxicated) are quite inconsistent with his own principles. Although Bentham called such punishments "inefficacious" because they are incapable of influencing those upon whom they are inflicted, he seems to forget his own teaching that punishment's primary utility consists in the influence it exerts, not on those receiving the punishment, but over those who witness it. Granted that punishing those not responsible for their actions (or possibly those who are entirely innocent) is ineffective in controlling their behavior before the punishment is inflicted, Bentham's principles force us to consider whether the actual punishment of the innocent (and the other undeserving agents) might provide a sufficient amount of utility to outweigh the "mischief" they cause. Hart explains this problem with Bentham's teaching with great insightfulness.

Bentham's argument is in fact a spectacular *non sequitur.* He sets out to prove that to *punish* the mad, the infant child or those who break the law unintentionally or under duress or even under "necessity" must be inefficacious; but all that he proves (at the most) is the quite different proposition that the *threat* of punishment will be ineffective so far as the class of persons who suffer from these conditions are concerned. Plainly it is possible that though (as Bentham says) the *threat* of punishment could not have operated on them, the actual *infliction* of punishment on those persons, may secure a higher measure of conformity to law on the part of normal persons than is secured by the admission of excusing conditions.[28]

On Hart's analysis, Bentham simply does not follow his punitive principles as far as they go. In discussing the punishment of those not responsible for their actions, he mistakenly concludes that his own theoretical justification of punishment would not allow a practice that nearly all people find morally unacceptable. Granted, Bentham is quite aware that his own opposition to punishing children and madmen is based upon a very different justification than that which would be provided by traditional jurisprudence (i.e., that such agents are not morally responsible for their actions and are therefore undeserving of punishment). Nevertheless, in attempting to claim that punishing such people is useless or harmful to the commonwealth, Bentham fails to consider the full scope of what his principles allow. We can see the force of Hart's objection by applying Bentham's principles to McCloskey's example mentioned earlier. To be sure, it would be absurd to think that punishing an innocent and law-abiding man would have any useful deterrent effect upon the one punished, but it may very well have a deterrent effect upon other potential murderers who believe in the guilt of the scapegoat (not even to mention its influence upon the lynch mob). When the morality of actions are determined solely by a cost/benefit analysis of their consequences, some things become justifiable that have hitherto been considered unthinkable by morally conscientious persons. The possibility that innocent and nonculpable agents may be punished is a sober reminder of what exclusive attention to utility might yield.

28. H. L. A. Hart, *Punishment and Responsibility* (Oxford: Oxford University Press, 1968), 19.

For precisely these reasons, Hart formulates a theory of punishment that attempts to correct Bentham's mistake while building upon his core utilitarian insight. Hart's main concern is that, if Bentham's principles do justify apparent travesties of justice such as the punishment of the innocent and the nonculpable, a purely utilitarian justification will be subject to a devastating reductio ad absurdam.[29] This is why Hart argues that, in providing a justification for the institution of punishment, philosophers must distinguish between the "general justifying aim" of punishment and the "distribution" of punishments that the law actually imposes. When he speaks of punishment's general aim, Hart refers to the justificatory reasons why the institution of punishment exists in the first place. In other words, how is it morally justified that a society chooses to have an institution of punishment instead of not having one? In Hart's view, this question must be distinguished from the related questions of who receives punishment and the extent to which punishments are inflicted for various kinds of actions. In short, whereas the general justifying aim of punishment pertains to the question "Why punish?" the distribution of punishment pertains to the questions "Who may be punished?" and "How much?" According to Hart, the very generality of the general justifying aim refers to the fact that, in discussing it, one may abstract from issues of applying punishment to specific types of crime, a question that presupposes that an institution of punishment already exists and at least should presuppose that such an institution has been satisfactorily justified.

29. Most utilitarian replies to this reductio ad absurdam argument attempt to show that utilitarian principles would never allow the punishment of the innocent because, in the final analysis, such an extreme measure would simply involve too much risk. One outstanding exception to this, however, is the celebrated philosopher and contemporary defender of utilitarianism, J. C. C. Smart, who responds to the reductio ad absurdam simply by embracing what is thought to be absurd. As Smart argues, if utilitarian principles justify the punishment of an innocent scapegoat, what needs to change is not utilitarianism, but rather our belief that punishing this innocent is always morally reprehensible. See J. C. C. Smart and Bernard Williams, *Utilitarianism: For and Against* (Cambridge: Cambridge University Press, 2007).

As Hart affirms, the general justifying aim of punishment can only be based upon utilitarian principles. Thus understood, when faced with the question of why we should have an institution of punishment in the first place, Hart openly rejects the answer, "in order to give criminals what they deserve."[30] In other words, Hart accepts the utilitarian (and Benthamite) position that the concept of desert offers no justification for the institution of punishment as a whole. The "general justifying aim" of punishment, therefore, can only include those goals outlined by Bentham, such as the protection of society from dangerous criminals, rehabilitation, and (most of all) deterrence. Where Hart breaks from classical utilitarian punishment theory, however, is that he reintroduces the role of desert when it comes to explaining the requirements of *distributing* punishments. Since the philosophical principles underlying punishment's general justifying aim are quite distinct from those governing punishment's distribution, Hart sees no contradiction in affirming that the punishment of the innocent (as well as those who commit crimes involuntarily) is wrong precisely because it is undeserved.[31] Hart thus avoids resorting to

30. Hart follows a well-known argument of S. I. Benn according to which appeals to desert "either avoid the question of justification altogether or are . . . disguised forms of utilitarianism" (*Punishment and Responsibility,* 9). Benn's classic argument for the UTP is stated in the following terms: "Appeals to authority apart, we can provide ultimate justification for rules and institutions, only by showing that they yield advantages." According to Benn, what the retributivist justification of punishment amounts to is the mere assertion that punishment is "fitting," or that fairness simply "requires" it. As he continues, "assertions of the type 'it is fitting (or justice requires) that the guilty suffer' only reiterate the principle to be justified—for 'it is fitting' means only that it ought to be the case, which is precisely the point at issue. Similarly, since justification must be in terms of something other than the thing in question, to say that punishment is a good in itself is to deny the need for justification. For those who feel the need, this is no answer at all" (Benn, "An Approach to the Problems of Punishment," *Philosophy* 33 [1958]: 326).

31. This characteristics of Hart's theory distinguishes it from so called "rule-utilitarian" theories of punishment. According to the latter, the punishment of the innocent may be excluded on the grounds that such an action violates a rule whose application is thought to result in the maximization of utility. Even though the rule-utilitarian may acknowledge that punishing the innocent would likely maximize utility in a particular case, therefore, he still disapproves of it because punishing the in-

Bentham's shaky reasoning for prohibiting the punishment of the innocent, according to which such punishments were considered "inefficacious." As Hart is now able to claim, even where such punishments are efficacious they are nonetheless unjustified by the chief principle of distributive justice in punitive matters, namely, that no one may be punished who has not committed a crime. Nor does Hart believe that affirming the concept of desert here commits him to the retributivist position that desert (or reestablishing the equality of justice) justifies (even partly) the institution of punishment as a whole. As he sums up, "retribution in the distribution of punishment has a value quite independent of retribution as justifying aim."[32]

In Hart's theory, the principle of desert only exists as a limitation upon the means by which the general justifying aim of punishment may be pursued. As he argues, fairness dictates that only those having committed crimes may be punished. Fairness also dictates that such persons may not be punished more severely than what they deserve. Hence, the state may not, in an effort to maximize utility, punish a jaywalker with the death penalty in order to eliminate all future traffic accidents associated with jaywalking. Even if such action would promise to result in a net gain of social utility, fairness would forbid such a disproportionately severe punishment from being inflicted. Introducing desert as a merely limiting principle, however, means that Hart does not accept the claim that legal authorities have the *duty* to punish, or that they have a duty to punish to a certain degree of severity, for retributive reasons. In other words, Hart introduces the no-

nocent, as a "rule," would be most harmful. As one can see, rule-utilitarianism's case against punishing the innocent is still made on utilitarian grounds; as opposed to that of Hart, who appeals to the fact that the innocent do not deserve punishment. Presumably, Hart would still object to punishing the innocent on grounds of justice even if it were shown that doing so as a rule would yield a net gain of utility. For a nice discussion of rule-utilitarianism as it applies to punishment, see Igor Primoratz, *Justifying Legal Punishment* (Atlantic Highlands, NJ: Humanities Press International, 1999), 118–28.

32. *Punishment and Responsibility,* 12.

tion of desert only to the extent that it prevents criminals from being punished more than they deserve, but he rejects the parallel insistence that criminals must be punished *so much as* they deserve. To make the latter claim would be (wrongly, in Hart's view) to include retribution among the general justifying aims of punishment, in which case Hart's position would become indistinguishable from that of any mainline retributivist. On the contrary, Hart remains a utilitarian inasmuch as he explicitly rejects the claim that criminals deserve to be punished. For Hart, the duty to punish exists only because of the good consequences (protection, rehabilitation, deterrence) that punishment promotes. Desert, therefore, should only be considered in order to prevent criminals (and even noncriminals) from becoming the sacrificial lambs of utility.

Unresolved Problems

One can see why the above theory of punishment has since been called a "compromise theory." Hart purports to reconcile the utilitarian–retributivist debate by claiming that each of their principles have a place, albeit in different dimensions of punitive justice. He does this by affirming what he considers to be the utilitarian insight that beneficial consequences provide the only meaningful goals for the institution of punishment, while simultaneously addressing the retributivist claim that pure consequentialism, when applied to the act of punishing itself, would result in unacceptable injustices. It is not enough for Hart to argue that the proper application of utilitarian principles would sufficiently rule out the punishment of innocent persons (as was claimed by John Rawls, who argued that punishing the innocent would always be too risky by utilitarian standards).[33] The fact that utililitarianism could even theoretically justify the punishment of innocent persons is enough, in Hart's mind, to show that utilitarian principles

33. John Rawls, "Two Concepts of Rules," *Philosophical Review* 64 (1955): 105–14.

are insufficient when it comes to the distribution of actual punishments.

The influence of Hart's theory of punishment is, perhaps, a large reason why purely utilitarian theories of punishment (strictly following Bentham) are so rare. Contemporary philosophers have mostly arrived at the conclusion that the notion of desert must be somehow introduced in order to exclude the absurd implications of the UTP. Furthermore, even if the punishment of the innocent would never ultimately be countenanced by the UTP, is now generally agreed that one's reasons for opposing such a travesty of justice must go beyond the claim that it is merely disadvantageous or that it involves too much risk.[34] What Hart's criticism of Bentham illustrates well is that punishing the innocent (and the criminally nonculpable) can only be morally wrong if it is undeserved. Only such a rationale can account for the kind of universal prohibition that such a practice seems to warrant and the kind of moral outrage that it rightly seems to elicit. But then we are faced with a question. Can H. L. A. Hart introduce the idea of desert in order to prevent unjust punishments without including it within the scope of punishment's general justifying aim? Can he, in other words, have it both ways? The compromise theory seen above has been praised to the point where it is claimed that Hart has once and for all settled the dispute between utilitarian and retributivist theories of punishment by retaining the insights and eliminating the defects of each. As Hart's critics have pointed out, however, what initially appears as a brilliantly designed balance between the best aspects of utilitarianism and retributivism is actually a confused attempt to combine two theories of punishment that are mutually exclusive.

Although it is not impossible to conceive of a purely utilitarian objection to Hart's theory,[35] the most pronounced criticisms

34. See Primoratz, *Justifying Legal Punishment,* 45–51.

35. Although not a utilitarian herself, Nicola Lacey articulates a possible utilitarian objection to Hart's theory of punishment which forbids the punishment of

have been rendered from the perspective of retributivism. As we have noticed above, Hart introduces the notion of desert into his theory of punishment only as a limiting principle. In other words, whereas the state is bound by justice not to punish criminals more than they deserve (or to punish the completely undeserving), they have no concomitant obligation to punish criminals so much as they deserve. As some have pointed out, whereas this solves one side of the problem by ruling out the punishment of the innocent and disproportionately severe punishments, it leaves open the possibility of not punishing those who truly deserve it or answering their crimes with disproportionate leniency. One may imagine cases where punishing a deserving criminal might not promise to serve social utility, or even where punishing a criminal might even be somewhat harmful from a utilitarian perspective. Since Hart's notion of punitive justice only extends to making sure such criminals do not receive more punishment than what they deserve, one must conclude that he would have to insist upon not punishing those who would seem to deserve it if the requirements of utility so dictated. Thus understood, Hart ends up allowing precisely what he set out to forbid, that is, the sacrificing of justice on the altar of utility. The only difference is that the injustice in question is that of undeserved leniency rather than undeserved harshness.[36]

---

the innocent on nonutilitarian grounds. As she observes, "there do appear to be emergency cases and possibly even less exceptional ones in which we are willing to some trade-off between justice and utility: for example, in the case of killing (perhaps through punishment) an innocent person in order to save a million lives." As Lacey continues, it is not clear how Hart would respond to this example. The defect in Hart's theory is that he leaves us no principles upon which to judge whether, when, under what circumstances, or to what degree justice may be sacrificed for the sake of utility (Lacey, *State Punishment: Political Principles and Community Values* [London: Routledge, 1994], 49).

36. This objection to Hart is advanced by Primoratz (*Justifying Legal Punishment,* 141–42). As Primoratz continues, the cases in which Hartian principles would require excessive leniency would be those in which failing to punish would seem to be the most egregious. For instance, one could imagine a Hartian objection to the punishment of Adolf Eichmann. If one is sufficiently persuaded that Eichmann

Whereas this objection would be embraced by those already persuaded of the value of retribution, it would be unlikely to convince someone already sympathetic to the Hartian theory. To point out that Hart would forbid the punishment of a criminal for purely retributive reasons (when utilitarian reasons are not forthcoming) is only a persuasive objection if one already believes that retribution is a valid motive for punishing criminals. But this, of course, is precisely what Hart denies. From his perspective, mild punishments for harsh crimes are not excessively lenient in the same way that harsh punishments for mild crimes are excessively severe. For the sake of illustrating this point, we may briefly recall the case of Texas criminal Karla Faye Tucker, who was sentenced to death for committing a gruesome murder in 1983 (unprovoked, she hacked a defenseless woman to death with a pickax). While awaiting execution, Tucker underwent a high-profile conversion experience and became a born-again Christian. Few people questioned the sincerity of her conversion, and, after Tucker received a stay of execution in 1995, she (unsuccessfully) made an appeal to have her death sentence remitted to life in prison. Let us assume, for a moment, that we have compelling evidence that Tucker's conversion was, indeed, genuine. Let us also assume that every indication points to the fact that she could be considered fully rehabilitated and fit for society. For the sake of argument, let us finally make the far less verifiable assumption that Tucker's execution would have no deterrent effect, perhaps because potential perpetrators of crimes like hers would be well beyond the deterrent threat of the criminal law. Following Hart's theory, one would be likely to grant Tucker the remission of her punishment, perhaps by lessening her sentence even beyond life imprisonment. If no utilitarian consequence is achievable, the only remain-

---

is (or can be rendered) no longer dangerous and that other "potential Eichmann's" are simply "beyond deterrence," it is difficult to see any justifiable reason to punish him other than the fact that he deserves it, a rationale to which Hart forbids us an appeal.

ing motive, on Hart's theory, to inflict the death penalty is that she deserves it, a motive that Hart explicitly repudiates. To object that Hart's theory would allow for lessening a punishment that strict retribution would require is not to refute that theory, but simply to observe one of its defining features.

A far more serious objection to Hart's theory, and one that I believe ultimately shows its incoherence, focuses upon Hart's use of desert as a merely limiting principle. According to the objection, the problem with Hart's theory of punishment is that he fails to recognize that the principle of desert, even when it is introduced in a limited role, logically entails a retributive theory of punishment that requires desert to be applied even to what Hart calls punishment's "general justifying aim." In short, Hart cannot have it both ways. We must remember that Hart's use of desert it not a mere *extension* of the utilitarian aims the institution of punishment should have. Hart is not arguing that utility will be ultimately best served when the law adheres to the rule that forbids punishing beyond what the criminal deserves. Instead, Hart insists upon desert as a *limitation* of utility, or that the law is bound by justice not to exceed desert even when utility (in the short or the long term) would require it. The problem, however, is that relying upon the actual concept of desert itself (as opposed to the mere appearance of desert for utilitarian reasons) commits Hart, whether he realizes it or not, to the very retributive theory of punishment he excludes at the outset. This point has been explained best by John Morison:

> Where Hart invokes a retributive principle for distributing liability to punishment it is clear that he desires a simple limiting principle—one that restricts punishment to the guilty only, but makes no further connection with retributivism. The problem is that this simply cannot be done. The basic retributive value, the idea of desert, cannot be accepted at one point in a theory without allowing in all the other retributive aspects. Hart may believe that he has summoned up the idea of desert to serve him in his compromise theory only at the point where liability is being considered, but in reality he has introduced an idea that

will become his master. This is the result of the nature of retributive theory.[37]

One may well ask Hart the following question: How is it consistent to condemn punishments that inflict more suffering than what the criminal deserves without acknowledging that they do in fact deserve some degree of punishment? To consider a punishment excessively harsh on the grounds that it exceeds the due amount, one cannot avoid the conclusion that there is actually some amount of punishment due. Hart's position is that because retribution is not part of punishment's general justifying aim, we should only consider desert insofar as it protects criminals (or noncriminals) from the excessively harsh punishments that utility might require. What Hart fails to consider is the inseparability between saying that criminals should not receive more punishment than what they deserve and saying that they deserve some amount of punishment. As Morison goes on to say, "the notion that the innocent do not deserve to suffer is presupposed by the idea that the guilty do deserve to suffer . . . the retributive justification and the retributive principle for distribution of liability are not only derived from the same basic proposition, they also entail each other. The reason why the retributivist restricts punishment to the guilty is because they, and only they, deserve it."[38] If one who subscribes to Hart's theory of punishment admits that desert is more than a mere fiction, and not just an extension of some version of rule-utilitarianism (from which Hart clearly distinguishes himself), he cannot avoid the conclusion that criminals, for the same reason that they should not be punished more than they deserve, do in fact deserve punishment. But if one recognizes this, it seems strange to exclude retributive justice from the realm of punishment's general justifying aim. If criminals truly deserve

37. John Morison, "Hart's Excuses: Problems with a Compromise Theory of Punishment," in *The Jurisprudence of Orthodoxy: Queen's University Essays on H. L. A. Hart,* ed. Philip Leith and Peter Ingram (London: Routledge, 1988), 125.

38. Ibid., 125–26.

to be punished, why would the goals of the institution of punishment ignore this important fact?

As we have seen, Hart's theory of punishment is an attempt to prevent the UTP from accepting the travesties of justice it would seem to allow by reintroducing an element of retributivism. Without this element of retributivism that acknowledges the role of desert, Hart argues, utilitarianism is subject to the objection that it may promote, in some instances, the punishment of the innocent and the excessively harsh punishment of the guilty. Hart's concern with strict Benthamite utilitarianism is certainly understandable, and although some utilitarians continue to defend the UTP, most contemporary philosophers of punishment seem to acknowledge that the objections against the UTP cannot be answered without significant modifications to the UTP. The problem with Hart's modification is that it cannot consistently acknowledge the value of retributivism in limiting punishment's distribution while not simultaneously embracing the central retributivist claim that punishment is (at least partially) justified simply because criminals deserve it. Hart's compromise theory of punishment, by rightly acknowledging the UTP's most serious defects, opens the door to a thoroughgoing retributivist theory of punishment. As we shall see, however, the version of retributivism that predominates among the contemporary philosophers has equally severe defects as the UTP and Hart's compromise theory. After a careful look at contemporary retributivism, we will be in a position to see clearly the need for an alternative, for which I propose a Thomistic theory of punishment.

2

THE PROBLEM WITH MODERN RETRIBUTIVISM

If, as the argument appealing to the possible punishment of the innocent seems to show, the UTP is ultimately untenable, and if Hart's attempt to save the UTP from itself cannot be consistently maintained, it is necessary to examine whether modern retributivism can provide a basis for the institution and practice of punishment. As we have seen, the difficulty with Hart's version of the UTP is that he attempts to introduce an element of retributivism without accepting the retributive theory as a whole. What this allows, however, is an acceptance of what the UTP (under Bentham) had traditionally excluded, namely, the notion of criminal desert. Whereas Hart intends only to introduce this notion in order to exclude the punishment of the innocent (or the severe punishment of the less culpable), he cannot offer a convincing answer to the question of why desert is not also valid as a concrete objective (if not *the* concrete objective) of punishment's "general justifying aim." Hart is thus unable to maintain reasonable grounds for his refusal to accept the full-fledged retributive theory of punishment in favor of his own compromise theory.

This difficulty inherent in Hart's argument is accentuated by an unmistakable reemergence of retributivism among English-speaking philosophers in the twentieth century. Prior to the 1960s, retributivism was hardly considered to provide a reasonable theory of punishment, and was widely thought to be little more than legitimization of irrational vengeance.[1] With the help of philosophers such as Herbert Morris, Jeffrie Murphy, and John Finnis, many participants in the discussion began to suggest, not only that the UTP is subject to a devastating criticism (as pointed out, for instance, by H. J. McCloskey), but that a purely retributive theory is capable of supporting the institution of punishment that utilitarianism, for its part, has failed to justify.

Whether or not it has been acknowledged by retributivists themselves, retributivism in its modern form originates in the moral and legal philosophy of Immanuel Kant. This is not to say that all contemporary retributivists adhere to the fully developed system of Kantian thought. To be sure, many do not even acknowledge the need to support their theories of punishment with a broader moral or political philosophical teaching.[2] It is also not to say that contemporary retributivism has not significantly improved upon the theory of punishment put forward by Kant himself.[3] Nevertheless, as I hope to demonstrate in this chapter, the core insights of the retributive view remain fundamentally Kantian, and so it will be helpful to precede our examination of retributivism in this chapter with an overview of Kant's theory of punishment. Only then can we formulate a clear understanding of modern retributivism's most serious flaws and the need to seek out an alternative

1. One noteworthy exception to this is the thought of late nineteenth- and early twentieth-century British philosopher Francis Herbert Bradley, who wrote: "Punishment is punishment, only when it is deserved. We pay the penalty, because we owe it, and for no other reason; and if punishment is inflicted for any other reason whatever than because it is merited by wrong, it is a gross immorality, a crying injustice, an abominable crime, and not what it pretends to be" (*Ethical Studies* [Oxford: Clarendon Press, 1967], 26–27).

2. For a debate as to whether such support is necessary, see M. Philips, "The Justification of Punishment and the Justification of Political Authority," *Law and Philosophy* 5 (1986): 393–416, and M. Davis, "The Relative Independence of Punishment Theory," *Law and Philosophy* 7 (1989): 321–50.

3. That Kant's theory of punishment is badly in need of improvement due to its lack of clarity and inconsistency, see Jeffrie Murphy's "Does Kant Have a Theory of Punishment?," *Columbia Law Review* 87, no. 3 (1987): 509–32.

theory of punishment that is neither utilitarian nor retributivist, but which (unlike Hart's theory) includes the genuine insights of each without retaining the defects of either.

Kantian Retributivism

The most revealing statement that Kant makes regarding punitive matters is his claim that punishment is a "categorical imperative." Although this remark comes deep within a treatise on legal philosophy, it hearkens back to the central principle of Kant's celebrated moral teaching. So that we may examine the significance of this claim in its proper context, let us (briefly) recall some of the fundamental aspects of Kant's moral philosophy of which his categorical imperative is the cornerstone.

First, Kant is emphatic that the principles of moral philosophy must not be taken from human experience. In other words, they must be derived a priori. This does not only mean that morality may not be derived from one's own experience, but also that one may not even derive moral principles from observations of human nature. To do so is to commit the fallacy of deriving how human beings *ought* to act from how they *happen* to act in reality, or, to use a more contemporary expression, to derive an "ought" from an "is." As Kant explains, most attempts to construct a moral philosophy before his own succumbed to the temptation of deriving moral principles from empirical considerations, especially those related to the pursuit of happiness. Such was, for example, the eudaimonistic moral philosophy of Aristotle as well as the hedonistic social contract theory of Thomas Hobbes. As different as these two systems are, both would be equally disqualified on Kantian principles. Regardless of how one defines happiness, as the attainment of the *summum bonum* (as in Aristotle) or the avoidance of the *summum malum* (as in Hobbes), morality can have nothing to do with its pursuit or, what amounts to the same thing, the inclinations of one's nature. Whereas the pursuit of happiness belongs to the realm of nature, morality belongs to the realm of freedom, and Kant never ceases to remind us how incompatible these two are.

Second, Kant argues that an action can have moral worth only if it is executed for the sake of duty alone, that is, solely out of reverence for the moral law. If the motivation for an action is self-interest, happiness, or even an amiable and sympathetic temperament, that action cannot be considered as worthy of moral praise. Another way Kant chooses to explain this is by insisting that the moral significance of an action depends not on the purpose for which it is executed, but rather on the maxim *by which* it is executed. As he argues, "an action done from duty has its moral worth *not in the purpose* that is to be attained by it, but in the maxim according to which the action is determined; the moral worth depends, therefore, not on the realization of the object of the action, but merely on the *principle of volition* according to which, without regard to any objects of the faculty of desire, the action has been done."[4] To act rationally from a maxim is to be motivated, not by inclination or the object of one's wishes, but by reverence for the moral law considered as an end in itself. As Kant says, "for an object as the effect of my proposed action I can have an *inclination,* but *never reverence.*" If one is motivated solely by a desire for the object or goal of one's action, therefore, one fails to act for the sake of duty and renders his action morally insignificant.

These first two aspects of Kantian moral philosophy lead to the categorical imperative itself. Unlike other moral principles (such as Bentham's principle of utility) that are derived from our common desire for some ultimate good, Kant's categorical imperative is formulated independently of any human desires or inclinations. In Kant's language, it follows not the form of any particular law that is based on particular ends but rather the nonparticular format of "universal law as such." Thus understood the categori-

4. Immanuel Kant, *The Groundwork for the Metaphysics of Morals,* trans. James Ellington (Indianapolis, Ind.: Hackett, 1993), 399–400.

cal imperative famously requires that one "ought never to act except in such as way that [one] can also will that [one's] maxim should become a universal law."[5] This, of course, does not mean that morally good actions are not oriented toward any ends whatsoever. Kant simply requires that the ends willed by an agent must be consistent with the universalizability of the maxim by which the action is performed. This means that the intended end of a morally good action must also be an end in itself (as opposed to a particular end of one's subjective desires). This eventually leads to Kant's well-known assertion that the objective end that makes possible genuinely moral behavior is nothing other than humanity itself. Hence, the same categorical imperative that requires a universalizable maxim also requires one to "act in such a way that you treat humanity, whether in your own person or in the person of another, always at the same time as an end and never simply as a means."[6]

Although Kant goes on to render additional formulations of the categorical imperative, the prohibition against using persons as a mere means to one's own subjective ends provides the principal basis for its association with punishment. If a criminal is punished for the sake of deterrence, such punishment would directly violate the categorical imperative by using the criminal to prevent future crime. Although Kant never ceases to remind us that criminals deserve punishment, he also holds that they are persons nonetheless, and may not be used by the state for its own subjective purposes, however beneficial those purposes may be. Kant concludes from these considerations that his categorical imperative forbids punishment from being inflicted under any other principal rationale than retribution:

5. Kant first introduces the categorical imperative in its negative or prohibitive form. Later in the *Groundwork,* he renders two additional formulations that emanate directly from it: "Act only according to that maxim whereby you can at the same time will that it should become a universal law." And subsequently, "act as if the maxim of your action were to become through your will a universal law of nature" (*Groundwork,* 421).

6. *Groundwork,* 429.

Punishment by a court (poena forensis) . . . can never be inflicted merely as a means to promote some other good for the criminal himself or for civil society. It must always be inflicted upon him *because he has committed a crime.* For a human being can never be treated merely as a means to the purposes of another or be put among the objects of rights to things: his innate personality protects him from this, even though he can be condemned to lose his civil personality. He must previously have been found *punishable* before any thought can be given to drawing from his punishment something of use for himself or his fellow citizens. The law of punishment is a categorical imperative, and woe to him who crawls through the windings of eudaimonism in order to discover something that releases the criminal from punishment or even reduces its amount by the advantage it promises, in accordance with the pharisaical saying, "It is better for *one* man to die than for an entire people to perish." For if justice goes, there is no longer any value in human beings' living on the earth . . . for justice ceases to be justice if it can be bought at any price whatsoever.[7]

Shortly after making these remarks, Kant asserts that the only reliable guide for determining the degree and the kind of punishment to inflict is the law of retribution *(ius talionis)*.

What kind and what degree of punishment does public legal justice adopt as its principle and standard? None other that the principle of equality (illustrated by the pointer on the scales of justice), that is, the principle of not treating one side more favorably than the other. Accordingly, any undeserved evil that you inflict on someone else among the people is one that you do to yourself. If you vilify him, you vilify yourself; if you steal from him, you steal from yourself. Only the Law of Retribution *(jus talionis)* can determine exactly the kind and degree of punishment.[8]

Kant's retributivism, already severe, goes even further. Not only is the state morally obliged not to punish its criminals merely as a means to some further end; it also, Kant says, has a categori-

7. Immanuel Kant, *The Metaphysics of Morals,* trans. Mary Gregor (Cambridge: Cambridge University Press, 1996), 6.331–32; see John 11.49–50 for Kant's scriptural reference.

8. Ibid., 6.332.

cal obligation to punish every person who commits a crime. That is to say, the state may not fail to punish a criminal, or even reduce the punishment, even for the sake of the criminal's or the community's welfare.[9] As a categorical imperative, the moral necessity to punish presupposes punishment as an end in itself so that the only legitimate reason for punishing a criminal is the mere fact, as Kant says, "that he has committed a crime." For Kant, criminal guilt is both a necessary and sufficient condition for punishing.[10] The absolute moral necessity of judicial punishment is expressed in its most explicit terms by Kant in the following passage:

> Even if a civil society were to be dissolved by the consent of all its members (e.g., if a people inhabiting an island decided to separate and disperse throughout the world), the last murderer remaining in prison would first have to be executed, so that each has done to him what his deeds deserve and blood guilt does not cling to the people for not having insisted upon this punishment, for otherwise the people can be regarded as collaborators in this public violation of justice.[11]

These words may constitute the strongest endorsement of retribution ever written, and they prompt one to wonder if a more emphatic retributivism is even possible. For the purposes of setting up a straw man, it would be easy to caricature Kant's teaching as nothing more than a legitimization of organized vengeance. We must notice, however, that, despite Kant's ominous appeal to the criminal's "blood guilt," his teaching on punishment is actually quite nuanced. Kant's retributivism is moderated by three factors, each of which helps to dispel the interpretation that Kant's theory of punishment amounts to little more than an endorsement

9. Admittedly, this claim which Kant clearly makes is difficult to reconcile with his justification of pardoning. For a discussion of this problem, see J. Angelo Corlett, "Foundations of a Kantian Theory of Punishment," *Southern Journal of Philosophy* 31 (1993): 277.

10. Cf. Corlett, "Foundations of a Kantian Theory of Punishment," 267, and J. Murphy, "Kant's Theory of Criminal Punishment," in *Proceedings from the Third International Kant Congress* (Dordrecht, Holland: D. Reidel, 1972), 434.

11. *The Metaphysics of Morals,* 6.333.

of bloodlust. First, it is important that his retributive remarks do not insist that utilitarian considerations are irrelevant in punitive matters. Kant's claim is that the criminal must be given his just deserts in a retributive fashion *before* any consideration is given to deterrence, rehabilitation, or some other beneficial consequence. This, of course, allows that utilitarian considerations may have a place, though this place can be only secondary.[12] Furthermore, even if one does punish for the purposes of deterrence or rehabilitation, this would only constitute a violation of the moral law and not a violation of the requirements of justice. A punishment is only unjust if it exceeds or falls short of what strict retribution demands, regardless of the motive behind the act of punishment itself (of course, Kant would probably add that punishing from a nonretributive motive is a likely way to render an unjust punishment, even though it does not make the punishment unjust ipso facto).

Second, it is important to realize that Kant's association of punishment with the categorical imperative actually eliminates vengeance in an important respect. If, by accusing Kant of giving in to vengeance, one means that he allows punishment to be an expression of public anger, one will have missed the central argument. Looking back at the categorical imperative, actions are morally praiseworthy only when they are performed from the motive of duty and not from any self-interested purpose and not even from any kind of natural inclination. If society punishes out of anger, even if the criminal objectively gets what he deserves, the punishment's motive will undermine the moral worth of the punishment itself. Kant's appeal to the categorical imperative includes an insistence that punishment be governed entirely by reason. When punishing from nothing more than a feeling or natural inclination of outrage, Kant would doubtlessly point out that the

12. For an interesting series of articles that explore the place of consequentialist considerations in Kant's retributivism, see Don Sheid, "Kant's Retributivism," *Ethics* 93 (1983): 272; Sharon Byrd, "Kant's Theory of Punishment: Deterrence in Its Threat, Retribution in Its Execution," *Law and Philosophy* 8 (1989): 153; and M. Tunick, "Is Kant a Retributivist?" *History of Political Thought* 17 (1996): 71.

justice of the punishment (if it indeed happens to be just) is only accidental. There is no guarantee, to say the least, that the degree of punishment demanded by an angry society will be the same degree required by retributive justice. To one who shares Kant's concern that criminals receive their just deserts, the motive of vengeance (in addition to having no moral value) provides no more of a guarantee that justice will be served than utilitarianism.

Third, Kant's retributivism clearly does not extend to all wrongdoing since he distinguishes between unjust actions and immoral actions. This is evident by his claim that punishment can be inflicted on someone "only on the ground that he has committed a crime." Certainly, these remarks exclude a primary concern with punishment's beneficial (or utilitarian) consequences by insisting upon the primacy of desert or guilt, but not just any sort of guilt. Kant's limitation of punishment to crime is also meant to remind us that there remains a realm of immoral actions that are not considered criminal because they do not infringe upon the freedom of others. Earlier in his *Rechtslehre* Kant defined justice as "the sum of the conditions under which the choice of one can be united with the choice of another in accordance with a universal law of freedom."[13] Hence, although all unjust actions are immoral, not all immoral actions are unjust, and certain freely chosen actions may be externally just even though they are executed with a morally wicked motive. Even though such actions violate the moral law, they cannot be punished because they do not violate justice in the narrow sense to which Kant restricts it. This is also why Kant insists that punishment, while distinguishing between voluntary and involuntary actions, must pay no attention to the *mens rea*. This means that a punishment must be only for the external action that constituted a violation of justice.[14] That a criminal acted with a more or less wicked motive is not only beyond the competence of the law to determine, it is also quite beside the point of

13. *Metaphysics of Morals*, 6.230.
14. *Metaphysics of Morals*, 6.218–21.

upholding public justice. Punishment is only *for* those who have committed a crime and only *on the grounds* that they have committed a crime. This excludes the punishment of moral (as opposed to criminal) guilt as forcefully as it excludes utilitarianism.

To summarize, although his retributivism is not unqualified, Kant's unwavering emphasis on the moral imperative of retribution sharply distinguishes his theory of punishment from anything resembling the UTP. He is clear that we have a categorical obligation to punish criminals, and that this obligation, as categorical, is not derived from consequentialist or utilitarian considerations. For Bentham, we must remember, consequentialist considerations provide the *only* basis from which to justify punishment. Certainly, for Kant, punishing criminals is necessary to protect society and to maintain peace and freedom, yet the moral law permits these factors only to play a secondary role. To allow them primary consideration is to sacrifice justice for the sake of some external benefit. This will not necessarily have the immediate effect of punishing criminals more or less than they deserve, but eventually the misplaced priorities of a utilitarian society may manifest themselves through grievous crimes against human dignity by using its criminals as mere means to its own submoral ends. What will prevent a society that prizes its general welfare over justice, Kant might ask, from punishing a criminal much more or much less than he deserves, and perhaps even punishing the innocent, if doing so will maximize the happiness of the community? Such utilitarian principles reflect a disgraceful lack of concern for legal justice. In Kant's words, "justice ceases to be justice if it can be bought at a price." Before the welfare of society is considered, all criminals must be punished *only* because they deserve it and *only* in accordance with what they deserve. Anything less fails to recognize the absolute necessity of maintaining strict legal justice within the state. As Kant says uncompromisingly, "if legal justice perishes, then it is no longer worth while for men to remain alive on this earth."

Contemporary Voices of Retributivism

To be sure, some aspects of Kant's theory of punishment have not been adopted by contemporary retributivists (e.g., Kant's reliance upon the *ius talionis*), whose formulations of retributivism have significantly refined that of Kant while nevertheless holding firm to what they understand to be his central insights. One such philosopher who deserves mention before any other is Herbert Morris, whose seminal article four decades ago provided the foundation of what is now called the "unfair advantage" theory of punishment. Morris entitled his article "Persons and Punishment,"[15] and in it he assumes the following perspective on political society and criminal law:

> Let us suppose that men are constituted roughly as they are now, with a rough equivalence in strength and abilities, a capacity to be injured by each other and to make judgments that such injury is undesirable, a limited strength of will, and a capacity to reason and to conform conduct to rules. Applying to the conduct of these men are a group of rules, ones I shall label "primary," which closely resemble the rules of our criminal law, rules that prohibit violence and deception and compliance with which provides benefits for all persons. These benefits consist in noninterference by others with what each person values, such matters as continuance of life and bodily security. The rules define a sphere for each person, then, which is immune from interference from others. Making possible this mutual benefit is the assumption by individuals of a burden. The burden consists in the exercise of self-restraint by individuals over inclinations that would, if satisfied, directly interfere or create a substantial risk of interference with others in proscribed ways. If a person fails to exercise self-restraint even though he might have and given in to such inclinations, he renounces a burden which others have voluntarily assumed and thus gains an advantage which others, who have restrained themselves, do not possess. This system, then, is one in which the rules establish a mutuality of benefit and burden and

15. The original article is from *The Monist* 52, no. 4 (1968): 475–501. However, I will cite here from its reprinting in Jeffrie Murphy's *Punishment and Rehabilitation*, 2nd ed. (Belmont, Calif.: Wadsworth, 1985), 24–41.

in which the benefits of non-interference are conditional upon the assumption of burdens.[16]

According to Morris, political society has the character of a joint enterprise in which individuals pursue their respective goals in cooperation with one another. At least in this respect, therefore, his theory of society shares an important characteristic with that of Kant, Bentham, and the liberal tradition; namely, that political society is primarily justified by its ability to serve individual interests better than would be served by human affairs conducted in its absence. According to Morris, each individual is expected to assume his or her fair share of "burdens" in exchange for the "benefits" that living and cooperating in society provides, the most important among which roughly correspond to the protection of what John Locke considered man's fundamental natural rights: life, liberty, physical security, and property.[17] Far from utilitarianism, Morris argues, what such a conception of society entails is an emphatically retributive understanding of punishment. This is so because crime may be understood as any action whereby a member of society, who already enjoys the benefits of the system, disregards his burdensome obligations of self-restraint and violates one of the "primary rules" under which he has (at least tacitly)[18] agreed to live. For example, let us suppose that one citizen is beaten and robbed by another citizen. Under Morris's conception of society, the criminal has failed to "play by the rules" by indulging in some benefit to which he is not entitled and by imposing an undue burden upon some other member of society. In so acting, he has also undermined the very purpose of the system of rules to which he

16. Ibid., 26.

17. Although Morris does not refer to Locke explicitly, he seems to have in mind something very close to the famous doctrine found in the *Second Treatise of Civil Government,* §6. To be sure, this is where Bentham, who famously called the notion of natural rights "nonsense on stilts," would part ways with Morris and the liberal tradition he represents.

18. For Locke's discussion of tacit consent, see the *Second Treatise of Civil Government,* §119.

belongs, namely, to "provide individuals with a sphere of interest immune from interference."[19] It is in this respect that Morris considers criminals to enjoy an "unfair advantage" over, not their victims only, but the rest of the law-abiding citizenry as well. "Matters are not even," he continues, "until this advantage is in some way erased. . . . Justice—that is, punishing such individuals—restores the equilibrium of benefits and burdens by taking from the individual what he owes, that is, exacting the debt."[20]

It is important to note that, according to Morris's theory of punishment, the unfair advantage that justice requires to be removed is not tantamount to any material benefits of the crime. To remove the unfair advantage, therefore, it would not be sufficient for a thief simply to return with interest a sum of money equivalent to what he originally stole. In addition to what a civil court might require of him, justice requires that the state impose an additional burden upon the criminal to eliminate the imbalance that his crime created. As Murphy elaborates, "if the law is to remain just, it is important to guarantee that those who disobey it will not gain an unfair advantage over those who do obey voluntarily. It is important that no man profit from his own criminal wrongdoing, and a certain kind of 'profit' (i.e., not bearing the burden of self-restraint) is intrinsic to criminal wrongdoing."[21] Therefore, in addition to eliminating the material benefits *from* the crime (such as the stolen goods from theft or robbery), the law must also eliminate the benefit *of* the commission of the crime itself. As John Finnis explains, the benefit of the crime may be understood as the wider exercise of one's will than what it permitted, an exercise that constitutes a real advantage for the criminal that needs to be removed through the imposition of punitive burdens for the sake of fairness:

19. Morris, "Persons and Punishment," 27.

20. Ibid., 26.

21. Jeffrie Murphy, "Marxism and Retribution," *Philosophy and Public Affairs* 2, no. 3 (1973): 228.

For when someone, who really could have chosen otherwise, manifests in action a preference (whether by intention, recklessness, or negligence) for his own interests, his own freedom of choice and action, as against the common interests and the legally defined common way-of-action, then in and by that very action he gains a certain sort of advantage over those who have restrained themselves, restricted their pursuit of their own interests, in order to abide by the law. *For is not the exercise of freedom of choice in itself a great human good?* If the free-willing criminal were to retain this advantage, the situation would be as unequal and unfair as it would be for him to retain the tangible profits of his crime (the loot, the misappropriated funds, the office of profit, the . . .).[22]

It is not difficult to see the appeal of the unfair advantage theory of punishment as explained by Morris, Murphy, Finnis, and its other proponents. Those intuitively persuaded by Kant's retributivism (and the shortcomings of the utilitarian theory) may be left wondering as to the precise reasons why justice requires punishment and what it accomplishes other than its useful consequences. Whereas Kant was able to explain why a strictly utilitarian theory of punishment violates certain important moral principles and risks the possibility of grave injustices, the unfair advantage theory offers an explanation as to why retribution is actually *required* by justice. One might say that Morris and his followers have reexplained Kantian retributivism in a way that eliminates its more untenable characteristics (such as the *ius talionis*) and replaced Kant's mere assertions with a careful articulation of retributivism's central insight, namely, that justice not only allows but requires the punishment of criminals independently of utilitarian considerations. Fairness, according to Morris's argument, is a real good of political society, just as real as health, property, food, and physical security. Although fairness is not strictly speaking tangible, its value in society should be clear even to those who require the most convincing of punishment's moral justification. Following

22. John Finnis, *Natural Law and Natural Rights* (Oxford: Oxford University Press, 1980), 262–63 (my emphasis).

Kant but with much greater clarity, the unfair advantage theory rebuilds retributivism upon the firm foundation of the liberal state, thus purifying it from the superstitious and metaphorical claims of premodern man that human justice should imitate divine justice which demands "an eye for an eye." Considered in this way, retributivism in its contemporary form provides a powerful response to Bentham's charge that retribution, while distracting us from punishment's "real" (i.e., utilitarian) benefits, is a mere chimera, a relic of a less enlightened age, or a disguise of our subrational desire for vengeance.

Is Modern Retributivism Defensible?

As one might expect, contemporary retributivism has not come without heavy criticism. It would be impossible within the confines of this chapter to survey the utilitarian–retributivist debate in its entirety, including all of the differing versions of retributivism.[23] It should prove helpful, however, to examine the most compelling contemporary criticisms of the unfair advantage theory in particular, since it clearly appears to be the strongest case for the retributive theory of punishment in the past half century. There are five such criticisms that deserve mention. As I shall argue, the first three of these, though important, are fully answerable and ultimately do not reveal any serious flaws in the theory itself. The final two, however, prove decisive. They show us that the unfair advantage theory of punishment is incapable of being coherently defended and point us in the direction of searching for a justification for punishment that no modern school of thought can provide.

The first criticism is that, by explaining punishment as the redistribution of society's "benefits and burdens," the unfair advantage theory has explained away the need for punishment al-

23. For a list of different versions of retributivism, see Cottingham, "Varieties of Retribution," *Philosophical Quarterly* 29 (1979): 238–46.

together and has conflated it with restitution. If all that fairness requires is the imposition of some burden upon the criminal proportionally equal to the victim's suffering, the punishment inflicted is more of a price than a penalty. Why not allow, on this view, for criminals to pay that price even before they commit the crime? So long as the price equals the benefit of their criminal behavior, fairness would seem to be satisfied either way. As Herbert Fingarette argues,

> On Morris' view . . . I would seem to have two equally legitimate options—paying my debts earlier in cash, or paying later in punishment. But surely that is not the intent of the law *prohibiting* stealing. The intent is precisely to deny us a legitimate alternative to paying the storekeeper for what we take. And even if I restore the balance by returning the stolen goods, and by paying back any incidental losses incurred by the storekeeper, it still remains intelligible and important—not only in principle but in the practice of the law—to ask whether I should also be punished. So Morris' kind of view . . . fails . . . to make intelligible the question of punishment as something over and above the equitable distribution of burdens and benefits.[24]

Another version of this criticism has been made by Richard Wasserstrom:

> For it remains to be seen [according to the unfair advantage theory] how it is that *punishing* the wrongdoer constitutes a taking of the wrongfully appropriated benefit away from him or her. . . . [C]ompensation or restitution to the victim by the wrongdoer, not his or her punishment, appears to be the natural and direct way to restore the balance in respect to wrongful appropriation of something that belonged to the victim.[25]

Although the above arguments rightly point to the importance of distinguishing between restitution and punishment, they are ultimately based upon a misconception of the unfair advantage theo-

24. Herbert Fingarette, "Punishment and Suffering," *Proceedings and Addresses of the American Philosophical Association* 50 (1977): 502.

25. Richard Wasserstrom, *Philosophy and Social Issues* (South Bend, Ind.: University of Notre Dame Press, 1980), 145.

ry's essential claim. When Morris and his disciples speak of the unfair advantage the criminal gains, it is not necessarily an advantage gained over the victim of his crime. They would most likely grant that the criminal very well may owe a certain degree of restitution such as he would be required to pay in a civil court. According to the unfair advantage theory, however, the compensation paid to a victim of assault (for example) for medical expenses, time lost from work, pain and suffering, and so on, is fundamentally different from the punishment required by retributive justice. The purpose of punishment is not to compensate for the burden suffered by the victim, but rather to eliminate the benefit enjoyed by the criminal. This benefit, moreover, is not identifiable with the material benefits of the crime (arguably, the most heinous crimes of rape and murder are those with the least material benefits), but rather derives from the criminal's overindulgent use of his freedom (as especially seen in the passage from Finnis above), a freedom not enjoyed by his law-abiding fellow citizens.[26] To attempt to pay for one's crimes ahead of time in cash, as Fingarette suggests, would do nothing to lessen the punishment required for a crime involving an injustice committed against the political community. No voluntary act of generosity can take the place of the state-imposed burdensome suffering of which punishment must consist in order to restore the equilibrium, not between criminal and victim, but between the criminal and the entire law-abiding populace.

The second criticism is that the unfair advantage theory, by insisting that burdens are inflicted of equivalent severity to the crime, would require inhumane and torturous punishment that no civilized society should allow. To some critics, this dimension of the unfair advantage theory represents a cruel irony, since it originates in a Kantian moral and legal philosophy that places a

26. As Richard Dagger explains, "the benefit is to be understood as the double advantage of not obeying the law when it suits one's purposes while also enjoying the advantages of the rule of law provided by the law-abiding citizens" ("Playing Fair with Punishment," *Ethics* 103, no. 3 [1993]: 478).

premium upon the respect due to persons, especially the person of the criminal by not allowing the state to use him as a "mere means." As Margaret Falls has argued, modern retributivism as defended by the unfair advantage theory mistakenly holds to two principles, namely, the principle of respect and the principle of proportionality, that are simply inconsistent with one another. According to Falls, "the principle of respect obligates us to respect persons as ends in themselves, as choosing beings capable of autonomous moral decision making. It forbids any acts which damage or destroy an individual's capacities for rational thought. In other words, certain acts, torture for example, are by their very nature forbidden by the respect principle. This is not true of the principle of proportionality. Any suffering the criminal mind can imagine and inflict, the proportionality principle allows in return."[27] So if a criminal, for example, not only kills, but rapes, dismembers, and cannibalizes his victims while they are still alive, proportionality is not satisfied with a sentence of life imprisonment or even the death penalty. The unfair advantage theory would seem to require a painful burden to be imposed upon the criminal equivalent to the severity of his crime. If, however, the state imposes the truly proportional punishment, according to Falls, it will be rightly accused of failing to respect the criminal's inherent personhood on which Kant, Morris, and retributivism's other defenders have insisted so emphatically.

Taken as a criticism of Kant, this objection may have some merit. As we have seen, Kant does seem to make the alarming claim that justice requires a proportional punishment regardless of the consequences or what this may mean; yet he later rules out punishments involving "maltreatment that would make an abomination of the humanity residing in the person suffering it."[28] What Falls seems not to acknowledge, however, is the possibility of the

27. M. Margaret Falls, "Retribution, Reciprocity, and Respect for Persons," *Law and Philosophy* 6, no. 1 (1987): 35.

28. Kant, *Metaphysics of Morals,* 6.335.

retributivist adjusting Kant's position by simply adhering to the principle of proportionality. This may very well not violate what Falls refers to as the "principle of respect," since one might make the Kantian argument that giving the criminal what he deserves *is* respecting him *even if this means torture.* Falls might respond that it is absurd to consider torturing someone (even if it is an appalling criminal such as the one described above) as consistent with respecting his human dignity. To a proponent of unfair advantage theory, however, such a claim may not seem so outrageous. On Kantian principles, one might argue, giving the criminal the punishment he deserves is essential to respecting his dignity because it implicitly respects the punishment that he willed upon himself when he freely committed a crime of proportional severity. So long as torturous punishments refrain from sinking to the motive of vengeance or using the criminal as a means to an end, one could respond, there is nothing subjecting it to the claim that fails to acknowledge human dignity. Whereas Falls might find such strict adherence to the principle of proportionality unpalatable, she surely cannot accuse it of inconsistency.

Falls's criticism is unpersuasive even if one does eliminate torturous punishments, simply because one need not insist upon the principle of proportionality in all cases to acknowledge it as a valid principle. For instance, a proponent of the unfair advantage theory may suggest that the state must inflict proportional punishments as much as possible without sacrificing some good of greater importance, such as the psychological and moral integrity of the person expected to carry out a torturous punishment.[29] To be sure, one need not abandon the principle of proportionality entirely in order to suggest lighter punishments when justice requires something of catastrophic consequences (Kant himself

29. Even for ordinary executions, for instance, Aristotle observed that a perpetual problem is finding someone suitable to be an executioner, since good men "do all they can to avoid it" while bad men "cannot safely be trusted with it" (*Politics,* 1322a 23–24).

allows for the state to withhold a deserved death penalty when inflicting it would reduce the commonwealth back to the state of nature).[30] This may still mean that punishing the perpetrator of heinous crimes with the simple death penalty may be somewhat unjust. By ignoring Kant's unreasonable insistence that such an injustice would make it "no longer worth while for men to remain alive on this earth," however, the proponent of the unfair advantage theory can quite comfortably, and with little compromise to his principles, concede that some goods are worth securing even at the cost of committing a certain degree of injustice. Again, this does not commit the retributivist to discarding the principle of proportionality altogether. It only means that retributivism may need to stop short of insisting upon it regardless of all implications. By attacking the unfair advantage theory only after assuming the strictest observance of proportionality, therefore, Falls has merely refuted a straw man.

The third criticism is that, even if the unfair advantage theory is defensible in principle, the view of political society it presupposes is so unrealistic as to render the theory altogether inapplicable. As many have recognized, this criticism of the unfair advantage theory is essentially Marxist. In explaining its persuasiveness, Jeffrie Murphy has relied upon the Marxist criminologist Willem Bonger, who argues that criminality is primarily a result of socioeconomic forces at work upon the criminal. If this is true, it makes little sense to understand the criminal's decision to break the law a free and rational choice to "get ahead" or to win some advantage over his fellow citizens. More commonly, a criminal breaks the law out of desperation or because he does not believe his society offers him any advantages in the first place. Even if the retributive theory is correct in principle, therefore, it is defective because it "fails to acknowledge that criminality is, to a large extent, a phenomenon of social class." As Murphy continues,

30. *Metaphysics of Morals,* 6.334.

Consider one example: a man has been convicted of armed robbery. On investigation, we learn that he is an impoverished black whose whole life has been one of frustrating alienation from the prevailing socio-economic structure—no job, no transportation if he could get a job, substandard education for his children, terrible housing and inadequate health care for his whole family, condescending—tardy—inadequate welfare payments, harassment by the police but no real protection by them against the dangers of his community, and near total exclusion from the political process. Learning all this, would we still want to talk—as many do—of his suffering punishment under the rubric of "paying a debt to society"? Surely not. Debt for what? I do not, of course, pretend that all criminals can be so described. But I do think that this is a closer picture of the typical criminal than the picture that is presupposed in the retributive theory—i.e., the picture of an evil person who, of his own free will, intentionally acts against those just rules of society which he knows, as a rational man, benefit everyone including himself.[31]

To be sure, one does not need to adopt a completely deterministic conception of human behavior according to which all human actions are products of socioeconomic influences (Murphy himself does not have such a conception) to see the force of this objection. One might even make the objection within the rubric of the unfair advantage theory itself. As we observed, the unfair advantage theory's essential claim is that punishment is necessary to restore the balance of benefits and burdens among individuals in society. If, however, there already exists a maldistribution of benefits and burdens before the crime is committed, the effect of a criminal action might in fact be to restore the preexisting imbalance. If it is true that the perpetrator of armed robbery described above by Murphy already suffers from an unfair disadvantage, the crime he commits will not put him "ahead" as the unfair advantage theory assumes.

It is beyond the scope of the present theoretical analysis to evaluate this criticism completely. To do so would require a careful examination of the Marxist claim that crime is a product of econom-

31. "Marxism and Retribution," 242.

ic disadvantage (or the extent to which it is so). Without becoming tangled in that thorny sociological issue, however, one might begin by questioning the relevance of economic inequalities for the unfair advantage theory itself. To give the Marxist objection its due, it is difficult to conceive of punishment as the rebalancing of benefits and burdens when criminals do not enjoy the benefits of the law in the first place. In such a case, the criminal cannot be said to enjoy a "double benefit" in committing a crime because the original benefit of the law's protection (assumed by the unfair advantage theory) does not exist. For example, in a society that enslaves a certain portion of its people the society itself would perpetuate an imbalance of benefits and burdens by not granting certain members an equal protection under the law and by simultaneously holding those members to an obligation of obedience. Such may even be the case in Murphy's example cited above, whereby the perpetrator of armed robbery is given "no real protection" from other harmful criminals in the community.

This having been acknowledged, however, one might respond that the unfair advantage theory is not upset by the mere existence of *economic* inequality even if such inequality exists unfairly. This is because the unfair advantage theory, properly understood, has only to do with the distribution of benefits and burdens consisting in the free exercise or restriction of human actions themselves. Even if great inequalities exist in material goods it is still possible to achieve an equality *under the law* whereby everyone is permitted the same sphere of noninterference with respect to one another.[32]

32. As one defender of the unfair advantage theory, Wojciech Sadursky, explains, "criminal law covers a rather narrow area of protected values: independence of persons from interference by others with their bodily integrity, with their property, and so on. It leaves outside its area of concern important spheres such as, for example, the sphere of economic well being. Criminal law, limited in scope as it is, builds upon the equality only of those benefits and burdens which relate to noninterference with human autonomy as the other values protected by criminal law. There are many other benefits and burdens which are distributed in a society in a manner inconsistent with the principle of equilibrium, but they are irrelevant to the discussion of punishment. As far as the benefits and burdens which are relevant to

Again, the equality required for the unfair advantage theory would surely be upset if not everyone enjoyed the protection of the law from criminal interference, and so to the extent which this is the case the Marxist objection is considerably persuasive. But unless it can be shown that a criminal's impoverishment leaves him *simply no choice* but to break the law, the unfair advantage theory is not affected by whatever economic stratification may exist in a society that relies upon it, regardless of whether that stratification is fair in itself.

This brings us to the fourth and fifth objections, which unlike the first three cannot be satisfactorily answered. The following arguments show us how the unfair advantage theory is ultimately incapable of providing a compelling rationale for criminal punishment. The fourth criticism is that the unfair advantage theory is fundamentally unable to account for the basic retributive insight that more serious crimes should be punished more severely and less serious crimes should be punished more leniently, that is, what Margaret Falls called the "principle of proportionality." More specifically, critics argue that any attempt to account for the principle of proportionality within the unfair advantage theory yields absurd results. How, we must ask, does one account for the severity of a crime under the benefits-and-burdens model of society and criminality that Morris (and others) have provided? One particularly tempting reply is as follows: since, according to the unfair advantage theory, the purpose of punishment is to eliminate the benefit derived from the criminal's action, the greater punishment would seem to correspond to the greater benefit. But surely this cannot mean *material* benefit. Granted that grand theft auto (where the material benefit is larger) should be punished more severely than petty theft, there are some particularly hei-

criminal punishment are concerned, it is not unrealistic to presuppose basic equality. This is equality with respect to a very narrow area of human values, yet this is all we need for a theory of punishment" ("Distributive Justice and the Theory of Punishment," *Oxford Journal of Legal Studies* 5, no. 1 [1985]: 58).

nous crimes, such as rape and murder, where there seem to be no material benefits whatsoever. If we follow Finnis's explanation of the benefits of crime, moreover, we see that material benefits are quite beside the point. As he explained, the benefit of committing a crime consists in the freedom to act in an unrestrained way and against the "legally defined common way-of-action." In other words, criminals enjoy the benefit of giving into the temptations of performing certain prohibited actions. If not by the material benefit of the action, then, perhaps one must judge the degree of the crime's benefit by the strength of the inclination to perform the crime. In other words, perhaps we should say that the criminal obtains more of a benefit by committing a crime that indulges a stronger temptation. Since indulging stronger temptations would naturally "feel better" than indulging weaker ones, one may surmise that actions indulging stronger inclinations provide a greater benefit and deserve, in turn, a greater punishment. And yet there is something deeply wrong with this analysis as well. As many have pointed out, it would mean that a criminal who felt very little temptation to commit murder, but did so regardless and merely "for the fun of it," would deserve a lighter punishment than the tax evader who gave into an overwhelming temptation to withhold a certain amount of his income on his tax return.[33]

To examine the unfair advantage theory with its best foot forward, therefore, we must consider some alternative way of assessing a crime's severity. Recognizing that the severity of a crime cannot be determined either by its material benefits or by the strength of the inclination to which the criminal gives in, George Sher (another defender of the unfair advantage theory) offers the following explanation.

> Consider again the murderer and the tax evader. Intuitively, our belief that these persons deserve different amounts of punishment has little to do with any empirically discoverable differences between them. In-

33. See, e.g., Richard Burgh's "Do the Guilty Deserve Punishment?" *Journal of Philosophy* 79, no. 4 (1982): 209, and David Dolinko's "Thoughts about Retributivism," 545.

stead, the crucial difference appears to be moral. If we believe that the murderer deserves a harsher punishment, it is surely because we regard murder as by far the more seriously wrong act. But if so, then the most natural candidate for what determines the murderer's degree of extra benefit is precisely the strength of the moral prohibition he has violated. By this criterion, the reason he has benefited more is not that he has indulged a stronger inclination, nor yet that he has received greater financial or psychic rewards. It is, instead, that he has violated a moral prohibition of far greater seriousness.[34]

Although more plausible because it does not result in the absurd consequences of establishing the severity of a crime by material benefits or the strength of the criminal's inclination, Sher's explanation is incoherent. Consider his central claim, namely, that a murderer has "benefited more" by violating "a moral prohibition of far greater seriousness." Granted that murder is a more serious moral offense than tax evasion, Sher's analysis is far from explaining how murdering involves a "greater benefit." Obviously, this cannot simply mean that murder deserves greater punishment, since this would render Sher's argument as circular. As he goes on to say (reiterating the fundamental thesis of the unfair advantage theory articulated by Finnis), criminals gain "extra liberty" in committing their crimes. It follows from this, according to Sher, that those who gain a liberty from the demands of a "stronger" moral prohibition somehow gain more. That is to say, they "get away with more."[35] But again, this provides no coherent explanation. Sher has still not made any meaningful connection between the "more serious crime" committed by the murderer and the greater benefit that the murderer appropriates to himself.[36] Sim-

34. George Sher, *Desert* (Princeton, N.J.: Princeton University Press, 1987), 81.

35. Ibid., 82.

36. Jeffrie Murphy offers the following criticism of Sher's explanation of proportionality in his review of *Desert*: "Sher himself puts the phrase 'gets away with more' in scare quotes (thereby indicating that even he finds it difficult to take literally) and, in my judgment, comes close to sacrificing whatever it was in the moral balance theory [unfair advantage theory] that initially made it seem preferable to simple intuitionism. We were supposed to get our intuition that serious wrongdoers deserve serious

ply to identify his greater benefit with a greater liberty is unhelpful. How exactly is one freer by violating the constraints of more serious prohibitions? Neither Sher nor any other proponent of the unfair advantage theory of punishment has provided a satisfactory answer to this question.[37]

The problem of accounting for proportionality is closely related to the fifth and most serious criticism of the unfair advantage theory, namely, that none of its proponents are able to explain in any compelling way how criminal actions constitute a "benefit" to the criminal himself. As we have seen, the benefits are described not as the material or psychological benefits of crime, but rather

---

punishment explained and justified in terms of an account of excess advantage; but, if the concept of excess advantage itself can be explicated only in terms of that very intuition, we have not moved very far. So it looks as though we may be forced to choose between a literal and clear notion of 'excess advantage' that will not yield the desired result or a notion that, though yielding the result, is strained, metaphorical, and obscure. I simply do not understand, for example, Sher's claim that 'as the strength of a prohibition increases, so too does the freedom from it which its violation entails.' Is this not simply a pun on 'strength'—freedom being a function of strength as irresistibility and moral gravity being a function of strength as importance or weight of supporting reasons?" (*Philosophical Review* 99, no. 2 [1990]: 282–83).

37. One proponent of the unfair advantage theory, Richard Dagger, has simply conceded that it cannot account for the principle of proportionality. As he says, "from this point of view [i.e., from the point of view of the unfair advantage theory] . . . all crimes are crimes of unfairness. . . . The murderer and the tax cheater are on par in this respect. Both are guilty of taking unfair advantage of those who obey the law, and both should be punished accordingly. Exactly how they should be punished is something fair play cannot tell us. That will depend upon the circumstances of the individuals in question, since what counts as an efficacious punishment at one place and time may not count at another." As Dagger continues, "this does not mean that [the unfair advantage theory] is unsatisfactory as a grounding principle. On the contrary, it simply means that reciprocity must be supplemented by other considerations—for example, deterrence, reform, moral education, restitution—when it is time to decide how exactly to punish wrongdoers" ("Playing Fair with Punishment," 483–84). Dagger's appeal to a punishment's efficacy is revealing. Whereas his explanation obviously avoids the problem of accounting for proportionality, he seems to undermine one of the very reasons why retributivism (and, by extension, the unfair advantage theory) seem attractive in the first place, namely, that it regrounds punishment upon principles of justice rather than a utilitarian conception of social hygiene. Whereas he might call it inefficacious, it is impossible for Dagger to explain coherently that punishing an unrepentant murderer with a small fine and a jaywalker with life imprisonment is *unjust.*

as the "extra freedom" enjoyed by the criminal by virtue of his unjust action. Upon careful analysis, however, this notion of extra freedom is extremely dubious. We have already noticed that John Finnis has described the criminal's unfair advantage as a freedom from the constraints of the law, something which the criminal's law-abiding fellow citizens do not enjoy. George Sher has explained matters in very much the same way, describing the criminal's advantage as "freedom from the demands of the prohibition he violates."[38] In focusing his criticism upon precisely this point, David Dolinko has put his finger upon the most serious flaw with the unfair advantage theory of punishment:

> It is hard to assign any meaning to Sher's claim that the criminal has gained "freedom from the demands of the prohibition he violates," unless it simply means that the criminal has in fact ignored the prohibition's demands. To make . . . [the unfair advantage theory] work, there must be something that a criminal necessarily "gains" from lawbreaking, which we can claim gives him the unfair advantage that punishment removes. Confronted with the difficulty of specifying what this "gain" is in a way that will make the theory come out right, Sher has, I think, simply reified the criminal's act of law-violation, misleadingly labeled it "freedom," and treated it as the "unfair advantage" to be taken away. Once we see this move clearly, Sher's analysis becomes virtually indistinguishable from Hegel's obscure claim that punishment somehow "annuls" the crime itself—a claim no more convincing in its new garb.[39]

To see the force of this criticism it is helpful to consider the most cold-blooded act of first degree murder, committed solely from the motive of recreation (i.e., for neither revenge nor material gain). In order for the unfair advantage theory to be defended, it must be explained how such a murderer either (1) has something he didn't have before committing the crime or (2) is "better off" than he was before he committed the crime. It is clearly false to say that, in murdering, the criminal gains the freedom to commit murder. The freedom to murder is not gained by the crime

38. *Desert,* 82.

39. "Some Thoughts about Retributivism," 548.

or murdering, but is rather presupposed by it. What defenders of the unfair advantage theory seem to mean is that such a murderer (and every other criminal) has opened for himself a wider range of actions to be performed by the *exercise* of his freedom. Instead of contenting himself with the range of actions permitted by law, he has taken an additional action the performance of which is not enjoyed by the rest of his fellow citizens. The pivotal question seems, then, to be this: Can the mere performance of an action prohibited by law, considered independently from that action's material benefits or any pleasure derived from it, constitute a meaningful benefit? Is, as Finnis argues, "the exercise of freedom of choice *in itself* a great human good?"[40] In considering the unjust action of a first degree murderer, it is quite difficult to go along with this aspect of the unfair advantage theorists' claim. Granted that a murderer has performed an action that most others do not perform, he only has an advantage over these others to the extent that the commission of murder is somehow beneficial (or that, concomitantly, refraining from murder is "burdensome"). It is difficult to avoid the conclusion that if such claims do not arise from a thoroughly perverse understanding of freedom and morality, they have at least distorted the concepts of "benefit" and "burden" so far beyond recognition as to render them meaningless.

As one examines this critical shortcoming of the unfair advantage theory, it is worth entertaining the possibility that the theory's problems may run deeper than the issue of punishment. Perhaps the problem lies at least partially in the understanding of political society that the theory presupposes. As we saw in Morris's seminal article, the political philosophy underlying the unfair advantage theory is generally derived from the liberal tradition and is loosely based upon a broad version of the social contract theory. That is to say, individuals actually or tacitly agree to assume the burden of living under certain "primary rules" in order to enjoy the benefits of security and prosperity that greatly out-

40. *Natural Law and Natural Rights,* 262 (my emphasis).

weigh the burdens of obedience. As some have argued,[41] however, an individualistic political theory that conceives of society as a "cooperative venture" for the sake of mutual, yet still individual, advantage, is neither self-evident nor beyond reproach. Especially if such a conception of society requires us to understand the most diabolical uses of human freedom as "advantageous," we may well wonder if the problem with contemporary retributivism is the political philosophy from which it is derived. To explore this possibility with due diligence, one has the option of suggesting a new approach to the philosophy of punishment not based upon liberal principles, or by rediscovering an approach absent from the contemporary debate that has been long neglected. In the present study, we will pursue the latter of these options by examining what the great premodern philosopher Thomas Aquinas can contribute to the philosophy of punishment and whether such a contribution is able to supply what is lacking in the utilitarian and retributivist theories that have prevailed throughout modernity.

41. See M. Falls's "Retribution, Reciprocity, and Respect of Persons," 30–32.

3

FOUNDATIONS OF THE THOMISTIC THEORY OF PUNISHMENT

In the foregoing analyses of the utilitarian theory of punishment and modern retributivism, I have indicated that each school of thought arrives at its conclusions regarding punishment from broader understandings of morality and political society. To be sure, Bentham's claim that punishments must be evaluated upon their beneficial consequences is immediately derived from his position that the morality of all actions must be so evaluated. Likewise, Kant's insistence that punishments may never use the person of the criminal as a mere means to the ends of the state echoes the core of his moral teaching and is explicitly linked to it when Kant declares that punishment "is a categorical imperative." Finally, the unfair advantage theory of punishment as articulated by Morris, Murphy, and Finnis is inseparable from the classically liberal teaching that explains political society as a "cooperative venture" of individuals coming together to pursue their personal ends more effectively (one may also include Bentham and Kant in this group if a historical depiction of the social contract is omit-

The middle two sections of this chapter, on Thomistic natural law and on the Thomistic theory of the common good, are partially taken from my previously published entry on Aquinas's political philosophy in the *Internet Encyclopedia of Philosophy.*

ted). Whereas chapters one and two were devoted to showing where utilitarianism and retributivism are lacking as punitive theories, I will attempt to demonstrate in what follows that Thomas Aquinas possesses a compelling theory of punishment that is immune to the devastating criticisms that the two modern schools of thought have leveled against each other. Before Aquinas's penal theory can be fully appreciated as an alternative, however, we must first understand at least in broad terms the moral and political teaching from which it is derived. Once we have done so, it will become clear that Aquinas's alternative teaching on punishment is fully explainable by his alternative approach to moral and political philosophy as such.

I will here endeavor to condense Aquinas's discussion of moral and political matters into a single chapter, not because I believe his moral and political thought may be so easily summarized, but in order to minimize any distraction from the issue at hand, namely, punishment, and to focus on what is foundational for Aquinas's theory of punitive justice.

We will begin this chapter by showing that while Aquinas's and Bentham's moral/political thought may broadly be construed as teleological, there are crucial differences that must be acknowledged between Aquinas's eudaimonistic teleology and Bentham's consequentialist teleology. Second, we will need to distinguish Aquinas's theory of natural law, derived from his teleological approach and upon which his theory of punishment is ultimately based, from Kant's notion of the categorical imperative that underpins his penal teaching. Third, in order to place the Thomistic theory of punishment in its properly political context, we must distinguish Aquinas's understanding of political society itself and of the common good from those proposed by Kant, Bentham, and the contemporary philosophers of punishment discussed in the first two chapters. Finally, we will examine Aquinas's conception of human law and consider some of the implications of his legal doctrine for his political thought as a whole. We should then be in a position to understand Aquinas's theory of punishment as he himself understood it, and to appreciate its application and contribution to the contemporary discussion.

Two Teleologies: Thomas Aquinas's Eudaimonistic Alternative to Utilitarian Ethics

From a strictly Kantian perspective, one might object to Aquinas's moral philosophy on the same grounds as one might object to utilitarianism. As we observed, Kant has famously argued that no moral principles may be derived from "anthropology" or from the natural inclinations of human desire. Following David Hume's famous prohibition against deriving an "ought" from an "is" (and prefiguring G. E. Moore's similar prohibition), Kant would have rejected both Bentham's attempt to derive a moral philosophy from the universal human pursuit of happiness and Aquinas's theory of natural law, which also derives moral principles from realities of human nature. Just as Bentham constructed his principle of utility upon pursuing the greatest happiness for the greatest number, Aquinas (following Aristotle and Augustine) argues that happiness is the ultimate end of all human actions and the principal reference point from which their moral goodness should be determined.[1] Nevertheless, the differences between Aquinas and Bentham are gargantuan. To illustrate these differences at their most fundamental level, we may begin by examining Aquinas's and Bentham's competing understandings of happiness itself. As we have observed, Bentham identifies happiness with pleasure and argues that it may only be measured in terms of quantity. What would become the classic utilitarian thesis is explicitly denied by Aquinas:

> Because bodily delights are more generally known, the name of pleasure has been appropriated to them (Ethic. vii. 13), although other de-

1. *Summa Theologiae (ST),* trans. The Fathers of the English Dominican Province (Westminster, Md.: Christian Classics, 1981), I-II, Q. 1., A. 7 (hereafter "1.7") (sed contra).

lights excel them: and yet happiness does not consist in them. Because in every thing, that which pertains to its essence is distinct from its proper accident: thus in man it is one thing that he is a mortal rational animal, and another that he is a risible animal. We must therefore consider that every delight is a proper accident resulting from happiness, or from some part of happiness; since the reason that a man is delighted is that he has some fitting good, either in reality, or in hope, or at least in memory. Now a fitting good, if indeed it be the perfect good, is precisely man's happiness: and if it is imperfect, it is a share of happiness, either proximate, or remote, or at least apparent. Therefore it is evident that neither is delight, which results from the perfect good, the very essence of happiness, but something resulting therefrom as its proper accident.[2]

From this passage we are given to understand that happiness is neither a feeling nor an experience to be maximized, but the ultimate *goal* of human life. One may say that the obtaining of this goal is supremely pleasurable, but it would be a mistake, Aquinas thinks, to identify the pleasure itself with the reaching of the goal. Whereas anyone is capable of experiencing pleasure, only human beings living morally upright lives and possessing both the moral and intellectual virtues can truly be called happy. This is why Aristotle had argued that, strictly speaking, children cannot be happy[3] and that happiness is only properly understood as the accomplishment of a life well lived. Under such a conception of happiness, it is even more understandable that Aquinas rejects the hedonistic thesis that happiness consists in *bodily* pleasure. As he explains, happiness must be defined according to the specific difference of human nature, which is the rational power of the human soul. Hence he argues that since "the rational soul excels the capacity of corporeal matter . . . that good which is fitting to the body, and which causes bodily delight through being apprehended by sense, is not man's perfect good, but is quite a trifle [*minimum quiddam*] as compared with the good of the soul."[4] In

2. *ST,* I-II, 2.6.

3. *Nichomachean Ethics,* 1100a2.

4. *ST,* I-II, 2.6.

explaining a teaching that Bentham would have found intolerable, Aquinas adds that human happiness can only be found in a rational activity of the highest order, namely, in the contemplation of the "uncreated" good which is none other than God Himself.[5] Only the participation in such an activity is capable of satisfying the rational desires inherent in human nature, and only by participating in such contemplation can humans achieve true happiness. Aquinas continually reminds his readers that, for this reason, perfect happiness is only possible in the next life, and yet we are still capable of imperfect happiness in the present life if we achieve at least a degree of contemplation and no serious impediments stand in our way (following Aristotle, Aquinas denied the Stoic thesis that the perfectly virtuous man could be happy in spite of any degree of suffering he undergoes).

For Aquinas, as for Aristotle, happiness is the ultimate reference point by which the moral status of all human actions should be evaluated. This may appear similar to Bentham's claim that the morality of actions should be determined according to what causes the greatest happiness for the greatest number, but again Aquinas means something quite different. The happiness at issue in evaluating the morality of an action is actually that of the agent himself. This is the respect in which Aquinas's moral theory may be said to be "teleological." The *telos* with which Aquinas is concerned is not the "end result" of an action, but the end or goal of a person's human life considered as such. Ultimately, all voluntary actions performed by human beings either promote the happiness of the agent or they do not. If they do, Aquinas often says that such actions are "according to reason" whereas those that do not are "contrary to reason." Reason, for Aquinas, is not an additional criterion for evaluating the morality of human actions, but another way of explaining how an action may or may not contribute to the ultimate purpose of one's life, namely, happiness.

It would be very easy to interpret these statements regard-

5. *ST,* I-II, 2.8.

ing Aquinas's moral teaching to mean that no actions are morally right or wrong in themselves, but that whatever happens to promote one's happiness is morally acceptable. Such an interpretation would make Aquinas's position similar to Bentham's, according to which no actions can be inherently right or wrong since there are only actions with good or bad, better or worse consequences. This conflation of Aquinas's teaching with that of utilitarianism, however, would be terribly misleading. In addition to underscoring the centrality of happiness, Aquinas also holds that certain actions are, by their very nature, immoral. Certain actions, in other words, are structured in such a way that they never contribute to the happiness of the one performing them. Regardless of the subjective feelings that might accompany them, some actions always hinder the agent from achieving the happiness that every human seeks. This fundamental difference between Aquinas and the utilitarian tradition is seen most clearly in a continual theme in Aquinas's ethical theory, according to which the morality of an action is primarily based not upon that action's foreseeable consequences, but upon the "object" of that action.[6] In discussing an action's "object," Aquinas does not mean the purpose or goal of an action (as one might refer in English, for instance, to the "object of the game"). The object of an action is deliberately distinguished by Aquinas from the action's "end" [*finis*], which is defined as the more remote purpose for which an action is ultimately chosen.[7] Although not perfectly consistent in his usage of these terms, Aquinas usually understands "object" to mean some actual thing upon which a human action is "brought to

6. For superb recent analyses, see Steven A. Long's *The Teleological Grammar of the Moral Act* (Naples, Fla.: Sapientia Press, 2007), and Steven J. Jensen's *Good and Evil Actions: A Journey through Saint Thomas Aquinas* (Washington, D.C.: The Catholic University of America Press, 2010).

7. Whereas "choice" [*electio*] is Aquinas's term for the act by which we will the means, "intention" [*intentio*] is that by which we will the end. If I intend the restoration of my health, I may therefore choose to see a physician (*ST*, I-II, QQ. 12–13). Therefore, this is how Aquinas would interpret such an action: The intention *is the willing of health*. The choice is *willing to see a physician*. The end is *health*. The object is the *physician*.

bear" [*circa quod est*].[8] To use Aquinas's own example, the object of the act of theft is, quite literally, *another man's possessions.* As he explains, the object is an indispensable factor in determining the all-important "species" of the action as well as whether the action is morally good or evil.[9] In other words, the object of the action, more than anything else, tells us *what the person is doing* and thus allows us to judge the action's moral worth. This, of course, does not mean that an objectively good action may not be evil by virtue of an immoral end. To give alms for the sake of vainglory or to volunteer at a soup kitchen in order to steal from it later on are morally evil actions in spite of having perfectly acceptable (or "suitable") objects: the man who gives alms for the sake of theft and one who does so from his love for the poor are both, strictly speaking, *giving alms.* Moreover, actions that are morally evil by their objects are not rendered acceptable because of good ends. For instance, to steal another man's possessions for the sake of giving the money to charity may be acting for a good end, but this does not excuse the fact that the object of the action, which establishes that action within the *species of theft,* lacks "due proportion" to the manner in which the agent acts upon it.[10] This is why Aquinas famously argues that morally good actions must be good "in every respect": "If therefore the will be good, both from its proper object and from its end, it follows that the external action is good. But if the will be good from its intention of the end, this is not enough to make the external action good: and if the will be evil either by reason of its intention of the end, or by reason of the act willed, it follows that the external action is evil."[11]

To illustrate this aspect of Aquinas's moral philosophy even

8. *ST,* I-II, 18.6. In this article, Aquinas also uses the term "object" to refer to the action's end. He does so in order to facilitate a distinction between two dimensions of the human act: the exterior act, the object of which is "that upon which the action is brought to bear," and the interior act of the will, the "object" of which is *end.*

9. *ST,* I-II, 18.2, 5 and 19.2.

10. As Aquinas explains, the objects of evil actions are not themselves evil, though they render an action evil by lacking "due proportion" to it (ST, I-II, 18.2, ad 1).

11. *ST,* I-II, 20.2.

more clearly, we may refer to the example of lying. Much later in the *Summa Theologiae,* Aquinas asks whether lying may ever be morally justified. In his response, he explains that lying, if defined as the deliberate telling of a falsehood, is always sinful. Any lies so defined are therefore understood, like the taking of another's possessions, to be morally wrong by virtue of the action's object. Just as the object of theft is another man's goods, the object of lying is the false statement itself, and when a person who is aware of a statement's falsity speaks it to another, Aquinas argues that such an act is "evil in respect to its genus, since it is an action bearing upon undue matter."[12] As he further explains, to lie is to use words in a way that contradicts their natural purpose, namely, to convey the thoughts of one's mind (this is why a lie is more than simply a false statement, since one may say what is false while thinking it to be true). Considered as such, a lie is an "inordinate act" regardless of the ultimate ends for which it may be told. Hence, Aquinas uncompromisingly claims that lying is never justified even to save someone's life:

> A lie is *sinful* not only because it injures one's neighbor, but also on account of its inordinateness. . . . Now it is not allowed to make use of anything inordinate in order to ward off injury or defects from another: as neither is it lawful to steal in order to give *alms*. . . . Therefore it is not lawful to tell a *lie* in order to deliver another from any danger whatever.[13]

Although refraining from telling a lie may have bad, even catastrophic, consequences, Aquinas remains committed to the position that any action with an unsuitable object is morally wrong regardless of any good ends the agent may have. This position stands in stark contrast to Bentham's claim that the goodness of an action's foreseeable consequences establishes the sole criterion of it moral worth. Again, this does not mean that Aquinas's teaching is not teleological. The moral wrongness of lying is entirely derived from the fact that it hinders the liar from his ulti-

12. *ST,* II-II, 110.3.
13. *ST,* II-II, 110.3, ad 4.

mate end. This is precisely what Aquinas means when he says that lying is an inordinate act, namely, that it contravenes the order to the end. If the end in question were the greatest happiness for the greatest number, it would be easy to justify certain lies that are necessary to "save lives" or to prevent some destructive event from taking place. As Aquinas sees it, however, the teller of the lie stifles his progress toward his own happiness in addition to whatever harm (and in spite of any external goods) his lies may cause. Simply stated, his lie makes him a worse person, less complete, and less capable of living a fulfilled human life. While remaining teleological to the core, therefore, Aquinas is committed to what Bentham's consequentialist teleology cannot allow, namely, that certain kinds of actions are always morally wrong in spite of their consequences and in spite of any good ends for which they are performed.[14]

Thomistic Natural Law and Kantian Ethics: The Role of Natural Inclination

In looking at Aquinas's universal condemnation of lying, it may seem that by distinguishing him from the utilitarian tradition we run the risk of conflating his moral teaching with that of Kant.[15] One need only consider the title of Kant's famous essay "On a Supposed Right to Lie for Philanthropic Concerns" to see the similarities between the implications of Aquinas's moral theory with the later deontological tradition. To help us evaluate these apparent similarities, we may recall from chapter two some of the

14. As Anthony Lisska points out, "Henry Veatch once suggested that one ought to call Aristotle and Aquinas 'teleologists' but to distinguish two kinds of teleology: one with non-moral ends to be obtained, which is common to utilitarianism, and the other with moral ends to be attained depending on the essence of the human person, which is appropriate for natural law theories" (*Aquinas's Theory of Natural Law: An Analytic Reconstruction* [Oxford: Oxford University Press, 1996], 100).

15. This is unfortunately one effect of Lisska's treatment of Aquinas's natural law theory, in which he says that "Aquinas would better be defined as a 'deontologist' than a 'teleologist'" (ibid., 100).

essential principles upon which Kant's moral theory is based. As we observed, Kant denies the validity of any moral theory that derives its principles from human nature or natural inclination. In other words, it is impossible to explain how human beings *ought to act* by simply observing, however perceptively, how they *happen to act.* Rather than human nature Kant emphasizes reason, which he believes can provide universally valid moral principles for all rational beings (including, but not necessarily limited to, humans). By following his strongest or most sublime natural desires, a man may very well find happiness, but he will be no closer to genuine moral goodness. If he follows reason, however, he will act in such a way as to conform to the requirements of morality whether this contributes to his happiness or not. As Kant famously argues, happiness and morality are at such odds that if humans were meant to pursue happiness above all else, they would not have been endowed with reason but would have simply been left to their natural instincts.

> In the natural constitution of an organized being, i.e., one suitably adapted to the purpose of life, let us take as a principle that in such a being no organ is to be found for any end unless it be the most fit and the best adapted for that end. Now if that being's preservation, welfare, or in a word its happiness, were the real end of nature in the case of a being having reason and will, then nature would have hit upon a very poor arrangement in having the reason of a creature carry out this purpose. For all the actions which such a creature has to perform with this purpose in view, and the whole rule of his conduct would have been prescribed much more exactly by instinct; and the purpose in question could have need attained much more certainly by instinct than it can ever be by reason.[16]

In spite of Aquinas's and Kant's shared emphasis upon reason (or, as Aquinas puts it, the "order of reason"), by considering the metaethical principles underlying Aquinas's teaching we may observe that his approach to morality is no less opposed to Kantian

16. Immanuel Kant, *Groundwork for the Metaphysics of Morals,* 395.

ethics than to utilitarianism. This is especially evident in Aquinas's theory of natural law, which provides a necessary complement to his theory of happiness described above. It may initially seem strange that after emphasizing the role of happiness and the order of reason to which humans must conform in order to achieve that happiness that Aquinas would later explain morality in terms of law. This apparent strangeness disappears, however, as one considers the perfect harmony between these two aspects of Aquinas's moral philosophy. While still within the "Treatise on Human Acts" and immediately after arguing that moral goodness requires adherence to the order of reason, Aquinas proceeds to argue that such goodness also requires adherence to the "eternal law."

> Wherever a number of causes are subordinate to each other, the effect depends more on the first than on the second cause: since the second cause acts only in virtue of the first. Now it is from the eternal law, which is the Divine Reason, that human reason is the rule of the human will, from which the human will derives its goodness. Hence it is written (Ps. iv. 6, 7): *Many say: Who showeth us good things? The light of Thy countenance, O Lord, is signed upon us:* as though to say: "The light of our reason is able to show us good things and guide our will, in so far as it is the light of (i.e., derived from) Thy countenance." It is therefore evident that the goodness of the human will depends on the eternal law much more than on human reason: and when human reason fails [*deficit*] we must have recourse to the Eternal Reason.[17]

The reference to Scripture in this passage may lead one to think that Aquinas is establishing a competing standard of morality from his earlier (and unmistakably Aristotelian) appeal to happiness and the order of reason. Upon examination, however, it becomes evident that Aquinas does not gainsay any aspect of that earlier teaching but rather adds an important new dimension to it. Far from introducing a theological claim (in the sense that such a claim would depend upon divine revelation), Aquinas explains that the eternal law is accessible to "natural reason which

17. *ST,* I-II, 19.4.

is derived from [the Divine Reason] as its proper image."[18] This is essentially the meaning behind his claim that, whereas reason is the "proximate" measure of human actions, the eternal law is the "remote" measure. Right reason should be considered only as the "proximate" measure of human actions precisely because the eternal law is the standard in reference to which right reason is judged as right. This is why Aquinas would not share Kant's claim that human beings, as rational, are autonomous.

Aquinas's teaching on these matters becomes clearer as one turns to those passages later in the *Summa Theologiae* where he takes up the question of the eternal law itself. As he explains there, everything in the terrestrial world is created by God and endowed with a certain nature that defines what each sort of being is in its essence. A thing's nature is detectable not only in its external appearance, but also and more importantly through the natural inclinations that guide it to behave in conformity with the particular nature it has. As Aquinas argues, God's authorship and active role in prescribing and sustaining the various natures included in creation may rightfully be called a *law*. After defining law as "an ordinance of reason for the common good, made by someone who has care of the community, and promulgated,"[19] Aquinas explains that the entire universe is governed by God who is the supreme lawgiver par excellence.[20] Even though the world governed by God's providence is temporal and limited, Aquinas nevertheless calls the law that governs it the "eternal law." Its eternal nature comes not from that to which it applies, but rather the source from whom the law is derived. As Aquinas explains,

> the very idea of the government of things in God the Ruler of the universe, has the nature of a law. And since Divine Reason's conception of things is not subject to time but is eternal, according to Prov. viii, 23 . . . this kind of law must be called eternal.[21]

18. Ibid., ad 3.
19. *ST,* I-II, 90.4.
20. *ST,* I-II, 91.1.
21. Ibid.

In the vast majority of cases, God governs his subjects through the eternal law without any possibility that that law might be disobeyed. This, of course, is because most beings in the universe (or at least in the natural world) do not possess the rational ability to act consciously in a way that is contrary to the eternal law implanted in them. Completely unique among natural things, however, are humans who, although subject to divine providence and the eternal law, possess the power of free choice and therefore have a radically different relation to that law. As Aquinas explains,

> among all others, the rational creature [*rationalis creatura*] is subject to Divine Providence in the most excellent way, in so far as it partakes of a share of providence, by being provident both for itself, and for others. Wherefore, it has a share of the Eternal Reason, whereby it has a natural inclination to its proper act and end.[22]

Because the rational creature's relation to the eternal law is so different from that of any other terrestrial thing, Aquinas prefers to call the law that governs him or her by a different name. In addition to saying that humans are under the eternal law, therefore, he further specifies that they are under the *natural* law, and yet "the natural law is nothing else than the rational creature's participation of the eternal law."[23] Another, equally accurate, way of stating Aquinas's position is that the natural law is *that part* of the eternal law that applies to human beings.

As the first "rule and measure" of human behavior, the natural law provides the only possible basis for morality and politics. Simply stated, the natural law guides human beings through their fundamental inclinations toward the natural perfection that God, the author of the natural law, intends for them. As we have seen, however, the human participation in the eternal law (called the natural law) is always concomitant with a certain awareness the human subject has of the law binding him. This awareness is crucial in Aquinas's view. Since one of the essential components of law is

22. *ST,* I-II, 91.2.
23. Ibid.

to be promulgated, the natural law would lose its legal character if human beings did not have the principles of that law instilled in their minds.[24] For this reason Aquinas considers the natural law to be a habit, not in itself, but because the principles (or precepts) of the natural law are naturally held in our minds by means of an intellectual habit, which Aquinas calls "synderesis." Synderesis denotes a natural knowledge held by all people instructing them as to the fundamental moral requirements of their human nature. As Aquinas explains, just as speculative knowledge requires there to be certain principles from which one can draw further conclusions, so also practical and moral knowledge presupposes an understanding of fundamental practical precepts from which more concrete moral directives may be derived. Whereas Aquinas calls the habit by which human beings understand the first moral principles (which are also the first principles of the natural law) *synderesis,*[25] he calls the act by which one applies that understanding to concrete situations *conscience.*[26] Therefore, by means of synderesis a man would know that the act of adultery is morally wrong and contrary to the natural law. By an act of conscience he would reason that intercourse with this particular woman that is not his wife is an act of adultery and should therefore be avoided. Thus understood, the natural law includes principles that are universally accessible regardless of time, place, or culture. In Aquinas's words, it is the same in all humans,[27] unchangeable,[28] and cannot be abolished from the hearts of men.[29] It is in light of this teaching that Aquinas interprets St. Paul's argument that the "[g]entiles who have not the law do by nature what the law requires, they are a law to themselves, even though they do not have the law. They show that what the law requires is written on their hearts."[30]

How are the precepts of the natural law derived? According to Aquinas, the very first precept is that "good is to be done and

24. *ST,* I-II, 90.4, ad 1.
25. *ST,* Ia, 79.12.
26. *ST,* Ia, 79.13.
27. *ST,* I-II, 94.4.
28. *ST,* I-II, 94.5.
29. *ST,* I-II, 94.6.
30. Romans 2.14–16.

pursued and evil is to be avoided."[31] As he explains, this principle serves the practical reason just as the principle of noncontradiction serves the speculative reason. Just as the speculative intellect naturally apprehends the fact that "the same thing cannot be affirmed and denied at the same time," the practical intellect apprehends that good is to be pursued and evil is to be avoided. By definition, neither the first principles of speculative nor practical reason can be demonstrated. Rather, they are principles without which human reasoning cannot coherently draw any conclusions whatsoever. Otherwise stated, they are first principles inasmuch as they are not derived from any prior practical or speculative knowledge. Still, they are just as surely known as any other knowledge obtained through demonstrative reasoning. In fact, they are naturally known and self-evident for the very same reason that they are not subject to demonstration. This is important from Aquinas's perspective because all practical knowledge (including the moral and political sciences) must rest upon certain principles before any valid conclusions are drawn. To return to the above example, a man who recognizes the evil of adultery will only know that *this* act of adultery must be avoided if he first understands the more fundamental precept that evil ought to be avoided in general. No one can prove this general principle to him. He simply understands it by the habit of synderesis.

Aquinas would be the first to recognize that the simple requirements of doing good and avoiding evil fail to provide human beings with much content for pursuing the moral life. How, one must ask, do we know what human actions *are* good and evil? In response to this Aquinas famously argues what unmistakably distinguishes his moral philosophy from that of Kant, namely, that human beings must consult their natural inclinations. In his response to the question as to whether the precepts of the natural law are one or many, Aquinas provides the following explanation. Beyond the mere knowledge that good is to be pursued and evil avoided

31. *ST,* I-II, 94.2.

our natural inclinations are the most fundamental guide to understanding where the natural law is directing us. In other words, our natural inclinations reveal to us what the most fundamental human goods are. What are these natural inclinations from which the precepts of the natural law are derived? As Aquinas explains, man first has natural inclinations "in accordance with the nature he has in common with all substances . . . such as preserving human life and warding off its obstacles." Second, there are inclinations we have in common with other animals, such as "sexual intercourse," the "education of offspring and so forth." And finally there are inclinations specific to man's rational nature, such as the inclination to "know the truth about God," to "shun ignorance," and to "live in society." Hence, Aquinas says, "according to the order of natural inclination, is the order of the precepts of the natural law."[32]

Two things should be mentioned with regard to Aquinas's connection between morality and natural inclinations. First, Aquinas is obviously not arguing that the natural inclinations *simply are* the precepts of the natural law. Such an interpretation would result in absurd conclusions. Just because human beings have an inclination to sexual intercourse, for instance, it does not follow that responding to this inclination is unqualifiedly good regardless of how they go about it. To appreciate Aquinas's true meaning it is helpful to refer back to what we observed earlier is the ultimate basis for morality, namely, human happiness. As we recall, such happiness is neither a subjective feeling nor an experience of pleasure, but the reaching of a goal that consists in the realization of the human person's full potential *as human*. Seen in this light, the inclinations that are most fundamental to our nature (and from which the precepts of the natural law are derived) must be pursued in accordance with the ultimate goal of happiness itself. Indeed, to pursue our inclinations in the best way means pursuing them in accordance, not with our own subjective preferences, but with the natural orientation of the inclinations themselves. Only by so doing will a person's

32. Ibid.

response to his inclinations be consistent with a proper ordering to the reaching of his true perfection, that is, his happiness. So, for example, in experiencing their sexual desires human beings must also realize that such inclinations are oriented toward some aspect of human fulfillment, in this case, toward the procreation of other human beings and the sustaining of the human race. Upon this realization, the reasonable person will further conclude that sexual activity that does not respect this natural orientation (such as homosexuality or contraception) is a hindrance to the very purpose of the inclination itself. This appears to be what Aquinas means when he adds, in a response to an objection included in the same article, that the natural inclinations belong to the natural law only "insofar as they are ruled by reason."[33] A properly functioning human being, for Aquinas, does not make choices that run counter to the inherent purposiveness in those inclinations fundamental to human nature. As we observed in the previous section, the "order of reason" is precisely that which guides the human being toward his fulfillment as a human. Hence, this method of deriving moral norms is not meant as a competing standard of morality against the ultimate goal of happiness. To be a properly functioning human being with respect to our inclinations is, for Aquinas, precisely to be happy (to the extent that one can be happy in this life). Responding to a natural inclination in a way that frustrates its natural orientation does not violate some abstract principle of "living according to nature" that is unconnected with one's happiness. On the contrary, such actions make the agent into a worse person and hinder him from reaching the completion and "proper human functioning" in which his terrestrial happiness chiefly consists.[34]

In light of these considerations, we may conclude that Aquinas would not accept the opposition insisted upon by Kant be-

33. *ST,* I-II, 94.2, ad 2.

34. Those familiar with modern commentators on Aquinas's ethics will recognize that my interpretation of *ST,* I-II, 94.2, is largely inspired by that of Ralph McInerny, who discusses this section of Aquinas's moral teaching on pages 40–62 of his *Ethica Thomistica* (Washington, D.C.: The Catholic University of America Press, 1982).

tween human reason and the direction of our natural inclinations. That for Aquinas there exists a fundamental harmony between reason and inclination is evident in the fact that one level of man's inclinations is precisely that which is "according to the nature of his reason," and that the very activity in which happiness consists, namely, contemplation, is a prompting of natural inclination at its highest level. Furthermore, Aquinas sees no difficulty in the claim that natural inclinations, properly interpreted, are signs as to what humans *ought to be doing* because of his emphatically teleological approach to morality. Aquinas would not say that he is "deriving an *ought* from an *is*" because human nature itself has the *ought* already built into it precisely in the form of natural inclinations.[35] As we have seen, this does not mean that actions are morally good regardless of how one may respond to their inclinations. Aquinas would recognize that just because certain men happen to murder each other is no indication that they should. But this does not mean that morality is not derived from human nature in the sense that it directs us toward that human perfection in which our happiness consists. If Aquinas can be accused of deriving a value from a fact, he derives it not from the facts of what human beings actually do, but rather from the facts of what human nature is capable of becoming if the true meaning of our inclinations are followed. The problem with Kant's moral philosophy, from the Thomistic perspective, is that it separates morality from the ultimate *good for man* and detaches reason from what is ultimately

35. This interpretation of Aquinas's natural law theory finds its antithesis in the interpretation of John Finnis and Germain Grisez. For an alternative interpretation of *ST,* I-II, 94.2, which denies that the natural inclinations are informative as to the content of morality, see Grisez's seminal article entitled "The First Principle of Practical Reason," *Natural Law Forum* 10 (1965): 168–201. For criticism of Grisez, see Ralph McInerny's "The Principles of Natural Law," *American Journal of Jurisprudence* 25 (1980): 1–15, and chapter 3 of his *Ethica Thomistica* (Washington, D.C.: The Catholic University of America Press, 1982). For a more recent version of the argument, see John Finnis's *Aquinas: Moral, Political, and Legal Theory* (Oxford: Oxford University Press, 1998), chaps. 3–4. For a critique of Finnis, see Jean Porter's "Reason, Nature, and the End of Human Life: A Consideration of John Finnis' *Aquinas,*" *Journal of Religion* 80, no. 3 (July 2000): 476–84.

befitting to human nature.[36] As we will eventually see, this is what allows Aquinas to provide the moral basis for the institution of punishment that Kantian principles fail to provide.

The Political Nature of Man and the Thomistic Theory of the Common Good

Now that we have established the incompatibility between Aquinas's moral thought and those of Kant and Bentham, it remains to consider the basis of his political philosophy as a foundation for his philosophy of punishment. Although he has little in common with Kant and Bentham regarding political matters, the most helpful point of contrast is between Aquinas's political thought and the principles underlying the unfair advantage theory of punishment discussed in the previous chapter. As we observed, the unfair advantage theory is based upon what most of its proponents agree to be the liberal tradition of political philosophy. The particular aspect of that tradition they seem to have in mind is the conception of political society as a "cooperative venture" of persons (Hobbesian and Lockean in origin) coming together to pursue their own individual interests more effectively.

36. As Anthony Lisska has skillfully argued, Aquinas's natural law theory is not subject to the Kantian (and contemporary analytic) criticism that an *is* may not be derived from an *ought* (or that a "fact" may not be derived from a "value"). The reason for this is that Aquinas begins with what Lisska calls an "ontology of dispositional properties." In other words, Aquinas is not pulling an *ought* out of thin air because he believes that human nature is already disposed toward a natural perfection that provides the content for morality from the beginning: "A human nature, of its very being, is composed of a set of dispositional properties metaphysically directed towards development. . . . The 'value' as end is not added on to the essence like paint to a bench. The value, as end, is the realization of the dispositional properties. End is to disposition as act is to potency. The concept of end is built into the very concept of the disposition. This is the significance of Aquinas's often-used passage that 'the good is an end.' If this end is what perfects the essence and if the perfection is what one means by 'well-being' or eudaimonia, then what does not lead to well-being hinders the development of the natural dispositions. The value is not derived from the fact. The value is built into the fact as actualization is built into potency" (*Aquinas's Theory of Natural Law: An Analytic Reconstruction,* 108).

Hence, Herbert Morris observes that membership in political society necessarily involves assuming a certain set of "burdens" in order to enjoy the "benefits" that society provides.[37] What justifies such membership, in turn, is that the benefits enjoyed outweigh the burdens shouldered, so that citizens may not complain that the restrictions of the law violate what is the fundamental moral reality of their existence, namely, their freedom. In some way, the tacit consent we give by living in society implies that the restrictions of the law, and the burdens that accompany them, are actually self-imposed. Hence, obedience to the law is not inconsistent with autonomy under the liberal conception of political society, which is something created by human beings and for human beings considered strictly as individuals.

In stark contrast to this is Aquinas's claim (following Aristotle) that political society is natural and that one of the most important natural goods to which human beings are inclined (as we saw in the last section) is "to live in society." This doctrine is taken primarily from the first book of Aristotle's *Politics* upon which Aquinas wrote an extensive commentary.[38] Following "the Philosopher" Aquinas believes that political society [*civitas*] emerges from the needs and aspirations of human nature itself.[39] Thus understood,

37. See "Persons and Punishment," 25–26.

38. Although the commentary is only completed through book 3, chap. 8, of Aristotle's *Politics,* Aquinas seems to have commented upon what he considered to be the *Politics's* theoretical core.

39. It should not go unmentioned that my interpretation of Aquinas's political thought, like my interpretation of the natural law, is contrary to that of John Finnis. According to Finnis, Aquinas's understanding of political society is merely instrumental. In many ways, Finnis's interpretation of Aquinas's political theory is closer to that of the unfair advantage theory we examined in chapter two and of which Finnis is one of the architects. According to Finnis, Aquinas, like the unfair advantage theorists and unlike Aristotle, understands political society as a cooperative venture at the service of individual interests. Hence, its limited scope should be that of securing justice (fairness) and peace (security). According to Finnis, Aquinas's theory of political society is "not readily distinguishable from the 'grand simple principle' (itself open to interpretation and diverse applications) of John Stuart Mill's *On Liberty*" (*Aquinas: Moral, Political, and Legal Theory,* 228). For criticism of this interpretation, more in keeping with my own reading of Aquinas, see Law-

it is neither an invention of human ingenuity nor an artificial construction designed to make up for human nature's shortcomings. It is, rather, a prompting of nature itself that sets humans apart from all other natural creatures. To be sure, political society is not simply *given* by nature. It is rather something to which human beings naturally aspire and which is necessary for the full perfection of their existence. The capacity for political society is not natural to man, therefore, in the same way as the five senses are natural. The naturalness of politics is more appropriately compared to the naturalness of moral virtue.[40] Even though human beings are inclined to moral virtue, acquiring the virtues nonetheless requires both education and habituation. In a similar way, even though human beings are inclined to live in political societies, such societies must still be established, built, and maintained by human industry. To live a full human life is to live in political society, and Aquinas makes a great deal of Aristotle's claim that one who is separated from society so as to be completely apolitical must be either subhuman or superhuman, either a "beast or a god."[41]

Aquinas admits, of course, that political society is not the only natural community. The family is natural in perhaps an even stronger sense and is prior to political society. The priority of the family, however, is not a priority of importance, since politics aims at a higher and nobler good than the family. It is rather a priority of development. In other words, politics surpasses all other communities in dignity while at the same time depending upon and presupposing the family. On this point Aquinas follows Aristotle's explanation of how political society develops from other lower societies including both the family and the village. The human family comes into existence from the nearly universal tendency of males and females joining together for purposes of procreation. Humans

---

rence Dewan's "St. Thomas, John Finnis, and the Political Good," *The Thomist* 64, no. 3 (2000): 337–74.

40. *Commentary on the Politics,* Book 1, Lesson 1 [40].

41. Aristotle's *Politics,* 1253a27; cf. Aquinas's *Commentary,* Book 1, Lesson 1 [39].

share with other animals (and even plants) a "natural appetite to leave after them another being like themselves,"[42] and immediately see the utility if not the necessity of both parents remaining available to provide for the needs of the children and one another. As families grow in size and number there also seems to be a tendency for them to gravitate toward one another and form villages. The reasons for this are primarily utilitarian. Whereas the household suffices for providing the daily necessities of life, the village is necessary for providing nondaily commodities.[43] What Aquinas and Aristotle seem to have in mind in describing the emergence of the village is the division of labor. Whereas humans can reproduce and survive quite easily in families, life becomes much more productive and affluent when families come together in villages, since one man can now specialize in a certain task while fulfilling his family's remaining material needs through barter and trade.

Despite the village's usefulness to man, it nevertheless leaves him incomplete. This is partly because the village is still relatively small and so the effectiveness of the division of labor remains limited. Much more useful is the conglomeration of several villages, which provides a wider variety of commodities and specializations to be shared by means of exchange.[44] This is one reason why the village is eclipsed by political society, which proves much more useful to human beings because of its greater size and much more elaborate governmental structure. There is, however, a far more important reason why political society comes into existence. In addition to yielding greater protection and economic benefits, it also enhances the moral and intellectual lives of human beings. By identifying with a political community, human beings begin to see the world in broader terms than the mere satisfaction of their bodily desires and physical needs. Whereas the residents of the village better serve their individual interests, the goal of the po-

42. *Commentary on the Politics,* Book 1, Lecture 1 [18].
43. *Commentary on the Politics,* Book 1, Lecture 1 [27].
44. *Commentary on the Politics,* Book 1, Lecture 1 [31].

litical community becomes the good of the whole, or the common good, which Aquinas claims (following Aristotle) is "better and more divine than the good of the individual."[45] The political community is thus understood as the first community (larger than the family) for which the individual makes great sacrifices, since it is not merely a larger cooperative venture for mutual economic benefit. It is, rather, the social setting in which man truly finds his highest natural fulfillment. In this sense, the political community, even though not directed to the individual good, better serves the individual by promoting a life of virtue in which human existence can be greatly ennobled. It is in this context that Aquinas argues (again following Aristotle) that although political society originally comes into being for the sake of living, it exists for the sake of "living well."[46]

Aquinas takes Aristotle's argument that political society transcends the village and completes human social existence to prove that the city is natural. Similar, but not identical, to this claim is Aquinas's further assertion that man is by nature a "civic and social animal."[47] To support this, Aquinas refers us to Aristotle's observation that human beings are the only animals possessing the ability to exercise speech. Not to be confused with mere voice [*vox*], speech [*loquutio*] involves the communication of thoughts and concepts between persons. Whereas voice is found in many different animals that communicate their immediate desires and aversions to one another (seen in the dog's bark and the lion's roar), speech includes a conscious conception of what one is saying.[48] By means of speech, therefore, human beings may collectively deliberate on core civic matters regarding "what is useful and what is harmful," as well as "the just and the unjust."[49] Whereas other animals exhibit a certain social tendency (as bees

45. *Commentary on the Politics,* Book 1, Lecture 1 [11].
46. *Commentary on the Politics,* Book 1, Lecture 1 [31].
47. *ST,* I-II, 72.4.
48. *Commentary on the Politics,* Book 1, Lecture 1 [36].
49. *Commentary on the Politics,* Book 1, Lecture 1 [37].

instinctively work to preserve their hive), only humans are social in the sense that they cooperate through speech to pursue a common understanding of justice, virtue, and the good. Since speech is the outward expression of his inner rationality, man is political by nature for the same reason he is naturally rational.

Although somewhat conventional, the above analysis of Aquinas's understanding of the political has been challenged by legal philosopher and Aquinas interpreter John Finnis. Instead of interpreting Aquinas's theory of political society as more or less Aristotelian, Finnis argues that Aquinas's political thought is actually closer to Finnis's own doctrine as explained in his celebrated 1980 study, *Natural Law and Natural Rights.* In that work, Finnis takes up the question of the common good as it applies to political society. After observing that one may speak of a common good with respect to a family, an athletic team, a business, or virtually any other community, Finnis identifies the common good of political society as "the securing of a whole ensemble of material and other conditions that tend to favour the realization, by each individual in the community, of his or her personal development."[50] With these remarks, Finnis suggests what he will later make explicit, namely, that the common good of political society is not an end in itself but rather an *instrumental* good in the service of the aspirations and goals held by the individuals who constitute the political community. Whereas smaller groups may have a common goal, therefore (as the sailors of a ship might share the common goal of reaching their destination), the political community cannot be said to have a "definite and completely obtainable objective."[51] Rather than a definite goal, the political community aspires toward, in Finnis's words, an "ensemble of conditions" necessary for the definitive goals of individuals. Hence, Finnis's early account of the political common good appears quite similar (if not identical) to that implied by Herbert Morris (seen in the previous chapter) according

50. *Natural Law and Natural Rights,* 154.
51. Ibid., 155.

to which political society is a cooperative venture by which individual goals are pursued more effectively than they are individually or within other smaller and less authoritative communities (such as the family). The essential point is that, for Finnis, political society is teleologically subordinate to the individual because it essentially exists for the sake of the individual's goals, that is, the fulfillments of the individual's "life-plan." Indeed, this is precisely what it means to say that it is an instrumental good.

According to Finnis's Aquinas, living and participating in political society is not a fundamental good to which humans are inclined by nature, but rather something that humans construct so as more effectively to pursue those things to which they are indeed naturally inclined (such as the goods of family life, knowledge, and religion). Finnis's explanation of his position is stated most clearly as he explains what he thinks Aquinas means when he says that political society is "natural."

> Contrary to what is often supposed, Aquinas's many statements that we are "naturally political animals" have nothing particularly to do with the *political* community. So they cannot be pressed into service as implying that the state or its common good is the object of natural inclination, is an intrinsic or basic good. . . . In human affairs which are matters of deliberation and choice, what is natural is settled by asking what is intelligent and reasonable. That in turn is settled by looking to the first principles of practical reason, to the basic human goods. So the *civitas* could be called natural if participation in it (*a*) instantiates in itself a basic human good, or (*b*) is a rationally required component in, or indispensable means to instantiating, one or more basic human goods. Aquinas's opinion, rather clearly, is that it is the latter.[52]

Finnis's attempt to steer Aquinas in the direction of the modern liberal tradition of political thought is, as he himself recognizes, very much at odds with more traditional interpretations of Aquinas's political thought.[53] According to Finnis, again, Aquinas's state-

52. *Aquinas: Moral, Political, and Legal Thought,* 245–46.

53. For an example of the more traditional interpretation, see Thomas Gilby, *The Political Thought of Thomas Aquinas* (Chicago: University of Chicago Press, 1958).

ment that humans are inclined to live in society has no reference whatsoever to *political* society. In Finnis's own words, Aquinas's remarks "do no more than assert our social not solitary nature, our need to have interpersonal relationships for necessities such as food and clothing, for speech, and in general for getting along together [*convivere*]; or the need for various social but not peculiarly political virtues, such as good faith in promising and testifying, and so forth."[54] Finnis's interpretation of Aquinas's statement that man is naturally inclined to "live in society," therefore, is not merely one that adds other forms of human society to the political, but rather one that deliberately excludes the political from its range of meaning. Political society thus becomes a "mere means" to realizing the full potential of human beings, which includes their membership in other forms of society such as the family and some form of religious society. Whereas membership in these other societies (or toward "interpersonal relationships" in general) is a basic good, political society "is not basic but, rather, instrumental to securing human goods which are basic . . . and none of which is in itself specifically political, i.e. concerned with the state."[55]

Is the above interpretation of Aquinas's political teaching correct? Shortly after Finnis's study of Aquinas was published, Fr. Lawrence Dewan, O.P., examined Finnis's interpretation of Aquinas's political teaching in some detail. Whereas Dewan takes issue

54. *Aquinas,* 246.

55. Finnis adds an interesting remark at the end of this statement: "If that proposition needs qualification, the qualification concerns the restoration of justice by the irreparable modes of punishment reserved to the state" (*Aquinas,* 247). What Finnis seems to mean by this is that Aquinas's retributivism prevents him from saying that all aspects of the political are instrumental, since doing so would commit him to some version of the utilitarian thesis that political punishment is only justified by its usefulness to individuals. This is, of course, however, a qualification rather than an exception to Finnis's point about Aquinas. Punishment's noninstrumental nature should not, Finnis would say, lead one to conclude that political society itself is noninstrumental, but rather that it possesses a noninstrumental dimension (i.e., retributive punishment) once it is established on purely instrumental grounds. As Finnis points out, no other society (such as the family) enjoys the qualifications or jurisdiction as political society to distribute punishment with a view to "restorative justice" (*Aquinas,* 252).

with several of Finnis's claims (especially Finnis's denial that, for Aquinas, the chief goal of political society is to lead its members to virtue), the core of his criticism relates precisely to the question of whether for Aquinas political society is, in itself, a basic human good to which humans have a natural inclination. Dewan begins his case against Finnis's interpretation in this regard by recalling a passage from Aquinas having to do with the virtue by which the proper amount of punishment is desired and inflicted, namely, *vindicatio*. Aquinas makes the following claim:

> As the *Philosopher* states (Ethic. ii, 1), aptitude to *virtue* is in us by *nature*, but the complement of *virtue* is in us through habituation or some other *cause*. Hence it is evident that *virtues* perfect us so that we follow in due manner our *natural* inclinations, which belong to the *natural* right. Wherefore to every definite *natural* inclination there corresponds a special *virtue*.[56]

The point that Dewan wishes to make has nothing to do with punishment per se, but rather with the connection in Aquinas's mind between virtues and natural inclinations. That *vindicatio* is the virtue that perfects the natural inclination to "remove harm" is an example of the fact that all virtues seem to pertain to some natural inclination or another (one may observe that, for example, the virtue of temperance perfects our inclinations to food, drink, and sexual intercourse; the virtue of studiousness perfects our inclination to obtain knowledge; the virtue of religion perfects our inclination to honor and worship God, etc.). With this Thomistic principle having been established, Dewan then moves on to highlight Aquinas's discussion of the virtue of legal justice. As Aquinas explains, the virtue of justice pertains to human beings' relations with one another, which "can happen in two ways." First, one may consider the relation to individual persons, which are governed by the requirements of what Aquinas calls "commutative" and "distributive" justice. Second, one may consider an individual's relation to the community as a whole, "in so far as a man who serves

56. *ST,* II-II, 108.2 (cf. Dewan, "Aquinas, Finnis, and the Political Good," 351).

a community, serves all those who are included in that community."[57] According to Aquinas, the latter relation is governed by the requirements of legal justice, which, contrary to commutative and distributive justice, is a "general virtue." By this Aquinas means that legal justice may embrace any virtue whatsoever so long as that virtue is referred to the common good (Aquinas's most frequent example of this is an act of a soldier's courage, which is also an act of general or legal justice when the fear of death is overcome for the sake of protecting the common good). The point that Dewan wishes to make from all of this is that, for Aquinas, legal justice is a very real and important virtue in Aquinas's mind, so important that Aquinas compares it with the highest virtue in his entire schema (and in the Christian tradition), namely, charity.[58] Whereas charity is a general virtue in the sense that any act of virtue whatsoever may be referred to the divine good (as when, for example, one exercises the virtue of temperance in fasting in order to honor God), legal justice is the virtue by which other acts of virtue may be referred to the *common* good. As Aquinas continues,

> Accordingly, just as *charity* which regards the Divine *good* as its proper object, is a special *virtue* in respect of its *essence*, so too legal *justice* is a special *virtue* in respect of its *essence*, in so far as it regards the common *good* as its proper object. And thus it is in the sovereign [*in principe*] principally and by way of a mastercraft, while it is secondarily and administratively in his subjects.[59]

One may thus far summarize Dewan's criticism of Finnis's position with the following syllogism:

> All virtues pertain to some natural inclination
> (from ST, II-II, 108.2).
>
> Legal justice is a virtue (from ST, II-II, 58.5).
>
> Therefore, legal justice pertains to some natural inclination.

57. *ST,* II-II, 58.5.
58. *ST,* II-II, 58.6 (cf. Dewan, "Aquinas, Finnis, and the Political Good," 353).
59. Ibid.

From this Dewan deduces that if legal justice must pertain to some natural inclination pertaining to the common good, it must be the inclination of which Aquinas speaks in ST, I-II, 94.2, to "live in society." Since this discussion, by Finnis's own analysis, marks out the basic goods of human nature, it would seem to follow that Aquinas holds there to be a natural inclination to the political good and that human beings are naturally political animals in precisely the sense in which Aristotle meant. Again, however, Finnis would respond by saying that when Aquinas speaks of the common good, he does not wish us to understand the *political* good, but rather the more generic good of sociability in general. As Dewan observes, therefore, Finnis wants to say that the virtue of legal justice perfects the individual person in his relations with any community to which he may belong, whether that community is political or not (thus, according to Finnis, one may exercise the virtue of legal justice as a member of the IBM corporation no less than as a member of some body politic). To be sure, Finnis does not object to there being a natural inclination to certain generic kinds of sociability, and so, in his mind, Aquinas's discussion of legal justice (to which there corresponds a natural inclination) in terms of the "common good" does not pose any particular difficulty. Even in the passage cited above comparing legal justice with charity in which Aquinas asserts that legal justice is primarily in "the prince" [*in principe*], Finnis could just as easily, in Dewan's words, "translate in a way which would make *princeps* apply even to the president of IBM."[60] In short, the texts considered thus far do not, in Finnis's mind, demonstrate that, for Aquinas, the virtue of legal justice implies a natural inclination toward the good of political society, but only to sociability and the cultivation of "interpersonal relationships" in general.

But is this really Aquinas's view? As unlikely as it may seem to some readers, Aquinas's use of the word *princeps* in the above passage does not necessarily need to have a political connotation. If, perhaps, he had said that the virtue of legal justice existed pri-

60. Dewan, "Aquinas, Finnis, and the Political Good," 353, n. 23.

marily in the *rex*, the *princeps civitati* or the *princeps regni*, the case against Finnis's interpretation would be much stronger, since legal justice would thus emerge as a primarily political virtue and indicate a corresponding political natural inclination. As Dewan continues his criticism, however, the plausibility of Finnis's position lessens dramatically as one proceeds to consider some important remarks made by Aquinas in his account of the virtue of prudence. Aquinas asks in ST, II-II, 47.10 whether the virtue of prudence extends to the ruling of many [*ad regimen multitudinis*], and he responds in the affirmative. As Dewan points out, Aquinas's reply to the first objection is very important for evaluating Finnis's interpretation. The objection states that, rather than prudence, it is actually the virtue of legal justice that constitutes the perfection of ruling a multitude, since legal justice is that which pertains to the individual's relation to the common good. Aquinas's reply is telling:

> Now just as every moral *virtue* that is directed to the common *good* is called legal *justice*, so the *prudence* that is directed to the common *good* is called political *prudence*, for the latter stands in the same relation to legal *justice*, as *prudence* simply so called to moral *virtue*.[61]

The analogy that Aquinas sets up is clear:

$$\frac{\text{“Political” prudence}}{\text{Legal justice}} = \frac{\text{Prudence “simply so called”}}{\text{Moral virtue}}$$

With these remarks, Aquinas does not explicitly state that the virtue of legal justice is primarily directed to the common good to a political community, but it is difficult to deny that this is the strong implication. If the virtue which "stands in the same relation" to legal justice as prudence simply so called stands in relation to moral virtue as such, it seems necessary, or at least extremely likely, to conclude that Aquinas understands legal justice to be a political virtue as well. If the two virtues really are analogous in the above sense, legal justice appears to be the general virtue that (primarily)

61. Cf. Dewan, "Aquinas, Finnis, and the Political Good," 354.

directs the other virtues to the common good of political society just as political prudence directs the practical intellect to the common good of political society. If the analogy holds up, therefore, it appears that that the *princeps* of which Aquinas spoke in his comparison between legal justice and charity is, after all, the *princeps* of a *civitas* or *regnum* rather than that of any community whatsoever. Even if one attempts to stretch Aquinas's use of the term "political" in referring to political prudence to include the governing of any sort of community whatsoever, that interpretation is proven false, as Dewan points out, in the following article where Aquinas distinguishes between prudence "simply so called," "domestic" prudence (which pertains to the governing of a household), and the "political" prudence he just mentioned, which, as he now says, is "ordered to the common good of a city or kingdom" [*ordinatur ad bonum commune civitatis vel regni*].[62] Taking these texts together, therefore, it seems extremely doubtful that Aquinas's understands the natural inclination to "live in society" in terms of any multitude whatsoever that could apply just as easily to an athletic team or a business association as to a political community. On the contrary, because legal justice is analogous to political prudence, and since political prudence refers exclusively to a political community, the common good which is the object of legal justice is to be interpreted as that of political society. Hence the corresponding natural inclination should also have political society as its object, which means that Finnis's denial that, for Aquinas, the political community is not a "basic good" is untenable. As Dewan concludes, "to make [the political good] more instrumental as regards such things as family common good, is to be rejected, if the goal is to interpret Thomas Aquinas."[63]

62. *ST,* II-II, 47.11; cf. Dewan, "Aquinas, Finnis, and the Political Good," 355; see also *ST,* II-II, 50.1 and Dewan's commentary on 356–57. In the latter passage, Aquinas presents "regnative" prudence by which one governs a city or a kingdom as the virtue of prudence in its "special and most perfect sense" [*secundum specialem et perfectissimam sui rationem*].

63. Dewan, "Aquinas, Finnis, and the Political Good," 357.

Human Law and the Limits of the Political

From these considerations, we may conclude that much of Aquinas's political teaching is, in fact, adapted from the Aristotelian political science which he studied in great detail and which he largely embraced. Perhaps the most central Aristotelian political doctrine in Aquinas's view is the inherent goodness and naturalness of political society. As we have seen, this profoundly important dimension of his political teaching distinguishes him from nearly all modern and contemporary political philosophers, including those who represent the various theories of punishment examined in the first two chapters. However, it is also necessary to understand, not least of all for Aquinas's own philosophy of punishment, that in addition to being good and natural political society is also limited in several important respects, not all of which were pointed out by Aristotle but are unique to Aquinas's teaching. As we have already seen, Aquinas believes that the human laws governing political societies must be somewhat limited in scope. For example, the fact that something like the practice of usury is unjust does not necessarily mean that political society can or should forbid it.[64] In other words, human law is incapable of regulating every dimension of social life. Perhaps he would elaborate that attempting to police the practice of usury may in some cases hinder a society's ability to prevent more serious crimes like murder, assault, and robbery.[65] As Aquinas explains, the attempt to police every aspect of social life would ultimately do more harm than good. This is due, in his view, to the limited nature of human law and political society itself and is one of the reasons why God has wisely chosen to apply his own divine law to human affairs. In addition to its infallibility and the fact that it applies to the "interior movements" of man's soul, divine law is able to punish all vices while making possible and demanding the moral perfection

64. *ST,* II-II, 78.1 ad 3.
65. *ST,* I-II, 96.2.

from humans that God expects.[66] Human law, on the other hand, must often settle for preventing only those things that imperil the immediate safety of those protected by it. This is not to say that human law does not also look to promote virtue, but the virtues it succeeds in instilling seldom fulfill the full moral capabilities of human citizens.

Moreover, Aquinas's definition of natural law as the specifically human participation in the eternal law indicates something emphatically transpolitical about human nature that cannot be found in the Aristotelian doctrine from which Aquinas develops important parts of his own. Whereas Aristotle had argued for the existence of a natural standard of morality, he never suggested an overarching human community with a supreme lawgiver, and yet this is precisely what Aquinas's teaching explicitly affirms.[67] Not only is the natural law a universally binding law for all humans in all places (something that Aristotle never recognized), it also points to the existence of a God that consciously and providently governs human affairs as a whole (also something absent from the Aristotelian teaching). Without such divine origins, the natural law would lose its legal character, since under Aquinas's own definition there can be no law that does not derive from someone who "has care of the community."[68] Hence the very existence of natural law implies a more universal community under God that transcends political society. This is also apparent by looking at the epistemological basis of Aquinas's natural law theory. As we have seen, human beings know the precepts of the natural law by a natural habit Aquinas calls synderesis. Whereas these precepts may be reinforced by the political community, they are first promulgated by nature itself and instilled in man's mind by the hand of God. They owe nothing, therefore, to political society for their content. This is considerably different from the Aristotelian doctrine that includes no teaching regarding the self-evident first principles of natural morality upon which Aquinas's natural law theory stands

66. *ST,* I-II, 91.4.

67. *ST,* I-II, 91.1–2.

68. *ST,* I-II, 90.3–4.

or falls and that seems to suggest (contrary to Aquinas's view) that no universally binding law even exists that is not somewhat subject to change from regime to regime.[69] This difference points out in a particularly striking way the un-Aristotelian character of Aquinas's insistence that all regimes, whether they realize it or not, are under God's supreme authority and owe the binding force of their laws to the more fundamental natural law of which God is the sole author.

Finally, political society as Aquinas understands it is limited in an even further sense. We may observe this by returning to Aquinas's claim that political society is natural. In one sense, of course, this affirmation of Aristotle's teaching constitutes a very high exaltation of the political. Only by living in political society is man capable of achieving his full natural potential. Thus understood, politics is no mere instrumental good (as in the teachings of Kant, Bentham, and the unfair advantage theory of punishment), but is part of the very fabric of the human person, and thus the individual's participation in political society is a great intrinsic good for the individual as well as for society. On the other hand, the characterization of politics as natural also means for Aquinas that it falls short of man's ultimate *supernatural* end. For this reason Aquinas never ceases to remind us that, although politics constitutes an important aspect of the natural law, "man is not ordained to the body politic [*communitas politica*] according to all that he is and has."[70] By this Aquinas means that beyond the fulfillment of the natural law, the active participation in political society, and even the exercise of the moral virtues, human beings find their complete perfection and happiness only in beatitude—the supernatural end to which they are called. As we observed, beatitude is only fully completed in the afterlife,[71] but even in his terrestrial existence man is called upon to exercise a supernatural perfection made possible through his active cooperation with

69. *Nicomachean Ethics*, 1134b33.

70. *ST*, I-II, 21.4 ad 3.

71. *ST*, I-II, 5.3.

God's grace. Precisely because it is a natural institution, political society is not equipped to guide human beings toward the attainment of this higher supernatural vocation. In this respect it must yield to the Church, which (unlike political society) is divinely established and primarily concerned with the distribution of divine grace and the salvation of souls.[72] Again, to say that political society is merely natural is not to suggest that it should only concern man's basic natural needs such as food, shelter, and safety. The common good that political authorities pursue includes the maintenance of a just society where individual citizens may flourish physically as well as morally. Politics thus ought to promote the natural virtues (most of all justice), which can contribute to the human soul's preparation for the reception of divine grace and the infusion of the supernatural virtues of faith, hope, and, above all, charity. The best one can hope from political society is that citizens will be well disposed to receive the grace available to them through the Church, which transcends politics both in its universality and in the finality of its purpose.

72. *On Kingship*, Book I, Chapters 14–15.

4

THE MORAL BASIS OF PUNISHMENT

Aquinas's Retributivism

The Metaphysics of Punishment

Everything that Aquinas says about punishment in the political order must be understood in relation to his concept of punishment itself. Following a common patristic doctrine, Aquinas argues that punishment is a kind of evil.[1] In fact, all evils that pertain to rational creatures (human beings and angels) must fall into one of two categories: punishment *(poena)* or fault *(culpa).* Aquinas's argument for this is very straightforward. There are two kinds of evil regarding the rational creature because there are two kinds of corresponding goods, one that pertains to man's actions and the other of which pertains to his "form and integrity." Naturally, the evil of fault is opposed to the goodness of a voluntary action. When such actions lack the due measure and order they ought to have, they may be called evil in this sense. As Aquinas explains, "a disordered act of the will has the nature of fault, for a person is blamed and rendered culpable inasmuch as he voluntarily does a disordered act."[2] On the other hand, punishment refers to any evil the rational creature "suffers" or "undergoes." Because all

1. *Summa Theologiae,* Ia. 48.5; *On Evil,* Q. 1, a. 4.
2. *On Evil,* Q. 1, a. 4.

evil consists in the privation of some good, Aquinas understands punishment to include all instances where rational creatures suffer *harm* of any kind. This would not only include the infliction of punishment by a court of justice, but all other so-called natural evils such as disease and physical disability. Aquinas's definition of punishment would even extend to the apparently moral evil of vice. Whereas a vice such as gluttony might be brought about by disordered voluntary actions (i.e., faults), the resulting vice itself consists in the lack of a perfection the gluttonous man ought to have (i.e., temperance regarding food and drink), and is therefore considered by Aquinas as a punitive evil from which he suffers.[3] Since punishment is defined as any evil affecting a rational creature's "form and integrity," the distinction between punishment and fault is intended to be exhaustive. Thus Aquinas approvingly cites Augustine, who taught that "fault is the evil we do, but punishment is the evil we suffer."[4]

Though Aquinas's definition of punishment is intended to be very broad, it would be an oversimplification to say that punishment refers to all evils not identifiable with fault. In that case there would be no special reason why punishment would have to apply only to the rational creature. As Aquinas explains, however, there are two additional characteristics of punishment (beyond the fact that it includes a certain kind of "suffering" [*passio*]) that further specify its nature and distinguish it from evil in the generic sense. The first is that punishment must be "contrary to the will" of the one being punished.[5] Since only the rational creature has a will (Aquinas defines the will as the "rational appetite"), only rational creatures can be "punished" in the proper sense.[6] This character-

3. *ST,* I-II, 87.2.

4. *On Evil,* Q. 1, a. 4; Cf. Augustine, *On Free Choice,* book 1, chap. 1.

5. Ibid.

6. According to Aquinas, all evils suffered by the rational creature are "contrary to the will" in some sense. If an evil is not contrary to the "actual will," of the one who suffers it, it will either be contrary to his "habitual will" or to the "natural inclination" of his will (*On Evil,* Q. 1, a. 4). By "habitual will," Aquinas means some-

istic of punishment is of particular importance when it comes to the punishment of sinners (by divine authority) or criminals (by human authority). As Aquinas argues, anyone who transgresses the order of justice (human or divine) has been "too indulgent to his will."[7] By this he means that actions are considered sinful when they voluntarily go beyond the sphere of permissibility determined by rightful authority. This is why it is fitting that such faults are answered by punishments that inflict something upon the criminal that is contrary to his overindulgent will. Without making the criminal suffer something "contrary to what he would wish," it is impossible to achieve the "restoration of the equality of justice." This remark shows us that Aquinas endorses a retributive theory of punishment of a kind. As we shall see, however, Aquinas's retributivism is quite different from those retributive theories discussed in chapter two. To cite one example, Aquinas does not adhere to a strict version of the *lex talionis* (as Kant does), which demands that punishment return the same *kind* of evil upon the criminal that he himself perpetrated. Instead, it is sufficient that the criminal's sinful will be repressed by the infliction of some contrary evil, not necessarily for the purpose of rectifying the criminal's will, but for repairing the order of justice that was damaged by the original criminal act. So insistent is Aquinas on this point, he even admits that if a reformed criminal freely submits to the punitive sentence imposed upon him, his penalty "loses somewhat the nature of punishment."[8] It is also why he recommends that wherever possible political authority ought to im-

---

thing like a hypothetical will. As he explains, a punitive evil is contrary to a person's habitual will when it consists in the loss of something "which he would grieve over if he knew [it was lost]." Likewise, a punitive evil may only be contrary to the will's natural inclination when a person loses a natural good of which he may not be fully aware. Thus understood, even if a reformed criminal embraces his punishment willingly (by means of his actual will) out of a concern for justice, his punishment remains contrary to his will by depriving him of something he naturally desires (such as his freedom).

7. *ST,* I-II, 87.6.

8. Ibid.

pose punishments "by depriving a man of what he loves most,"[9] with the extent of the punishment corresponding to the severity of the crime. Again, this dimension of Aquinas's understanding of punishment has emphatically retributive overtones, and the notion of suppressing the criminal's will for the restoration of justice would surely resonate with Kantians and representatives of the unfair advantage theory of punishment. How Aquinas understands the infliction of punishment to have the effect of repairing the order of justice, and how this differs from the rationale provided by Kant and the unfair advantage theory, is something we must take up in detail later on.

The second essential property of punishment, which also explains why only rational creatures can be punished in the proper sense, is that punishment must have "regard to fault." As Aquinas argues, "someone is properly said to be punished when he suffers evil for some act he has committed."[10] When we examine punishment in political society it is not difficult to see why this must be the case. Even if a person is harmed by legitimate political authority, it would not make sense to call it punishment unless he is harmed on account of some voluntary action he performed that has been deemed punishable. Without this condition being met, the infliction of harm is merely an act of aggression. This certainly does not mean that all punishments must be carried out exclusively for retributive reasons. A punishment has "regard to fault" even when the punisher attempts to instruct a criminal by correcting his behavior. Regarding this point, Aquinas persistently reminds us that "punishment may be considered as a medicine, not only healing the past sin, but also preventing from future sin, or conducing to some good."[11] The "good" to which Aquinas refers, moreover, need not even be the good of the criminal on account of whose fault the punishment is inflicted. It may simply be the good of deterrence that the spectacle of punishment provides.

9. *ST,* II-II, 108.3. 10. Ibid. 11. *ST,* II-II, 108.4.

As Aquinas explains, "the punishment that is inflicted according to human laws, is not always intended as a medicine for the one who is punished, but sometimes only for others . . . that at least they may be deterred from crime through fear of punishment."[12] It would be a mistake, of course, to conflate Aquinas's approbation of deterrence with that of the utilitarian theory of punishment. When Aquinas insists that punishment has "regard to fault," he does not mean that deterrence is something that political authorities may pursue at the expense of justice, and the concept of "medicinal punishment" is one that presupposes that the criminal has been found guilty of an offense for which punishment is due.

This is considerably different, one should notice, from Aquinas's notion of divine punishment, whereby God sometimes inflicts punishments with no retributive intentions whatsoever. Hence, Aquinas explains that the blind man of John's gospel was punished neither because of his own sins nor the sins of his parents, but that "the works of God may be manifested, and from them that God be known."[13] And yet even this punishment, in an extended way, is inflicted "regarding fault," not in any retributive sense, but on account of the fault of original sin. For "the very fact that man is in such a condition that he must be helped, either to avoid sin, or to advance in virtue, by means of these misfortunes or defects, pertains to the weakness of human nature, which derives from the sin of our first parent."[14] Of course, human beings are not at liberty to punish criminals for such exclusively therapeutic reasons. When Aquinas, speaking in terms of political affairs, says that punishment must essentially have "regard to fault," he appears to mean that it may only be inflicted as a response to crime (notwithstanding whatever additional reasons God may have for punishing humans). In this sense, Aquinas

12. *ST,* I-II, 97.3 ad 2.

13. Thomas Aquinas, *Commentary on the Gospel of St. John,* vol. 2, trans. James A. Weisheipl, O.P., S.T.M., and Fabian R. Larcher, O.P. (Petersham, Mass.: St. Bede's Publications, 1998), 1301.

14. *On Evil,* Q. 5, a. 4.

does have a conception of criminal punishment that may be considered as a subdivision of the broader definition of punishment which includes all harm suffered by rational creatures.

The Basis of Punishment in Natural Law

The above preliminary observations are primarily descriptive, and the question to which we must now turn is whether Aquinas has a compelling moral justification of punishment. As we have noticed in the previous chapter, the core of Aquinas's moral philosophy is found in his celebrated doctrine of natural law. If the institution of punishment can be morally justified, therefore, it will need to be done primarily in this context. As we also observed, the natural law that lies at the heart of human morality is accessible through the natural inclinations that direct human beings to the most fundamental goods that constitute their happiness. Without the inclinations revealing these most basic goods of human nature, the first precept of the natural law that "good is to be pursued" would have no content and little meaning. As we saw, Aquinas does not argue that the natural inclinations constitute precepts of the natural law themselves. Simply to act upon a natural inclination is no guarantee that one is acting in a morally upright fashion. His purpose was rather to demonstrate the multiplicity of the natural law's precepts by pointing to the multiplicity of human nature's most fundamental inclinations. However, these basic inclinations take on a profoundly moral dimension when viewed in light of the "order of reason," something to which Aquinas refers constantly in his various discussions of morality. We observed in the previous chapter that an ideal example of Aquinas's teaching may be taken from the inclination toward "sexual intercourse" *(coniunctio maris et feminae)*. As he argues, "the order of reason consists in its ordering everything to its end in a fitting manner."[15] Thus, by reflecting upon this particular natural inclination, a rational agent will con-

15. *ST,* II-II, 153.2.

clude not only that sexual intercourse directs one toward a fundamental good of human nature, but will also see that sexual activity has a certain role and purpose within the broader context of human affairs, that is, that it exists for the propagation of the species, within the context of marriage, and so on.[16] By understanding this, all human beings should conclude that pursuing this inclination outside the context of its natural end will result in a fundamentally disordered action. Thus are derived certain moral precepts requiring modesty, purity, and chastity (all of which Aquinas considers under the virtue of temperance), and forbidding such things as fornication and adultery. Only by discerning, in the above manner, the true purpose for which an inclination exists can human beings follow their inclinations in a morally acceptable way that results in genuine human flourishing.

Given Aquinas's assertion as to the central role of natural inclination, it stands to reason that he would identify the moral basis of punishment by pointing to some kind of a natural inclination to punish wrongdoers. If such an inclination exists, it would provide a starting point from which to establish something very much at issue in the philosophy of punishment, namely, the naturalness and goodness of punishment. To be sure, though punishment by its nature is always a certain kind of evil for the one suffering it, it may be considered as a good from the point of view of the institution inflicting it. Now although Aquinas never mentions the word "punishment" in his enumeration of the natural inclinations during his discussion of natural law (in I-II, 94.2), he does identify the all-important inclination for preserving human life and "warding off its obstacles." This, one will recall, is one of the inclinations that man shares with "all substances," not only including other animals but also nonsentient and even inanimate beings as well. It may seem strange that inanimate things exhibit inclinations at all, especially the inclination to "ward off obstacles." It may seem even stranger that such an inclination, experienced by humans,

16. Ibid.

could provide a basis for the institution of punishment. Nevertheless, Aquinas's most explicit argument justifying the punishment of wrongdoers relies precisely upon this phenomenon.

> It has passed from natural things to human affairs that whenever one thing rises up against another, it suffers some detriment therefrom. For we observe in natural things that when one contrary supervenes, the other acts with greater energy, for which reason hot water freezes more rapidly, as stated in *Meteor.* i.12. Wherefore, we find that the natural inclination of man is to repress those who rise up against him. Consequently, whatever rises up against an order, is put down by that order or by some principle thereof. And because sin is an inordinate act, it is evident that whoever sins, commits an offence against an order: wherefore he is put down, in consequence, by that same order, which repression is punishment.[17]

To be sure, this passage raises questions. What could hot water's tendency to "freeze more rapidly" possibly have to do with punishment? Why is the behavior of "natural things" relevant at all to a human institution in need of moral justification? Clearly, Aquinas's appeal to the subrational world is not intended to imply that natural things that are devoid of reason should serve as models for human behavior. The inclination to punish is not natural because it is found in other natural things, but rather because it is part of *human* nature. In this regard it may be compared to other natural inclinations motivating humans to pursue food, drink, and sexual intercourse. Whereas these inclinations direct us to fundamentally good things that are necessary for our survival (either as individuals or as a species), so also the natural inclination to punish criminals directs us to preserving the common good by retaliating against those who threaten it. Much earlier in the *Summa Theologiae,* Aquinas related each of these inclinations to the two faculties of man's "sensitive appetite." On the one hand, all human beings possess a "concupiscible faculty," which refers to that part of the soul whereby man experiences his bodily desires and which is partially constituted by his sexual inclinations used

17. *ST,* I-II, 87.1.

in the above example. According to Aquinas, "concupiscence" is that which drives man "to the acquisition of what is suitable and to the avoiding of what is harmful"[18] in accordance with the desires and aversions of his five senses (especially those of touch and taste). On the other hand, the sensitive appetite also exhibits what Aquinas calls an "irascible faculty," which offers "resistance against corruptive and contrary agencies" and "are a hindrance to the acquisition of what is suitable, and productive of harm."[19] Thus understood, the irascible faculty follows upon the concupiscible and could not exist without it, since the "obstacles" it "fights against" *(impugnet contraria)* are precisely those which stand to prevent us from attaining our concupiscible desires. This is why Aquinas argues that the irascible faculty is the "champion and defender" *(propugnatrix et defensatrix)* of the concupiscible, and is expressed primarily in passions such as hatred and anger, the latter of which naturally seeks to inflict a punitive evil upon its object.[20] Again, the irascible faculty exists in all animals possessing a sensitive appetite, and even a semblance of it is found in inanimate things such as fire, which "resists whatever destroys or hinders its action." When compared with the strikingly similar example of hot water that "freezes more rapidly," Aquinas leaves little room for doubt that the natural inclination to punish, having "passed from natural things to human affairs," is none other than the irascible faculty of the human soul.

Understood strictly as a function of the irascible faculty, the desire to "repress" one's assailants has no special moral significance. When seen as a function of the irascible faculty of the *human* soul, however, the inclination to which Aquinas refers takes on a whole new dimension that is absent in other animals. Like the concupiscible faculty and the inclinations lying at the heart of the natural law, the irascible faculty and the passions associated with it are subject to the judgment of reason.[21] Because of this Aquinas argues that

18. *ST,* Ia. 81.2.
19. Ibid.
20. *ST,* I-IIa. 46.1–2.
21. *ST,* Ia. 81.3.

anger, though a natural and necessary passion of the human soul, becomes evil "if it sets the order of reason aside."[22] In other words, anger becomes sinful when it desires the punishment of "one who has not deserved it, or beyond his deserts, or again contrary to the order prescribed by law, or not for the . . . maintaining of justice and the correction of defaults [*conservatio iustitiae et correctio culpae*]."[23] In this regard the inclination to "repress those who rise up" against us is perfectly analogous to the concupiscible inclinations by which humans pursue sexual intercourse. In both cases, the desires and the ensuing actions are subject to the natural end for which the desires have been given by nature in the first place. In the case of the concupiscible sexual inclinations, human actions must be directed to the goal of human procreation within the context of a true and loving marriage. When they are so directed, the rational agent acts within the order of reason and according to the virtue of chastity. In the case of the irascible inclination to "resist harmful attacks," human actions must be oriented to the natural goals for which this inclination is given, namely, the "maintaining of justice and the correction of defaults." If the order of reason is observed in this case, the virtue manifested is something Aquinas calls "vindication" *(vindicatio)*, a subvirtue of justice by which the correct degree of punishment is desired and pursued. Once again highlighting the role of natural inclination, Aquinas's description of this virtue makes the connection between punishment and the irascible faculty of the human soul unmistakable.

As the Philosopher [Aristotle] states, aptitude to virtue is in us by nature, but the complement of virtue is in us through habituation or some other cause. Hence it is evident that virtues perfect us so that we follow in due manner our natural inclinations, which belong to the natural law. To every definite natural inclination there corresponds a special virtue. Now there is a special inclination of nature to remove harm, for which reason animals have the irascible power distinct from the concupiscible. Man resists harm by defending himself against wrongs, lest

22. *ST,* II-II, 158.2.
23. Ibid.

they be inflicted on him, or he avenges those which have already been inflicted on him, with the intention, not of harming, but of removing the harm done. And this belongs to [the virtue of] vengeance [*vindicatio*], for Tully says that by "vengeance we resist force, or wrong, and in general whatever is obscure (i.e., derogatory), either by self-defense or by avenging it."[24]

By considering this passage alongside Aquinas's explanation of the debt of punishment in I-II, 87.1, we are given to understand that the primary moral basis of punishment rests upon the naturalness of man's inclination to inflict it. As is the case with all of the natural inclinations, of course, this comes with profound moral qualifications when understood in light of virtue and the order of reason which instructs us how to follow our inclinations "in due manner." In other words, the punitive inclination to which Aquinas refers is only enough to determine punishment's naturalness and goodness, not the specific conditions under which punishment may be inflicted. Still, in Aquinas's mind it would be impossible to defend the legitimacy of an institution that deliberately inflicts harm without being anchored in the natural inclinations which, as we have seen, provide the only possible basis of the natural law and of morality itself.

Inclination, Irascibility, and Anger: Implications of a Natural Law Justification of Punishment

Aquinas's appeal to the irascible faculty may seem like a strange way of providing a moral basis of punishment, and modern readers of Aquinas may have some appreciation for Jeremy Bentham's ridicule for this aspect of natural law, something he argued was governed by the principle, not of utility, but of "sympathy and antipathy." According to Bentham, those who appeal to natural law are approving of certain actions and disapproving of others (whether they realize it or not) based solely upon their

24. *ST,* II-II, 108.2.

positive or negative sentimental reactions to those actions. As he states mockingly,

> A great multitude of people are continually talking of the Law of Nature; and then they go on giving you their sentiments about what is right and what is wrong: and these sentiments, you are to understand, are so many chapters and sections of the Law of Nature.[25]

Whereas it is doubtful that Bentham has Thomistic natural law specifically in mind when he makes these remarks, his repudiation of natural law ethics would likely be just as severe when confronting Aquinas's appeal to the natural inclinations. Applied to punishment, appeals to natural law and natural inclination amount to the ridiculous assertion that society should punish actions merely because those actions create the feeling of antipathy in the hearts of onlookers. Rather than a punishment's usefulness, appeals to natural law require an irrational and sentimentally motivated principle that amounts to the following: "If you hate much, punish much: if you hate little, punish little: punish as you hate."[26]

In order to clarify Aquinas's claim that punishment's moral basis rests upon the natural inclination to punish, we must examine more carefully what he means by natural inclination. If such inclinations are merely urges or instincts identical with what may be experienced by irrational animals, Bentham's criticism has considerable force. As Aquinas uses the term in his discussion of the natural law, however, the meaning of natural inclination is quite different. Throughout Aquinas's writings, the notion of natural inclination is inseparable from that of natural appetite or natural desire, and those things to which one has a natural inclination are, in his view, desirable by nature. It is no accident, therefore, that just as Aquinas distinguishes between the three levels of inclinations in humans (those that we share with all substances, those that we share with all living things, and those that are specific to our ratio-

25. *Introduction to the Principles of Morals and Legislation,* chap. 2, sec. 15 (n. 6).
26. Ibid., chap. 2, sec. 13.

nal nature), he also distinguishes between three ways in which a natural appetite may be observed in created things.

> Some [things] are inclined to *good* by their *natural* inclination, without *knowledge*, as plants and inanimate bodies. Such inclination towards *good* is called "a *natural appetite*." Others, again, are inclined towards *good*, but with some *knowledge*; not that they *know* the aspect of *goodness*, but that they apprehend some particular *good*; as in the sense, which *knows* the sweet, the white, and so on. The inclination which follows this apprehension is called "a sensitive *appetite*." Other things, again, have an inclination towards *good*, but with a *knowledge* whereby they perceive the aspect of *goodness*; this belongs to the *intellect*. This is most perfectly inclined towards what is *good*; not, indeed, as if it were merely guided by another towards some particular *good* only, like things devoid of *knowledge*, nor towards some particular *good* only, as things which have only sensitive *knowledge*, but as inclined towards *good* in general. Such inclination is termed "will."[27]

It is important not to interpret the distinction in the above passage as identical with the distinction Aquinas makes in I-II, 94.2, when discussing the derivation of natural law precepts. In that passage, Aquinas discusses the three *kinds* of natural inclinations experienced by humans. In the passage above, Aquinas is speaking of three distinct *ways in which* creatures experience their natural inclinations. As he explains, humans are inclined to the various goods toward which their nature directs them while intellectually perceiving the "aspect of goodness."[28] In other words, even the objects of natural inclinations that humans share in common with "all substances" (such as the desire to "preserve oneself in being") are also apprehended by the human intellect as being good. Whereas a dog may defend its life as fiercely as a man, only the man recognizes and is conscious of the fact that his life is good and worth defending. This is precisely what Aquinas means when he says that humans "perceive the aspect of goodness," for it is impossible to judge that something is good without an intellectual comparison

27. *ST,* Ia. 59.1.
28. See also *ST,* Ia. 80.1.

between a particular good thing and the general idea of goodness itself (just as it is impossible to judge something as beautiful without some concept of beauty). The point is that all the goods to which humans are inclined are desired along with the intellectual recognition of their goodness, which illustrates the further important point that, for Aquinas, natural inclinations in humans are far more than blind urges or instincts.

When we apply the above distinctions to Aquinas's discussion of the natural inclination to punish (from ST, I-II, 87.1), a clear pattern emerges. Substances at all levels (those substances possessing an intellectual power, those possessing only the powers of sensation, and those possessing neither) exhibit the natural tendency to repress a "supervening" contrary force. Hence the tendency of hot water to "freeze more rapidly"[29] and of fire to "resist whatever destroys or hinders its action."[30] Although Aquinas's nonhuman examples are taken from the subsentient world, one may observe the phenomenon he describes even more clearly in the animal kingdom. The horse that instinctively jerks up its head when its nose is pulled toward the ground, the dog that snaps at a perceived threat, and the bees that swarm and sting an animal that disturbs its hive would all qualify under the same natural tendency described by Aquinas. Because these animals are possessed of an irascible faculty, they act (unlike fire and water) against those things that threaten them based upon their sense experience of the "supervening" object. Only in humans, however, is the natural inclination of which Aquinas speaks "punitive": only humans are capable of intellectually judging the infliction of harm upon someone as deserved and the punishment itself as good. The claim that humans exhibit a natural inclination to punish wrongdoers, therefore, does not at all constitute a denial of reason's role in recognizing the goodness and propriety of the punishment inflicted. In pointing out the similarities between humans and the subrational

29. *ST,* I-II, 87.1.
30. *ST,* Ia. 81.2.

world, Aquinas is far from arguing that one should take the behavior of the subrational as a model for human morality. Because natural inclinations in humans also include an act of reason, Aquinas has a firm basis for distinguishing between punishment and blind retaliation.

Whether or not Bentham had Aquinas's natural law theory in mind, therefore, it is certainly a caricature to say that Aquinas's appeal to natural inclination commits him to the argument that humans should simply "punish as they hate" or to the degree that they feel the passion of anger or resentment. One may see this with even greater clarity if one examines Aquinas's theory of anger itself, which he argues is experienced by humans in a profoundly different way than by other animals with a merely sensitive appetite. One may say that, for Aquinas, anger is of considerable moral significance when considered as a human passion. In the *Summa Theologiae,* Aquinas considers anger in two sections, first under the topic of passion and second under the topic of moral vice. In the latter discussion, the question arises as to whether it is ever lawful to be angry, and in his response Aquinas identifies a well-known position that he will oppose.

> The Stoics designated *anger* and all the other *passions* as emotions opposed to the order of reason; and accordingly they deemed *anger* and all other *passions* to be *evil*, as stated above when we were treating of the *passions*. . . . But, according to the Peripatetics, to whose opinion *Augustine* inclines, *anger* and the other *passions* of the *soul* are movements of the sensitive *appetite*, whether they be moderated or not, according to reason [*sive sint moderatae secundum rationem sive non*]: and in this sense *anger* is not always *evil.*[31]

Predictably, Aquinas prefers the position of Aristotle and Augustine to that of the Stoics (the main representative of which, when it comes to the question of anger, is Seneca).[32] According to Aquinas, it is wrong to say that anger is always illicit because,

31. *ST,* II-II, 158.1, ad 1.
32. See esp. Seneca's *On Anger.*

properly speaking, anger is a movement of the sensitive appetite.[33] In one sense, then, anger, like all passions, is morally neutral, since the mere fact that one is angry leaves open the question as to whether one's anger conforms to the order of reason. Since anger essentially desires the punishment of someone perceived to be a wrongdoer, it remains to be seen whether such a desire is out of accord with what the wrongdoer actually deserves. The connection between anger and punishment is, according to Aquinas, what distinguishes anger from hatred. Whereas hatred simply wishes evil upon the one hated, anger (while also wishing such evil) does so under the aspect of its desire for justice.[34] While it is true that anger is a passion of the sensitive appetite, therefore, Aquinas argues that it inherently presupposes a judgment of reason. Simply put, a human being cannot be angry (at least for long) without *believing* that the object of his anger is deserving of punishment and by rationally comparing the "punishment to be inflicted" with the "hurt done."[35] Of course, anger is not rational in the sense that this prior judgment is necessarily correct, but when exhibited in human beings it always involves, at least over time, more than a subrational urge. One might even say that anger is good in the sense that, when it does conform to the order of reason and to what its object truly deserves, it assists the angry person in being well disposed to some act of injustice.

This is why Aquinas argues (in true Aristotelian fashion) that just as excessive anger is sinful, so also is a lack of anger toward someone whose actions warrant an angrier reaction. Stated more precisely, since anger is a natural result of the judgment that one deserves punishment, a lack of anger where punishment is due may also constitute a disordered response. As Aquinas explains, when confronted with injustice, "the movement of *anger* in the sensitive *appetite* cannot be lacking altogether, unless the movement of the *will* be altogether lacking or weak."[36] Understood in

33. *ST,* II-II, 158.1.
34. *ST,* I-II, 46.6.
35. *ST,* I-II, 46.4.
36. *ST,* II-II, 158.8.

this light, the passion of anger is an important dimension of the natural inclination to repress those who commit injustice. As part of an inclination directing us to something that is good and fitting to human nature, anger may actually be understood as reason's ally (just as sexual desire may be understood as the ally of reason with respect to the good of procreation). For Aquinas, those in whom the angry response to injustice is stifled or deliberately resisted are also likely to be those in whom the virtue of justice itself is lacking. It is in this sense that anger, as a manifestation of the irascible faculty, is of profound moral significance. It reveals a dimension of the natural law that men might even neglect if they relied solely on the judgment of reason. Hence, when Aquinas speaks of the natural desire in man to "repress those who rise up against him . . . which repression is punishment," it is difficult to deny that anger, considered along with the judgment of reason it either leads to or presupposes, is an important part of the irascible inclination linking punishment with the natural law.[37]

Given that Aquinas's appeal to the natural inclination of the irascible faculty is not simply an appeal to subrational instinct, and that the natural inclination to punish includes the intellectual apprehension that punishment is deserved, an important question arises: Is Aquinas's treatment of punishment's moral basis question begging? As we observed in Bentham's complaint of natural law theory, proponents have the tendency to assume that the moral standards of the natural law are simply identical with their own personal "sentiments about what is right and what is wrong." From this perspective, it may seem highly questionable that Aquinas supports the claim that punishment is deserved for injustice

37. For an insightful contemporary treatment of anger's significance for the institution of punishment, see W. Berns's *For Capital Punishment: Crime and the Morality of the Death Penalty* (Lanham, Md.: University Press of America, 1991), chap. 5. For similar and equally insightful treatments of the related concepts of vengeance and resentment, see Robert Solomon's "Justice v. Vengeance: On Law and the Satisfaction of Emotion," in *The Passions of Law,* ed. Susan Bandes (New York: New York University Press, 1999), 123–48, and Jeffrie Murphy's *Getting Even: Forgiveness and Its Limits* (Oxford: Oxford University Press, 2003), chaps. 2–3.

on the sole basis that humans have the natural inclination to believe that punishment is so deserved and to desire punishment as a fundamental good. Because it is so closely associated with natural inclination, it appears as though Aquinas is arguing that the inherent goodness of punishment is a precept of the natural law and thus a self-evident principle that cannot itself be demonstrated (just as the goodness of procreation, knowledge, and life itself is self-evident). To one such as Bentham, however, who holds that punishment has no inherent goodness (but is only "good" inasmuch as it may prevent some greater evil), Aquinas's argument may seem to demonstrate nothing, and is agreeable only to those who already share his conclusions and circular to those who do not. What, Bentham may ask, is preventing someone from using a similar argument to assert the inherent goodness of cannibalism or incest on the questionable premise that human beings have a natural desire for such things? If the fact that many do not share such a natural desire is irrelevant to the persuasiveness of the argument, Aquinas's line of reasoning that supports the goodness and desirability of punishment is no more convincing.

Aquinas would respond to his criticism by pointing out that the natural desire to punish is not on the same level as any other desire. Whereas he would grant that the desire to punish may be perverted by being pursued outside the order of reason, the desires to cannibalize another human being or to perform incest are already themselves perversions of other more fundamental natural desires (i.e., the desire to eat and to have sexual intercourse).[38]

38. Aquinas touches upon this distinction in *ST,* I-II, 91.6, where he discusses "whether there is a law in the *fomes* of sin." Aquinas grants that one may speak of certain sinful "inclinations" caused by man's fall from original justice (original sin). As he explains, however, the "law of sin" is only a law in a secondary or metaphorical sense, since it is not according to reason and not for the common good. We are given to understand that, unlike the fundamental natural inclinations discussed in *ST,* I-II, 94.2, which guide us toward fundamental goods in accordance with our nature, the sinful inclinations associated with the "fomes" are, by definition, perversions of those same inclinations. Hence, Aquinas states that whereas even such sinful inclinations leads man in the general direction of some good, such as the "preservation of

Though he does not seem to have anticipated the objection mentioned above, Aquinas might further argue that those who deny that there exists a natural inclination to punish (unlike those who deny the natural inclination to cannibalize and perform incest) fail to recognize their very own belief that punishment is good. To explain this further, we may return to Aquinas's discussion of anger. Even someone who denies the inherent goodness of punishment will have considerably more trouble denying that they ever experience anger. If Aquinas's analysis of anger is correct, however, rational beings undergoing this passion cannot avoid the belief that the punishment of those to whom their anger is directed is good. To be sure, one who is persuaded by contrary philosophical arguments (such as that of Bentham) may consciously resist this belief. Nevertheless, Aquinas would likely insist that the power and universality of the punitive inclination make such a denial extremely difficult. Will a utilitarian still believe, for example, that punishment has no inherent goodness when someone close to him has been murdered? Or when the same murderer escapes punishment, can the utilitarian be entirely honest with himself in saying that the only regrettable aspect of such a situation is the missed opportunity to maximize utility? Perhaps the utilitarian will claim that, regardless of how strongly one is inclined to believe something, beliefs that are unsupportable by the principle of utility must simply be resisted as much as possible. It is here, in all likelihood, that we reach the fundamental metaethical disagreement between Aquinas's natural law theory and the modern moral philosophies examined in the first two chapters. For Aquinas, our fundamental natural inclinations and the natural goods they cause us to desire are to be trusted. Without them, morality is simply impossible to conceive of because there are no human goods that give content to the first self-evident precept that "good

---

nature in the species or the individual" (ad 3), they incline him to do so in a perverse manner that is out of accord with the attaining of those goods themselves. For the law of sin "is called the 'fomes' insofar as it strays from the order of reason."

is to be pursued and evil is to be avoided." Because the natural law is the human participation in the eternal law, a natural inclination as universal and powerful as the one inclining us to desire the punishment of wrongdoers cannot be dismissed as morally insignificant or accidental. Whatever the criticisms of Aquinas's approach, his appeals to natural inclination and natural law make his theory of punishment a decisive alternative, not only to utilitarianism, but to that of Immanuel Kant as well. It is this latter comparison that will occupy us in the final section of this chapter.

Thomistic versus Kantian Retributivism

The above account identifies Aquinas's theory of punishment as at least partially retributive.[39] One may begin to see this by merely observing the language used by Aquinas in connecting punishment with the natural law and natural inclination. As he says, the natural inclination in man to repress those who rise up against him is evidence of the *reatus poenae*. Aquinas's use of *reatus* is often translated as "debt," but a more accurate (though clumsier) rendering might be something like "guilt" or "deservingness" (such a rendering would help to underscore Aquinas's decision not to use the more common *debitum*). Whereas the inclination to repress harmful attackers may have no moral significance in other animals, therefore, the fact that humans are inclined to inflict harm upon their assailants is taken by Aquinas as an indication that such harm is actually deserved. To speak of a *reatus poenae* is to say more than that punishment is necessary (and hence justified) as a kind of self-defense. Punishment is deserved on account of a criminal's harmful action in such a way that society is not only permitted, but obliged, to inflict it as a matter of justice.

But what, according to Aquinas, is the essence of a criminal's

39. The observations in this present section are taken from my own "Two Theories of Retributive Punishment: Immanuel Kant and Thomas Aquinas," *History of Philosophy Quarterly* 22, no. 4 (October 2005): 319–38.

deservingness to be punished? As we have already seen that punishment is justified as a fundamental human good by its connection with natural inclination and natural law, the precise nature of a criminal's liability to punishment needs further explanation. To unfold this aspect of Aquinas's teaching, we must consider the following important remarks from the *Summa Theologiae:*

> [T]he act of sin makes man deserving of punishment, insofar as he transgresses the order of divine justice, to which he cannot return except he pay some sort of penal compensation, which restores him to the equality of justice [*ad aequalitatem iustitiae reducit*]; so that, according to the order of divine justice, he who has been too indulgent in his will, by transgressing God's commandments, suffers, either willingly or unwillingly, something contrary to what he would wish. This restoration of the equality of justice by penal compensation is also to be observed in injuries done to one's fellow men.[40]

Later on, Aquinas argues that the restoration of the "equality of justice" gives punishment its defining character.

> Punishment may be considered in two ways. First, under the aspect of punishment, and in this way punishment is not due save for sin, because by means of punishment the equality of justice is restored [*reparatur aequalitas iustitiae*], insofar as he who by sinning has exceeded in following his own will suffers something that is contrary to his will. . . . Secondly, punishment may be considered as a medicine [*medicina*], not only healing the past sin, but also preventing from future sin, or conducing to some good.[41]

As we have already seen, the essence of punishment involves the infliction of something "contrary to the will" of the person being punished. To be sure, the necessity that punishment must be against the criminal's will may be considered from a merely prudential or utilitarian standpoint, and this is why Aquinas himself argues that the most effective punishments deprive a man "of what he loves most," such as his riches, his country, his freedom,

40. *ST,* I-II, 87.6.
41. *ST,* II-II, 108.4.

or even his life, since otherwise the fear of punishment would not deter potential criminals from committing crime.[42] What Aquinas has in mind in the two passages above, however, is something quite different. Punishment must be contrary to the will of the criminal, not for the sake of deterrence, but because this is precisely what its ability to restore justice requires. Why is this so?

According to the first passage, punishment's contrariety to the will is necessary to answer the "overindulgent" will of the criminal act. Because the essence of crime involves a transgression of the will by which someone voluntarily goes "too far" in following his criminal intentions, the essence of punishment represses that will by inflicting some kind of harm upon the criminal. By focusing so much upon the criminal's will, it may seem that Aquinas is addressing punishment's rehabilitative function, as if the criminal's will is "corrected" by the punishment he undergoes. In point of fact, however, the passages above have nothing to do with rehabilitation. What needs correcting, according to the above argument, is not the criminal's will itself, but a certain kind of inequality that comes about as a result of the crime. Even if the criminal is not rehabilitated, therefore, suffering a proportionate punishment that represses his will places him back upon "equal terms" with the rest of the law-abiding community. When a kidnapper is deprived of his freedom by being imprisoned, the harm he suffers against his will balances his willful transgression of the law and assault upon the common good. The more culpable the transgression of the criminal's will, the more "repression" is required to bring the equality of justice back into balance.[43]

Considered from this perspective, punishment is emphatically retributive, since the equality of justice is a dimension of the common good that is quite independent of any other goals that legislators may hope to bring about through the criminal law, such as deterrence, rehabilitation, or the protection of society. From

42. *ST,* II-II, 108.3.

43. IV Sent. D. 20, Q. 1, A. 2, QC 1 (corpus).

the second passage, one might even conclude that the retributive function of punishment is that which Aquinas considers most important, since punishment restores the equality of justice when considered "under the aspect of punishment." To be sure, punishment has a "medicinal" purpose as well (which we shall discuss more fully in the following chapter), which Aquinas broadly characterizes as "healing the past sin . . . preventing from future sin, or conducing to some good." Since medicinal punishments are not considered by Aquinas "under the aspect of punishment," however, we are given to understand that they are not punishments properly speaking. Whereas medicines are intended to heal the person receiving them, punishment (considered "under the aspect of punishment") is essentially intended to inflict some kind of harm without which the inequality caused by crime cannot be removed. This is not to say that retributive punishment (distinguished from medicinal punishment) looks "backward" upon the crime (as some critics of retributivism suggest). When someone who harms society is punished by political authority, the equality of justice having been restored, in Aquinas's view, is a real good that has come from the punishment. From the point of view of a legislator or judge about to render a punitive sentence, it is a future good worth pursuing just the same as maintaining peace, inculcating virtue, or securing any other constitutive element of the common good.

While Immanuel Kant expresses an emphatically retributive theory of punishment as well, there are three important dimensions in which his rationale of punishment differs from that of Aquinas. As we observed in chapter two, Kant insists that punishment is a "categorical imperative." This does not only mean that political and legal authorities have an obligation to punish criminals, but also that they have a moral obligation to do so for the sake of the obligation itself. In other words, a judge or lawgiver may not punish for the sake of deterrence or rehabilitation, since to do so would be to use the criminal as a means to the ends of the state. Equally disqualified, therefore, would be to punish from a natural inclination. According to Kant's moral teaching, natural inclination tells us nothing more than our own subjective desires and aversions and has nothing to do with the requirements of morality. To punish for the sake of satisfying one's natural desire for vengeance, for instance, would also be to use the criminal as a means to an end. To be sure, punishing from natural inclination or for deterrence does not automatically make a punishment unjust (what is necessary to deter or to satisfy natural inclination may *happen* to be the same as what justice requires), but it does render the act of punishing to be morally illicit.

Several aspects of Kant's invocation of the categorical imperative in this context are troubling. First, whereas the categorical imperative seems to provide an intelligible rationale for prohibiting acts of punishment in a way that uses the criminal as a means to an end, it is much more difficult to say how the categorical imperative implies a positive obligation to punish. When it comes to other kinds of actions required by the categorical imperative, Kant is much clearer. One has a categorical obligation to tell the truth, for instance, because a world in which no one told the truth would make lying effectively impossible. One has an obligation to develop one's talents, moreover, because it would be impossible to will a world in which no persons developed their talents. According to Kant's teaching, the impossibility or undesirability of the imagined world in which a morally illicit maxim is universalized cannot be the motive behind the choice to tell the truth or develop one's talents. Such impossibility or undesirability is, rather, the *test* by which one discovers that truth telling and talent developing are duties required by the moral law. One's motive, therefore, should not be to promote any desirable states of affairs, but strictly to conform one's actions to the moral law itself. Now one might argue that, for Kant, the punishment of criminals is morally required because no rational agent would desire a world in which criminal actions went unpunished. In other words, no one could rationally and consistently universalize one's maxim in choosing not to punish someone who has committed injustice. To be sure, this first formulation of the categorical imperative would seem to be the most likely candidate for establishing a positive categorical obligation to punish criminals (at least when compared with formulations involving the treatment of humanity as an end in itself, the formula from autonomy, and the kingdom of ends). Unfortunately, however, Kant does not provide us with anything resembling such a rationale.[44] Granted that Kant could provide some formulation of his categorical imperative that provided a moral obligation to punish criminals (equally binding as, say, the requirement to develop one's talents), a second problem nevertheless remains. To say that punishment is a categorical imperative, in Kant's moral thought, is to say that it is not morally justified by any good that it brings about (those familiar with Kant's thought will recall that this is precisely what distinguishes categorical imperatives from hypothetical imperatives). For Kant, punishment is not, strictly speaking, a good to be pursued. It is simply right or just. To say that punishment is good would be to say that it brings about some desirable state of affairs or that it is desirable in and of itself, but for Kant neither of these facts (assuming they are true) provides any ground for punishment's *moral* justification. If punishment is a categorical imperative, it is morally required by the law of pure practical reason, which is to say that its morality is derived independently from human desire, considerations of utility, or any understanding of human nature or the human good. To one already committed to the Kantian system

44. One interpretation of Kant's assertion that punishment must be inflicted as a categorical imperative emphasizes the categorical imperative's first formulation, but in a much different way. As Fleischacker suggests, the act of punishing forcibly universalizes the *criminal's* maxim so as to apply the evil he has committed against another to himself. Although this is a very interesting interpretation of Kant's retributivism in light of his moral theory, it enjoys practically no explicit textual support, and therefore deserves here consideration only in passing. For this view, see Samuel Fleischacker, "Kant's Theory of Punishment," in *Essays on Kant's Political Philosophy* (Chicago: University of Chicago Press, 1992), 191–212.

of morality, this observation will certainly not be understood as a weakness of Kant's theory of punishment (though Kant's inability to link punishment with any one formulation of the categorical imperative might very well be seen as a weakness to Kantians). On the other hand, one does not need to be a committed utilitarian to find something lacking in a moral justification of punishment completely detached from the human good.

By contrast, Aquinas's retributive theory of punishment is profoundly rooted in his understanding of the human good. Though he reaches the same conclusion that the primary justification of punishment (at least considered "under the aspect of punishment") is retributive, it is extremely important for Aquinas that punishment is also good. As we have seen, Aquinas's understanding of punishment's moral justification is inseparable from the human desire to inflict punishment as a response to injustice. Thus understood, punishment is morally acceptable and even required precisely because, by the natural constitution of the human person, it is necessary for preserving the fundamental good of justice desired by human beings. As we have seen, the desire for punishment is not merely an instinctual retaliatory urge brought on by the desire for self-preservation. Whereas it may be accompanied by subrational desires (such as the passion of anger), the natural inclination to punish is also a desire of the rational appetite (or the will). As the practical intellect understands that the punishment of criminals is good, the will is moved to desire that good under the aspect of goodness itself. Because we are led to it through our natural inclinations, the good of punishment is desired as a constitutive element in the overall happiness of the human person and human society. Just as humans will not be completely happy if they ignore some other good to which they are directed by their natural inclinations (e.g., the good of knowledge), so also, according to Aquinas, they cannot be completely happy by ignoring their natural desire to punish criminals. Rather than a conclusion of pure practical reason that owes nothing to human nature, therefore, Aquinas's justification of punishment is explained in the only way that Aquinas understands how to make any moral argument, namely, by showing its connection with human happiness and the human good. Any additional moral parameters concerning punishment discovered by reason would be meaningless, Aquinas would say, without first establishing punishment's goodness in the natural inclinations and the natural law. Whereas Aquinas and Kant reach a similar conclusion regarding the retributive dimension of punishment, therefore, the moral perspectives which lead them to this conclusion could hardly be more opposed.

A second weakness of Kant's retributivism stems from his famous (or infamous) appeal to the *ius talionis*. As we observed in chapter two, Kant argues that criminals be punished, not only to the same *degree* as the severity of their crime, but also with the same *kind* of suffering they inflicted on their victims. As he explained, "any undeserved evil that you inflict on someone else among the people is one that you do to yourself. If you vilify him, you vilify yourself; if you steal from him, you steal from yourself; if you kill him, you kill yourself." Kant's insistence upon this principle is especially evident in a revealing section of the *Metaphysical Elements of Justice* where he discusses the appropriate penalty for a case in which a member of the upper class commits a "verbal injury" against a social inferior. Pointing out the inadequacy of fining someone for such an offense (since a wealthy aristocrat would hardly notice such a fine), Kant suggests that the perpetrator should be forced publicly to kiss the hand of his victim. Only in this way, Kant thinks, can the humiliation suffered by the victim of the verbal offense be matched by the humiliation of the punishment. For Kant, it seems, the *ius talionis* means more than mere proportionality, but additionally includes a strange kind of poetic justice.

As it has been pointed out on numerous occasions, the *ius talionis* upon which Kant relies is not always applicable. Whereas following it would be fairly straightforward in punishing crimes such as theft, assault, and murder (these might be punished, respectively, with fines, stripes, and the death penalty), how would one treat crimes such as embezzlement, kidnapping, or the use of illegal substances? Furthermore, what about particularly heinous crimes in which victims are not only killed, but raped, tortured, dismembered, or cannibalized? Would Kant really insist that the state should treat its criminals with the same grizzly barbarism carried out by the criminals themselves? Strictly speaking, the death penalty for a man who slowly dismembers someone until his victim finally dies would be too lenient according to a literal interpretation of the *ius talionis*. Perhaps Kant would qualify his argument by saying that a perfectly equal retribution should be abandoned if it requires society to inflict gruesome suffering upon its criminals. Surely, the moral and psychological integrity of citizens is more important than insisting upon the kind of poetic exactness that the *ius talionis* requires. And yet, if Kant were to make this concession, does he not admit that realizing the exact equality of justice can be sacrificed for other nonretributive goods like the moral integrity and/or psychological wellness of those responsible for punishing? If, however, the state can deviate from the *lex talionis* and its categorical obligation to punish for the sake of these nonretributive goods, why not also for others like rehabilitation or deterrence? Unfortunately, Kant leaves these questions unanswered.

Turning to Aquinas's theory of retribution, we can immediately observe that he avoids the problems associated with the *ius talionis*. The reason for this stems from his emphasis, not upon the external details of the wrongdoer's crime, but upon the will of the criminal being punished. Since the essential requirement of retribution, for Aquinas, is that criminals experience a loss commensurate with the degree to which they indulged their wills beyond the boundaries of legality, there is no need to require the poetic justice recommended by Kant. As we noticed, Kant's focus was entirely upon the criminal's external act (or the "crime"), taking little or nothing of the criminal's *mens rea* into consideration.[45] This is not the case for Aquinas, whose central requirement for equal retribution is only that criminals suffer the same degree as that which they contravened by the inordinate act of their wills. What criminals deserve, in other words, is determined by estimating the seriousness of the criminal act and is realized by imposing a correspondingly serious penalty within the parameters of a reasonable determination of what will place the criminal back upon equal terms with the rest of the law-abiding citizenry.[46] Under Thomistic principles, therefore, punishment need not conform to the impossible demand that criminals receive a punishment exactly equal in both severity and kind with the harm inflicted by their crimes.

The purpose of this chapter has been to expose the first principles of Aquinas's theory of punishment. By establishing the link between punishment and natural law (something about which

45. Whereas Kant is perfectly clear that punishment should be based upon a criminal's external action and should take no consideration of the criminal's motive (*Metaphysics of Morals,* 6.218–21), he is less clear as to what extent his emphasis upon externality rules out the possibility of determining the varying degrees of voluntariness or culpability for the same external crimes. To be sure, degree of voluntariness is a different concept from that of motive. One might argue, however, that the same principle that forbids a judge from considering a criminal's motive, namely, that no one is privy to the inner workings of the *mens rea,* would also prevent that judge from attempting to discern whether a crime of murder (for example) was committed more or less voluntarily. For Aquinas, however, ascertaining the degree of a criminal's culpability is essential for imposing a just punishment. Since a criminal is liable to punishment precisely on account of the overindulgence of his will, a more voluntary crime (even if it is carried out in the same type of external act) is inherently more deserving of punishment than a less voluntary crime. On Thomistic principles, therefore, the judge must do his best to determine culpability with the evidence available to him and within the limitations of his human condition (we will examine Aquinas's treatment of these limitations more fully in the next chapter).

46. It is important to note that whereas Aquinas's concern is with redressing the inordinate act of the criminal's will rather than "matching" the criminal's crime, he does not go so far as to recommend that criminal justice should have anything to do with a wrongdoer's overall character. That would be considerably more difficult to determine than the volition of a single criminal act, not to mention, in Aquinas's view, quite beside the point in reestablishing the equality of justice.

Aquinas is not always explicit), we have shown how the question of punishment is situated within Aquinas's moral teaching as a whole. To be sure, this account of punishment's moral basis leaves many questions unanswered. Granted that punishment is justifiable in principle, what sort of *institution* of punishment does Aquinas recommend to carry out the actual punishment of criminals? Related to this, granted that Aquinas's theory of punishment rests upon different principles than those of Kant, how may we distinguish his rationale for punishment from the unfair advantage theory discussed in chapter two? On the face of it, Aquinas's claim that punishment inflicts something against the will of the criminal for the purpose of reestablishing justice makes his teaching sound very similar, if not identical, with those of Herbert Morris and John Finnis. Finally, other than the retributive aspects of punishment that Aquinas highlights, is there room for the nonretributive purposes of punishment such as deterrence, rehabilitation, the protection of society, or other similar goals? As a retributivist, what legitimacy does Aquinas grant such motives for punishing and what, may we say, is their moral status? It is these, and other related, questions to which we now turn.

5

BEYOND RETRIBUTION

Punishing Criminals in Civil Society

Punishment and Political Authority

As we observed in the last chapter, Aquinas's argument for the "debt of punishment" *(reatus poenae)* rests upon his claim that man has a "natural inclination to repress those who rise up against him . . . which repression is punishment." Whereas Aquinas's appeal to natural inclination provides the crucial link in his argument between punishment and natural law, he makes equally important remarks in the same article relating to the agencies by which punishment is properly administered.

Now it is evident that all things contained in an order, are, in a manner, one, in relation to the principle of that order. Consequently, whatever rises up against an order, is put down by that order or by the principle thereof. And because *sin* is an inordinate act, it is evident that whoever *sins*, commits an offense against an order. . . . Accordingly, *man* can be punished with a threefold punishment corresponding to the three orders to which the *human will* is subject. In the first place a man's *nature* is subjected to the order of his own reason; secondly, it is subjected to the order of another *man* who governs him either in *spiritual* or in temporal matters, as a member either of the state or of the household; thirdly, it is subjected to the universal order of the Divine government. Now each of these orders is disturbed by *sin*, for the sinner acts against his *reason*, and against *human* and *Divine law*. Wherefore he incurs a threefold punishment; one, inflicted by himself, viz. remorse of *conscience*; another, inflicted by *man*; and a third, inflicted by *God*.[1]

The threefold distinction mentioned in the above passage (I-II, 87.1) harkens back to, and is further explained by, a distinction Aquinas made earlier in the *Summa Theologiae* (I-II, 72.4). In the earlier passage, Aquinas argued that all sins are "fittingly divided against God, against oneself, and against one's neighbor," although the distinction is not perfectly even in the sense that some sins are included in more than one category. As Aquinas explains, most sins are violations of the "rule of reason" inasmuch as sin is properly defined as an inordinate act.[2] Hence, when one sins by straying from the order of reason (e.g., by eating or drinking more than what is necessary for sustaining one's life and health), the rational power of one's soul is able to render a judgment as to the action's sinfulness. The specific power responsible for doing this is what Aquinas calls "conscience," which not only "prods," "urges," and "binds" us to act in certain ways (by applying the more general principles of morality known by *synderesis* to concrete situations), but also "accuses" and "causes remorse" when "that which has been done is found to be out of harmony with the knowledge according to which it is examined."[3] Although a remorseful conscience clearly causes its possessor a certain kind of discomfort, it is necessary to view it analogously when considering it as an agent of punishment. Since punishment is, by definition, an evil suffered by a rational agent, it is difficult to see what evil, what loss of good, is constituted by remorse. Since one can only be just to oneself in a metaphorical sense,[4] moreover, the remorse of conscience must not be understood as necessary for reestablishing the just balance of equality as other forms of punishment do. As Aquinas continues to explain, the order of reason is itself embraced by the "order of divine law," whereby God inflicts punishment upon sinners for vio-

1. *ST,* I-II, 87.1.
2. Cf. *ST,* I-II, 71.1 and 6.
3. *De Veritiate,* 17. 1.
4. Cf. *Commentary on the Nicomachean Ethics,* book 5, lecture 17.

lating his commandments. Strictly speaking, all sins are transgressions against God, since divine commandments relate to every aspect of human life.

Rather than examining the long list of reasons that Aquinas gives to explain the phenomenon of divine punishment, what is important for our purposes is rather to notice that Aquinas understands punishments, like the sins for which they are inflicted, within the context of an "order." Whether a sinful act contravenes the order of reason or the order of divine law only (most sins contravene both),[5] punishment is inflicted by some principle of the order that was violated. The inseparability between punishment and an order is essential for understanding Aquinas's conception of the punishment of human beings by other humans. With a few exceptions,[6] such punishments may only be inflicted within the context of the *political* order, which is added to the order of reason and the order of divine law. Aquinas's explanation of the political order and the punishments inflicted on its behalf recall his political teaching examined in chapter three: "If *man* were by *nature* a solitary animal, this twofold order would suffice. But since *man* is *naturally* a civic and social animal, as is *proved* in Polit. i, 2, hence a third order is *necessary*, whereby *man* is directed in relation to other men among whom he has to dwell."[7]

As we noticed in chapter three, Aquinas's claim that humans are political animals sets him apart from most philosophers in the modern tradition of political thought, including (but certainly not only) the architects of utilitarianism and modern retributivism. For Aquinas, political society is not an invention of human beings,

5. Aquinas appears to list "heresy, sacrilege, and blasphemy," perhaps because of unaided reason's inability to determine their wrongness, as examples of sins that violate divine law but not the order of reason (*ST,* I-II, 72.4).

6. From I-II, 87.1, the exceptions appear to be the punishments administered by those representatives of the Church with "spiritual authority" or parents. As Aquinas explains elsewhere, however, the authority to inflict more serious punishments (i.e., those causing death and permanent bodily injury) belongs exclusively to those with "public authority" (*ST,* II-II, 65.1).

7. *ST,* I-II, 72.4.

but something to which the author of human nature inclines us as a constitutive element in our fulfillment. This teaching also has a bearing upon the origins of political authority. Whereas modern philosophers in the social contract traditions of Hobbes, Locke, Rousseau, and Kant identify political authority as deriving from those who freely or tacitly agree to subject themselves to it, Aquinas understands political authority as a natural extension of divine authority. As he himself explains it, this fact is most important for the justification of punishment. Since "the men who are put in positions over other men are like executors of divine providence," those who punish criminals on behalf of the state are not to be judged as those acting of their own accord. As Aquinas explains, "God through the order of His providence directs lower beings by means of higher ones." And since "this order of divine providence requires the good to be rewarded and the evil to be punished . . . men who are in authority over others do no wrong when they reward the good and punish the evil."[8] As far as Aquinas is concerned, the divine origin of political authority is not a specifically Christian doctrine (as opposed, one might observe, to the divine right of kings doctrine held by Sir Robert Filmer and criticized by John Locke). It comes, as the above remarks indicate, from the observation that the universe is governed by divine providence embodied in the eternal law.[9] Since the natural law is nothing other than the eternal law as it applies to human beings, and since the inclination to "live in society" is one of the fundamental inclinations included in the natural law, the political nature of man is derived from and embraced under the much broader cosmopolis that God providently directs. This is why Aquinas is not nearly as concerned as modern political philosophers are with the question of a regime's legitimacy. Much more

8. *Summa Contra Gentiles (SCG),* III. 146 (2).

9. For an excellent treatment of the naturalness of political authority and how this doctrine is distinguished from those of the liberal tradition, see Yves Simon's *A General Theory of Authority* (South Bend, Ind.: University of Notre Dame Press, 1980).

central for Aquinas is whether or not a regime is just, and in some sense all regimes are legitimate whether they rule justly or not.[10] The situation with the political order is thus very much analogous, one might say, to what Aquinas believes about the order of reason. Just because an individual person's reason may lead him astray from the order of reason itself, this does not take away from the fact that that same person's reason is the rightful authority[11] over his or her actions and the other parts of his or her soul. Analogously, an oligarchical regime exercises a rightful authority over its subjects even when its laws are not designed to promote the common good. To be sure, Aquinas holds that citizens of such a regime must not obey the law when it commands them to do something explicitly forbidden by divine authority (or not to do something explicitly commanded by divine authority), but this is not because the commanding regime is illegitimate.[12] It is rather because its authority is trumped by the broader and more authoritative eternal law that provides the basis of the rightful political authority that all regimes enjoy regardless of whether it is rightfully used.

The importance of political authority for the institution of punishment is particularly evident when we examine Aquinas's distinction between punitive sanctions and private self-defense. As he argues, killing someone in self-defense is only justifiable under certain conditions. If one's life is threatened, Aquinas says, defending oneself even to the point of inflicting a lethal blow is lawful so long as "one's intention is to save one's own life" rather than "the slaying of the aggressor."[13] To use the phraseology of more contemporary analyses of the subject, Aquinas is saying that when a private citizen inflicts death upon an aggressor the

10. Aquinas does allow for tyrannicide on rare occasions, but is always quick to warn that such drastic measures can often harm the common good more than help it (cf. *ST,* II-II, 42.2, ad 3). It is worth observing that, even in his allowance for tyrannicide, Aquinas's argument is not that the tyrant does not rule legitimately (or that his authority is not genuine), but merely that he does not rule justly.

11. Cf. *ST,* I-II, 19.3.

12. Cf., *ST,* I-II, 96.4.

13. *ST,* II-II, 64.7.

aggressor's death must be something like a foreseen but unintended consequence of the defensive action. Hence, directly intending to kill an attacker is morally unlawful for Aquinas even when such killing is necessary to save one's own life. It matters not that the person killed is in the wrong or that protecting oneself is the ultimate goal of one's action. In stark contrast to this, however, Aquinas clearly believes that those acting with public authority may directly intend to kill those whose death is deemed necessary for the preservation of the common good. Because "the care of the common *good* is entrusted to *persons* of rank having public authority . . . they alone, and not private *individuals*, can lawfully put evildoers to death."[14] This is not exactly to say that persons holding public authority are held to a different moral standard as compared with private individuals. Whether one holds public authority or not, it is never morally right to intend the death of another human being on one's own initiative (we shouldn't forget that public authorities are *also* private individuals when they do not act in their public capacity). What makes the infliction of death morally legitimate in the cases of judicial punishment (and also, for Aquinas, the waging of a just war) is precisely the fact that one does *not* kill on one's own initiative. As a public authority, one is an instrument of a higher agent from whom one's authority is derived. This is true, for Aquinas, not only in the case of a political sovereign acting as the instrument of God, but also in the cases of a soldier acting on the authority of a general, or a general acting on the authority of a king. The notion of instrumentality is crucial for understanding Aquinas's theory of punishment because it is precisely such instrumentality that distinguishes one's action from private defense and makes, not just the infliction of death, but the direct and voluntary infliction of any evil upon another human being to be justifiable at all.[15] Again, Aquinas does not intend his teaching on these matters to imply an argument for theocracy.

14. *ST,* II-II, 64.3.
15. *ST,* II-II, 64.7.

The divine origins of political authority to punish is detectable, not only in observing the political nature of man, but also in understanding the philosophical doctrine that all human affairs are subject to the eternal law.[16] Whereas Christian revelation, Aquinas thinks, confirms the derivative status of political and judicial authority from the divine, his teaching implies that natural reason alone may conclude that rightful political authority, and the authority to punish that comes with it, comes from "above" just as Thomas Hobbes and John Locke believed they could show that it derived from the consent of the governed.[17]

Punishment and the Law

Aquinas's claim that political authority is derived from divine authority is paralleled by his well-known teaching that all laws issued by human beings (he calls them "human laws") are derived from the natural and/or eternal law. Because they naturally are part of a political body, it is not sufficient for human beings to live simply under the natural law. According to Aquinas, there must also be human laws to determine the details of how a given political society will live. Since "human reason needs to proceed to the more particular determination of certain matters,"[18] rightful

16. Cf. *ST,* I-II, 93.6.

17. This aspect of Aquinas's philosophy of punishment is explained with particular clarity by Steven Long: "Insofar as the state serves justice, the state participates in divine authority by its very nature—for, as St. Thomas always and definitively insists, the natural law is nothing other than the rational participation of the eternal law—indeed it is not other than the eternal law, but merely the limited and natural, rational participation of the same. Hence the state participates in divine authority not by some theocratic *superadditum* or religiosity, but simply by its natural ordination toward securing justice: for just law is by its very nature and being a rational participation of eternal law. Just ordinances are so by virtue of conformity to the eternal law. *Hence, the primal jurisdiction over life belongs to God alone, and all political authority of the state to execute, and even to punish, is delegated by God as a function of the participation of genuine human law in the eternal law: without which metaphysical participation, there is no authentic law.* That is to say, this reaches to the very being of law. *Mala lex, nulla lex*" (*The Teleological Grammar of the Moral Act,* 59–60).

18. *ST,* I-II, 91.3.

authorities must decide how the natural law will be applied to the concrete affairs of political life. As Aquinas explains, this happens in either one of two ways. First, a human law may be a "conclusion" of the natural law. In such a case, the human law would forbid something that directly violates one of the natural law's precepts, such as the prohibition against murder. Thus understood, human laws that constitute conclusions of the natural law may not be changed according to the decision of a legislator. Any political authority that composes a law permitting (or, even worse, requiring) murder, for example, would be in such direct breech of natural justice that his decision would lose any binding force it was perceived to have. Conversely, laws prohibiting murder, theft, and other fundamentally unjust actions are essentially different than those Aquinas labels as "determinations" of the natural law. Unlike conclusions, determinations of the natural law may be decided one way or the other. For instance, the law requiring drivers to stay on the right side of the road is something that could just as rightfully have been decided in the reverse. Of course, once it has been decided, such a law has the same binding force as any conclusion of the natural law. Nevertheless, there is nothing intrinsically unjust about driving on the left as there is about murder or theft.

Relating this distinction to the institution of punishment, Aquinas makes the following observation: "The natural law has it that the evil-doer should be punished; but that he be punished in this way or that way, is a determination of the law of nature."[19] As we saw before, man's natural inclination to repress those who rise against him is what grounds the institution of punishment in the natural law. From there, however, prudent legislators (or judges) may presumably impose differing punishments according to the various contingencies with which they are faced. To use the analogy Aquinas cites, the need for some institution of punishment pertains to political society as certain essential features pertain to the "general form of a house." Carrying this analogy further, a

19. *ST,* I-II, 95.2.

society without any sort of penal law would be like a house without doors, windows, or a roof. In other words, the failure to punish criminals would frustrate one of the essential purposes for which political society naturally exists, namely, to protect its citizens from the unjust aggression of others. Beyond that, however, individual punishments may be decided as the general form of a house is determined to "some particular shape." Hence, a murderer may be exiled, imprisoned, or killed, according to various considerations just as a house may be sturdily build upon various kinds of foundations.

Now despite Aquinas's assertion that selecting a particular punishment is a determination (rather than a conclusion) of the natural law, he does not simply hold that for a given crime any punishment will suffice. Although the natural law does not specify the exact form of punishment due to each crime, legislators and judges are not free to punish misdemeanors with the death penalty as they are to have drivers stay on the right or the left side of the road. To cite once again Aquinas's analogy from architecture, the fact that one is more or less free to "determine" the size and shape of a house's front door does not mean that one may install a door that is only one foot high. To do so would be almost as bad as not having a door at all, which would violate something fundamentally important with respect to a house's "general form." Likewise, because punishment is essentially a political and legal act, to inflict a punishment that hinders the basic function of human law or frustrates the purposes of the institution of punishment itself would constitute a violation of the natural law the same as having no institution of punishment at all. This point becomes clearer as one examines what Aquinas argues the purposes of human law actually are. The following passage contains Aquinas's most explicit statement on this crucial question.

As stated above, *man* has a *natural* aptitude for *virtue*; but the perfection of *virtue* must be acquired by *man* by means of some kind of training. Thus we observe that *man* is helped by industry in his necessities, for instance, in food and clothing. Certain beginnings of these he has from *nature*, viz. his *reason* and his hands; but he has not the full complement, as other animals have, to whom *nature* has given sufficiency of clothing and food. Now it is difficult to see how *man* could suffice for himself in the *matter* of this training: since the perfection of *virtue* consists chiefly in withdrawing *man* from undue pleasures, to which above all *man* is inclined, and especially the young, who are more capable of being trained. Consequently a man needs to receive this training from another, whereby to arrive at the perfection of *virtue*. And as to those young people who are inclined to acts of *virtue*, by their *good natural* disposition, or by custom, or rather by the *gift* of *God*, paternal training suffices, which is by admonitions. But since some are found to be depraved, and prone to *vice*, and not easily amenable to words, it was *necessary* for such to be restrained from *evil* by force and fear, in order that, at least, they might desist from *evil*-doing, and leave others in peace, and that they themselves, by being habituated in this way, might be brought to do willingly what hitherto they did from fear, and thus become *virtuous*. Now this kind of training, which compels through fear of punishment, is the discipline of laws. Therefore in order that *man* might have peace and *virtue*, it was *necessary* for laws to be framed: for, as the *Philosopher* says, "as *man* is the most noble of animals if he be perfect in *virtue*, so is he the lowest of all, if he be severed from *law* and righteousness"; because *man* can use his *reason* to devise means of satisfying his lusts and *evil passions*, which other animals are unable to do.[20]

Although the good habits of living in society are usually instilled from within the family, Aquinas explains that some people must be restrained from evil by "force and fear." This means that a primary purpose of the law is to prevent those who are "prone to vice" and "not easily amenable to words" to "leave others in peace." Not content to stop there, Aquinas further adds that once these potential criminals are sufficiently subdued the law may even look to make them virtuous by bringing them "to do willingly what hitherto they did from fear." From these remarks we may conclude that Aquinas considers the maintaining of peace and the instillation of virtue to be two the primary purposes of law. It nec-

20. *ST*, I-II, 95.1.

essarily follows that punishment, too, should have these goals, especially since Aquinas explicitly mentions the "fear of punishment" as the primary means by which they are to be achieved. As he elaborates in a subsequent passage, "men who are evilly disposed are not led to virtue unless they are compelled."[21] Later on Aquinas clarifies that human laws should not attempt to lead people to the absolute perfection of virtue, but only to those virtues upon which the stability of political society depends. Hence, "human laws do not forbid all vices, from which the virtuous abstain, but only the more grievous vices, from which it is possible for the majority to abstain; and chiefly those that are to the hurt of others, without the prohibition of which human society could not be maintained, [such as] murder, theft and suchlike."[22] In this passage as well, "peace" and "virtue" (albeit a limited virtue) constitute two primary purposes for which human law exists and against which the propriety of punishments may be judged.

Punishment and the Requirements of Justice: Aquinas's Retributivism Reconsidered

If securing peace and promoting virtue were the only two goals of human legislation, punishment would have, in Aquinas's language, an exclusively "medicinal" function. During his discussion of human law, however, he adds that "a lawgiver [also] prescribes certain things pertaining to good order."[23] Again mentioning "peace" as one aspect of this good order, Aquinas now also mentions "justice." As we observed in the previous chapter, Aquinas understands punishment as necessary to restore a kind of equality by inflicting some harm upon the criminal against his will. Through punishment, in other words, the criminal is placed back upon equal terms with the rest of the law-abiding citizenry. Again, this does not necessarily mean that the criminal's will is redirected to the common good or a life of virtue. The equality

21. *ST*, I-II, 95.1 ad 1.

22. *ST*, I-II, 96.2.

23. *ST*, I-II, 96.3.

of justice may be restored, on Aquinas's account, whether or not such a moral rehabilitation takes place. By examining again this aspect of Aquinas's theory of punishment, it is very important to raise the question as to whether or not Aquinas's understanding of punishment's retributive dimension is substantively different from the unfair advantage theory that was found to be flawed in chapter two. According to that theory as well, punishment is necessary for the restoration of justice, or, as Herbert Morris argued, for the redistribution of benefits and burdens among citizens. We must now ask whether, for Aquinas also, criminal actions create the same kind of "unfair advantage" described by Morris and his followers. It should come as no surprise that John Finnis, who is both a proponent of the unfair advantage theory of punishment and one of the foremost interpreters of Aquinas's moral and political philosophy, has virtually identified Aquinas's view with that of Morris and himself. Finnis's interpretation, to be sure, has its merits. In fact, his discussion of this subject contains a very insightful explanation of some of the same important aspects of Aquinas's retributivism discussed in the previous chapter. The following passage constitutes the core of Finnis's interpretation and requires extensive quotation.

> In any state of affairs capable of being improved by it, punishment's justifying point is to make an improvement. In Aristotle's phrase, which Aquinas everywhere adopts, punishment is "a kind of [or: like a] *medicine* [remedy, cure]." But in Aquinas's thought this "cure" involves far more than the possible reform of the offender, and includes also the restraining and the sheer deterrence of the offender and everyone else who needs deterring from wrongdoing and coercive inducement to decent conduct. Above all, it includes the healing of a disorder—an unjust inequality, a *defectus in statu reipublicae*—introduced into the whole community by the wrongdoer's conduct. It is the remedying of this social disorder that gives punishment its defining characteristics. . . . For it is of the essence of punishments that they subject the offender to something *contrary to their wills* (contra voluntatem). This, not pain, is of the essence. Why? Because the essence of offences is that in their wrongful acts offenders "yielded to their will more than they ought,"

"followed their own will excessively," "ascribed too much to their own preferences"—the measure of excess being the relevant law or norm for preserving and promoting the common good. Hence the proposition foundational for Aquinas's entire account of punishment: the order of just equality in relation to the offender is restored—offenders are brought back into that equality—precisely by the "subtraction" effected in a corresponding, proportionate suppression of *the will which took for itself too much* (too much freedom or autonomy, we may say). In this way, punishment "sets in order" the guilt whose essence was wrongful willing; and this (re)ordering (ordinativa) point of punishment can either be accounted remedial (medicinalis), or contrasted with the remedial (deterrent, reformative). The debts from which just punishment liberates the offender are not debts to the victims whom the offender has indeed wronged (in one way or another *willfully*) and who therefore might be plaintiffs in a civil proceeding or might understandably but wrongly desire revenge. Rather, we may say, those debts are the advantage—the inequality—which, in the willing of an offence, is wrongly gained *relative to all the offender's fellows* in the community against whose law, and so whose common good, the offence offends: the advantage of freedom from external constraints in choosing and acting.[24]

To be sure, there are several points highlighted by Finnis that shed important light upon Aquinas's approach to punishment. First, it is crucial to note the importance of Aquinas's teaching that punishment is contrary to the will of the one suffering it. As we saw earlier, contrariety to the will is one of punishment's essential characteristics in addition to its being an evil suffered by a rational agent on account of some fault. As we saw in the previous chapter, moreover, it appears to be precisely punishment's contrariety to the will that enables it to restore the equality of justice, "in so far as he who by *sinning* has exceeded in following his own will suffers something that is contrary to this will."[25] Second, Finnis helpfully distinguishes between Aquinas's understandings of punishment and restitution. Although he is well aware that

24. *Aquinas: Moral, Political, and Legal Theory,* 213–14.
25. *ST,* II-II, 108.4.

Aquinas does not explicitly distinguish between civil and criminal law, Finnis points out the important Thomistic idea that, whereas restitution deals with individuals' relations with one another, punishment deals with the criminal's relation to political society as a whole. Punishment is primarily necessary, in other words, not to settle the score between the criminal and his victim, but between the criminal and the body of citizens of which his victim is a part. Finally (and perhaps most importantly), Finnis captures a crucial aspect of Aquinas's retributivism. Not only does he acknowledge that, for Aquinas, punishment's primary justifying rationale is its ability to remove the inequality caused by the criminal's crime, but he also (albeit subtly) defends Aquinas against the consequentialist charge that retribution is inherently "backward looking" and hence (as Bentham would argue) both gratuitous and pointless. As Finnis describes Aquinas's position, punishment is necessary for a real "improvement" in the state of affairs upon which it is brought to bear. This is because the inequality caused by crime is a real "defect" from which society suffers, no less real than the defect in a person's soul that may stand in need of rehabilitation. This point is accentuated even more by Finnis's observation that, in his *Commentary on the Sentences,* Aquinas even goes so far as to include reestablishing the equality of justice (or the "ordering of fault by penalty") within punishment's "medicinal" capacity (something he avoids doing in the *Summa Theologiae*).[26] Far from looking backward, therefore, Aquinas's retributivism looks ahead to a real good to be achieved as a result of the infliction of punishment.

In spite of these ways in which Finnis can help us understand some of the crucial dimensions of Aquinas's theory of punishment (especially in its retributive aspects), however, there is reason to have serious misgivings about some of the finer points of his interpretation, especially regarding his tendency to conflate Aquinas's

26. Cf. Commentary on the Sentences of Peter Lombard, Book II, D. 36, A. 3, ad 3 with *ST,* II-II, 108.4.

penology with that of his own unfair advantage theory. More specifically, it is quite hasty to equate Aquinas's claim that punishment restores the equality of justice by inflicting an evil upon the criminal against his will with Finnis's claim that punishment restores the balance of benefits and burdens within society by negating the advantage the criminal has gained as a result of his crime. To see this we must begin by reminding ourselves of the differences (observed in chapter three) between Aquinas's theory of political society and that of the unfair advantage theorists. According to Herbert Morris in "Persons and Punishment" and John Finnis in *Natural Law and Natural Rights,* political society is a cooperative venture of individuals who live together in such a way as to advance more effectively their individual interests. This is why Morris describes the "primary rules" of society as those that protect the "benefits" of living in society (primarily that of physical protection) while simultaneously imposing burdens upon its members to respect the "spheres of noninterference" around others that those rules establish. Obedience to the law is thus understood as a burden because it requires the restraining of those inclinations that, in the absence of society, one would perhaps like to act upon. Since the benefits of living in society greatly outweigh the burdens, most people willingly agree to live under the primary rules offering them protection. It is also why violating the aforementioned primary rules entitles society to punish the offender. The crime essentially consists in "renouncing the burdens" of compliance to the primary rules and creates an unfair advantage that can only be erased by imposing a burden upon the criminal sufficient to outweigh his crime.

As we observed in chapter two, however, the unfair advantage theory of punishment is fatally flawed by its inability to explain coherently the benefits or advantages that committing a crime produces for the criminal and which thus need to be "erased" or "negated" by punishment. According to the unfair advantage theory's representatives, the benefits of crime are not to be confused with any material benefits (such as those that a civil court would forcibly return to a victim), but rather constitute the benefits or advantages of freedom from the constraint of the law. Let us recall Finnis's explanation of "criminal advantage," which he later attributes to Aquinas:

> When someone . . . manifests in action a preference . . . for his own interests, his own freedom of choice and action, as against the common interests and legally defined common way-of-action, then in and by that very action *he gains a certain sort of advantage* over those who have restrained themselves . . . in order to abide by the law.[27]

As we recall from chapter two, what is problematic in this account of crime is the highly doubtful nature of the claim that a criminal "gains freedom" from his transgression of the law, and no defender of the unfair advantage theory has intelligently been able to explain how criminals have something they did not have or are better off than they were before their crime was committed. As we observed in David Dolinko's criticism of George Sher (a criticism that could be applied to any proponent of the unfair advantage theory), "confronted with the difficulty of specifying what this 'gain' [or 'benefit'] is in a way that will make the theory come out right, Sher has . . . simply reified the criminal's act of law-violation, misleadingly labeled it 'freedom,' and treated it as the 'unfair advantage' to be taken away."[28] With this crippling objection in mind, the crucial point to understand is this: although Aquinas shares a retributive theory of punishment with those proponents of the unfair advantage theory, he does not share the view that crime constitutes an *advantage* to the criminal that must be, or can be, taken away by the infliction of punishment. To read him in this way is to impute to him a meaning he does not wish to convey and to bring his theory of punishment into conflict with the rest of his approach to moral and political philosophy.

Let us begin to distinguish Aquinas's penology from that of the unfair advantage theory by comparing the latter with Aqui-

27. *Natural Law and Natural Rights,* 263 (emphasis added).

28. "Some Thoughts about Retributivism," 548.

nas's teaching with regard to man's political nature and especially the virtue of legal justice. If Aquinas is right to say that human beings are naturally inclined to the good of political society in a way that does not imply the political community to be an instrumental but rather a basic good of human nature, it is quite difficult to believe that crimes against the common good constitute an *advantage* to the criminal who performs them. On the contrary, antisocial actions that violate the common good are, according to Aquinas's view, not only harmful to the person or persons attacked, stolen from, murdered, or defrauded, but are also (and perhaps even more severely) harmful to the perpetrator himself. To become a criminal who prefers his own immediate interests to those of others is actually to frustrate one's own happiness as a "naturally civic and social animal." Just as the virtue of legal justice that directs us in the service of the political common good is inherently perfective of the individual possessing it, a lack of concern for the political community (reinforced by actions that actually harm that community) stifle one's own progress toward a uniquely human happiness. Hence, the value of legal justice is much greater and more profound for the one who possesses that virtue than it is for the remainder of the community that benefits from its usefulness. Following the Aristotelian and even Socratic traditions, Aquinas (as we have interpreted him here) suggests that the virtue of justice is even better *for the just person* than it is for those to whom justice is demonstrated. This point has been recently made with particular eloquence by Mary Keys in her detailed study of Aquinas's theory of the common good.

> Justice is thus a human virtue that is especially perfective of the person as a rational as well as a social and civic animal (cf. *Pol.* I.2). To the Socratic and Thrasymachean query as to whose good justice really is, Aquinas responds in effect "*yours;* but even more so *mine;* and ultimately, in legal justice that seeks the common good, *ours.*" He argues that justice is a better good for the person practicing and possessing it than for the persons who are the immediate beneficiaries of just deeds or policies. They benefit from the justice of others only insofar as they are

not harmed through being deprived of a good that is already rightfully theirs. The lover and doer of justice, by contrast, stands to gain something much more valuable: a great perfection of his or her own soul, or at least an opportunity to strengthen and exercise this perfection if it is already possessed.[29]

According to Keys, one might say, Aquinas understands one's membership in political society in terms of "enlightened self-interest" in an emphatically classical, as opposed to modern, sense of that expression. Instead of living justly because doing so will ultimately promote one's own interests, the primary incentive to live justly is the fact that the virtue of justice is a constitutive element in living a fulfilled human life. In this sense, Aquinas's just man is "enlightened" in a much higher sense than the rational man of the social contract who tolerates the requirements of justice (or, as Morris puts it, the requirements of "self-restraint") in order to enjoy their material benefits. Justice is truly "its own reward," for Aquinas, in a much stronger and more immediate sense than the reasons for which Hobbes warned "the fool" to live justly lest he suffer the fate of those who underestimate the power of the sovereign.[30] In any case, if the interpretation presented here is correct, it is quite wrong to suggest that, for Aquinas, actions that deliberately harm the common good constitute, in themselves, an advantage or a benefit to the criminal. Criminals are, on the contrary, supremely *disadvantaged* by their criminal actions which, precisely because they fly in the face of one's natural inclination to serve and promote the political common good, make those who perform them into *a worse person.* To be sure, Aquinas is well aware of certain material advantages that may come as a result of crimes (e.g., the money or goods stolen), but it is fundamentally false to suggest that Aquinas considers the crime *itself* to constitute an advantage of any kind.

29. Mary Keys, *Aquinas, Aristotle, and the Promise of the Common Good* (Cambridge: Cambridge University Press, 2006), 196–97.

30. Cf. *Leviathan,* chap. 15 [4].

But what can be said, therefore, of the passages cited by Finnis alleged to show that Aquinas understands punishment as necessary to erase the criminal's advantage? As Finnis reminds us of Aquinas's teaching, "it is of the essence of punishments that they subject offenders to something *contrary to their wills* [*contra voluntatem*]. . . . Why? Because the essence of offences is that in their wrongful acts offenders 'yielded to their will more than they ought' [*plus voluntati suae indulsit quam debuit*],[31] 'followed their own will excessively' [*peccando nimis secutus est quam voluntatem*],[32] ascribed too much to their own preferences' [*plus suae voluntati tribuens quam oportet*][33]—the measure of excess being the relevant law or moral norm for preserving and promoting the common good."[34] If we examine these important phrases carefully, however, it becomes apparent that whereas Aquinas is definitely saying that crimes consist in "excessive," "misguided," or "inordinate" acts of the will, he does not indicate that crimes in themselves yield any sort of advantage of benefit to the criminal. To say that the unchecked or unrestrained act of the will *itself* constitutes a benefit, in such a way that the criminal "gains more freedom" than what is enjoyed by his law-abiding compatriots, coheres with Finnis's teaching in *Natural Law and Natural Rights* and Herbert Morris's doctrine in "Persons and Punishment," but it cannot be extrapolated from Aquinas's remarks without doing great violence to the text. On the contrary, a more faithful reading of Aquinas will have us draw the opposite conclusion, namely, that in spite of whatever material benefits a crime may bring, the criminal act itself causes a great and immediate harm to the one who performs it.[35]

31. *ST,* I-II, 87.6. 32. *ST,* II-II, 108.4.

33. *Compendium of Theology,* I.121 [237].

34. *Aquinas: Moral, Political, and Legal Theory,* 212–13.

35. This is not to say that the criminal act is harmful to the agent completely in and of itself. This would be to confuse, in Aquinas's language, the *malum culpae* with the *malum poenae.* On Aquinas's account, the sinful act is not its own punishment, since sins are necessarily voluntary and punishments are necessarily involuntary (*ST,* I-II, 87.2). Nevertheless, the sinful dispositions or vices immediately following from sins are to be counted as punitive, i.e., harmful to the sinner or criminal.

If the above interpretation of Aquinas is correct, what do we make of statements such as this one taken from his *Commentary on Aristotle's Nicomachean Ethics*?

[According to Aristotle] if one of two contestants receives a wound and the other inflicts it, or even if one commits murder and the other is murdered, this division of action and passion brings about inequality because the assailant and the murderer have more of what is esteemed good, inasmuch as they have done their own will and so seem as it were to have gained. But the man who is wounded or murdered has more of evil insofar as he is deprived against his will of well-being or life, and so he seems as it were to have suffered loss. The judge tries to equalize this by subtracting from the gain and allotting compensation for the loss, inasmuch as he takes away something from the assailant and the murderer contrary to their will and bestows it to the gain or honor of the person wounded or murdered.[36]

Although it is only cited by Finnis in passing,[37] this passage might seem to confirm his interpretation and to refute the interpretation offered here, since he explicitly mentions the unfair "gain" of the criminal that needs to be deleted in order for the equality of justice to be restored. The problem with interpreting this passage as an illustration that Aquinas's theory of punishment is akin to that of the unfair advantage theorists, however, is that Aquinas is not here specifically speaking about punishment.[38] The discussion rather concerns the issue of commutative justice more generally, and the particular issue at stake in the example provided by Aristotle is that not of punishment, but of what Aquinas will later call "restitution." In the *Summa Theoloigae,* Aquinas explains that restitution differs from punishment in that the former is an act of justice whereby one individual renders what he owes to another individual. As we have already seen, however,

36. *Commentary on the Nicomachean Ethics,* book 5, lectio 6 [952].

37. *Aquinas: Moral, Political, and Legal Theory,* 213, n. 153.

38. One might also argue that Aquinas is not advancing his own view, but rather summarizing Aristotle's, but I take this to be a much weaker argument since his discussion of justice throughout book five of the *Commentary* appears to be approving.

punishment has to do not so much with individuals' relations with one another but rather with the criminal's relation to the political community as a whole. Since, in the above passage from his *Commentary on the Nicomachean Ethics,* Aquinas speaks of a judge who "subtracts from the gain" of the murderer or assailant and "bestows" it upon the victim, he appears to have restitution in mind rather than punishment.[39]

Unlike punishment, restitution in itself does not actually presuppose any unjust action, but only rather a kind of imbalance that exists when an exchange is in the process of taking place. For instance, if one person renders a service that is worth a certain amount of money, there exists a debt that inheres in the recipient of the service until the amount is paid in full. The amount of money owed in this case is what Aquinas calls the "ius," which he defines as the "object" of any just transaction.[40] As Aquinas explains, criminals may owe something to their victims in a number of ways, all of which constitute requirements, not of punishment, but of restitution. First, one must restore what is taken from another or, in the case of an exchange, something of equal value. Second, the person who takes something from another may also be bound to restore something to him "on account of the taking," by which Aquinas means in addition to the value of the thing itself. For instance, in renting a house from my landlord it is not sufficient simply to return the house after I am done using it, but I must also pay him rent to compensate him for having "taken" the house for a given time.[41] Because this may also embrace what

39. According to Finnis's interpretation, Aquinas is "dealing simultaneously but to some extent distinctly with criminal punishment and civil compensation" (*Aquinas,* 213, n. 153). Although this interpretation is not impossible, since Aquinas sometimes classifies punishment under commutative justice (which is the subject at issue in this lecture of the *Commentary*), I find it to be unlikely. No form of the word "punishment" is ever mentioned in the entire lectio, and the example provided clearly deals with what is owed by one individual to another, something which (by Finnis's own observation [*Aquinas,* 213, n. 150]) characterizes restitution rather than punishment.

40. *ST,* II-II, 57.1.

41. *ST,* II-II, 62.6.

Aquinas calls examples of "injurious" taking, this aspect of restitution can easily be confused with punishment. As he says, in the case of theft and robbery, "the *thief* is bound to restitution not only by reason of the thing, but also by reason of the injurious action, even though the thing is no longer in his possession."[42] In other words, compensating the victim of robbery is not accomplished simply by returning the goods that were robbed, but requires a further payment to account for the injurious taking itself (analogous to the additional payment of rent in the previous example). Such a payment is thus required even when no material goods are taken at all, as in the case of assault. "For just as a man who strikes another, though he gain nothing thereby, is bound to compensate the injured *person*, so too he that is guilty of *theft* or robbery is bound to make compensation for the loss incurred, although he be no better off. . . ." Although what Aquinas is discussing is often described today as "punitive damages" paid to the victim, he clearly distinguishes between such payment and punishment as he adds "and *in addition* [*ulterius*] he [the perpetrator of injurious taking] must be punished for the *injustice* committed."[43] In other words, punishment is required over and above the requirement to compensate the victim of crime for his losses, even when such losses are, as in the case of assault, intangible. The "gain" assumed by the criminal of which Aquinas spoke in his *Commentary on the Nicomachean Ethics* must, therefore, be seen in its proper context. First, it is only a gain in a very extended sense of the term, since it corresponds only to the metaphorical sense in which one "takes" something from the victim of assault. Second (and more importantly), even if one interprets the gain of the assaulter quite literally, Aquinas makes it clear that such gain is taken away by restitution, not punishment, since even after one is forced to pay one's victim for damages one must still be punished "in addition." Moreover, the gain of which Aquinas speaks

42. Ibid.

43. Ibid. (emphasis added).

in his *Commentary* cannot be a gain that is taken away through punishment, since Aquinas holds that it must be paid (by order of the judge) *directly to the victim* of the crime whose losses need to be compensated. If Aquinas was speaking of punishment, he would not be talking about what is paid to the victim but rather what is inflicted upon the criminal by the political community as a whole (of some representative thereof).[44] To say that *punishment* takes away that criminal's gain, therefore, is to conflate punishment with restitution, which requires the return of stolen goods plus a payment that erases the metaphorical "gain" that criminals appropriate to themselves on account of their injurious taking. Because he distinguishes both of these from punishment, however, Aquinas gives us no reason to believe that punitive sanctions have anything to do with negating a gain, a benefit, or an advantage enjoyed by the criminal.

Examining one final text should make the point perfectly clear. In his discussion of the virtue of justice in the *Summa Theologiae,* Aquinas affirms the classical dictum that the act of justice is "to render to each his own" *(reddere unicuique quod suum est).* In the third objection, however, the point is raised that this definition is insufficient because acts of justice not only assign goods to those entitled to them, but also "repress" injurious actions to those deserving. The word for punishment is not used, but the meaning of the objection is clear. Acts of justice seem to include, not only the distribution of good things, but also the infliction of punitive evils where necessary, an aspect of justice that the classical definition appears not to capture. Aquinas's reply is very telling:

44. Although punishment is primarily inflicted by the political community as a whole, Aquinas does speak about ways in which individuals are given their due when criminals are punished. First, it is sometimes the accuser's right that a criminal be punished if the person accusing was harmed by the crime committed (*ST,* II-II, 67.4). Second, the victim of the crime is secondarily entitled to the criminal's punishment inasmuch as its infliction upon the one who injured him helps in restoring his "honor" (*ST,* II-II, 67.4 ad 3). Nevertheless, the primary way in which punishment restores justice is to reestablish the equality between the criminal and the political community.

As the *Philosopher* states (Ethic. v, 4), in matters of *justice*, the name of "profit" [*lucrum*] is extended to whatever is excessive, and whatever is deficient is called "loss." The reason for this is that *justice* is first of all and more commonly exercised in *voluntary* interchanges of things, such as buying and selling, wherein those expressions are properly employed; and yet they are transferred to all other matters of *justice*. The same applies to the rendering to each one of what is his own.[45]

We are thus given to understand that applying the traditional formula of justice to punitive matters requires a significant "extension" of the terms and concepts employed. The reason for this is that punishment simply does not neatly fit into the textbook example for a just transaction, namely, the exchange of goods or services of relatively equal value. In such a textbook example, the concept of profit or gain is central. Since I profit by receiving a service (e.g., having my driveway snowplowed), I must return something equally profitable to the renderer of that service (usually in the form of monetary payment). To be sure, something similar is taking place in the case of punishment. A criminal is being "paid back" for something he has done (as the snowplow operator is being paid for his service rendered). But as Aquinas fully acknowledges, the language we use to speak about the act of justice falls short in the case of punishment precisely when we incorporate the notion of profit. Aside from any monetary gain that may be appropriated to oneself in committing a crime, the commission of the crime itself involves no profit in any real sense whatsoever. If I murder someone, I certainly deserve punishment and I certainly have *taken* something extremely valuable from someone. But unlike cases of monetary taking I have neither gained anything for myself nor do I now enjoy an advantage over anyone in any sense of the term. This appears to be why Aquinas states that the concepts of profit and gain are "properly" used in cases of voluntary interchanges such as buying and selling, the direct implication of which is that to apply profit and gain to acts of criminality (and

45. *ST,* II-II, 58.11, ad 3.

by extension to criminal justice), would be to use such concepts *improperly.* Such improper use of the concepts of profit or gain is precisely what is done in speaking of punishment as necessary to remove the criminal's "unfair advantage." For this reason, it clear again that Aquinas's theory of punishment simply cannot be identified with the unfair advantage theory and is therefore not subject to the same devastating criticisms already discussed.

Beyond Retribution: The Death Penalty and Punishment's Medicinal Function

It remains to consider Aquinas's treatment of the death penalty, on which his most direct statement is the following:

> Now every part is directed to the whole. For this reason we observe that if the health of the whole body demands the excision of a member, through its being decayed or infectious to the other members, it will be both praiseworthy and advantageous to have it cut away. Now every individual person is compared to the whole community, as part to whole. Therefore, if a man be dangerous and infectious to the community, on account of some sin, it is praiseworthy and advantageous that he be killed in order to safeguard the common good, since "a little leaven corrupteth the whole lump."[46]

In light of his theory of punishment, it should come as no surprise that Aquinas appeals to the common good in his argument for the death penalty. It is also not surprising that he reminds us that punishment (capital or otherwise) presupposes a relationship between individual citizens and the political "whole" of which they are part. Nevertheless, Aquinas's justification for the death penalty introduces a slightly new argument that is absent from his discussion of the institution of punishment in general; and it conspicuously leaves out certain elements of the more general discussion as well. For these reasons, a careful look at Aquinas's treatment of the death penalty allows us to see his entire

46. *ST,* II-II, 64.2.

penology in a different light. Rather than the need to restore the equality of justice, Aquinas emphasizes protecting society from the criminal. Just as a gangrenous limb must be cut away to save the life of the whole body, so also must some criminals be cut away from society. Presumably, such criminals are so "infectious" that they must be banished, not just from the political community, but from the land of the living altogether. Clearly, one way of interpreting Aquinas's defense of capital punishment is to see his argument as an appeal to the physical protection of society. Some criminals are simply so dangerous that political authorities must execute them to protect the safety of those entrusted to their care. This is not difficult to imagine in cases where criminals may become so dangerous, corrupt, and powerful that even a sentence of permanent incarceration would be insufficient to protect the innocent from their potentially deadly reach.[47]

Looking back upon the text, however, one may also observe that his argument may not be restricted to society's *physical* protection. One indication of this is Aquinas's reference to St. Paul's Letter to the Corinthians, which warns that "a little leaven corrupteth the whole lump."[48] The context of this passage (of which we can only assume Aquinas was aware) pertains to the moral danger that certain sinners present to the Christian community. In the chapter from which the quotation is taken, St. Paul is discussing the ill effects of an incestuous adulterer within the Corinthian Church (whom he apparently saw fit to excommunicate). Since the sinful person in this case is identified by St. Paul as a "fornica-

47. To be sure, this argument should not be confused with Aquinas's treatment of legitimate self-defense. As he later argues, even a private citizen may deliver a lethal blow in order to protect himself from a dangerous assailant. So long as the defender does not directly and intentionally kill (and provided that he does not use "more than necessary violence"), his lethal action may be entirely blameless (*ST*, II-II, 64.7). This is quite different from the case of capital punishment, which involves the direct infliction of death carried out by legitimate public authorities. Because such persons are charged with the protection of the common good, they (unlike private citizens) may intentionally kill certain criminals just as a soldier intentionally kills an enemy combatant in the line of duty.

48. 1 Cor. 5.6.

tor," we may surmise that he must be removed for the protection of the community's moral and spiritual, rather than its physical, welfare. This at least is what the next sentence seems to indicate, when St. Paul insists that the community must "purge out the old leaven, that you may be a new paste, as you are unleavened." Assuming that Aquinas is not quoting St. Paul out of context, therefore, it is not unreasonable to suggest that he understands the death penalty in similar terms. When a criminal becomes "dangerous and infectious to the community on account of some sin," his dangerousness may also stem from the moral corruption his sinful character might spread.[49] To be sure, how to deal with sinful and dangerous criminals is not for anyone to decide. Aquinas makes it quite clear in the following article that since "the care of the common good is entrusted to persons of rank having political authority . . . they alone, and not private individuals, can lawfully put evildoers to death."[50] Still, the extreme measure of killing one of the community's own citizens appears to be justified by the need to preserve society's moral integrity. This would cohere well with Aquinas's position that "virtue," in addition to "peace" and "justice," is an aspect of the common good requiring the attention of the law. Apparently, preserving the virtue of citizens is so important that it warrants the killing of certain criminals who, "on account of some sin," may facilitate the moral demise of others. When confronted with the objection that such killing violates the solemn commandment binding us to "have charity toward all men," Aquinas again appeals to the moral corruption, and not only the physical dangerousness, of the criminal.

> By sinning man departs from the order of reason, and consequently falls away from the dignity of his manhood, in so far as he is naturally free, and exists for himself, and he falls into the slavish state of the beasts, by being disposed of according as he is useful to others. . . . Hence, although it be evil in itself to kill a man so long as he preserve his dignity,

49. See Long, "*Evangelium Vitae,* St. Thomas, and the Death Penalty," 534.
50. *ST,* II-II, 64.3.

yet it may be good to kill a man who has sinned, even as it is to kill a beast. For a bad man is worse than a beast, and is more harmful, as the Philosopher states.[51]

Unfortunately, the thought of punishing someone for sins like fornication gives the reader the impression that Aquinas is licensing the coercive arm of the law to conduct a witch hunt. We must remember, though, that Aquinas quotes St. Paul, not to imply that fornication ought to be punished by the state in addition to excommunication, but to convey the more general point that one of punishment's medicinal purposes is to protect the moral integrity of those in the community who have knowledge of the crime. Though Aquinas may certainly also mean that criminals must be restrained or even killed in order to defend society from physical harm, his words are also open to the interpretation that punishment has a way of publically denouncing the criminal's action, uplifting the moral rectitude of society, and ensuring that criminal actions are not regarded as normative. To be sure, this considerably expands the concept of "protection," but we get an indication that

51. *ST,* II-II, 64.2 ad 3. John Finnis argues that Aquinas's argument here is deeply flawed. As Finnis observes, Aquinas himself acknowledges that even perpetrators of heinous crimes are still human and thus deserving of humane treatment (*Aquinas: Moral, Political, and Legal Theory,* 282). One, indeed, wonders why Aquinas, in answering the objection that the death penalty contradicts our obligation to act with charity toward all human beings, does not rely on the argument that public officials simply have the authority to inflict evils upon people that private citizens do not. Aquinas could have simply reiterated arguments made elsewhere by saying that public officials are "executing divine justice" by killing those who deserve it and/or who perilously threaten the common good. For his part, Finnis would argue that Aquinas's own principles would not allow the intentional infliction of death (or any permanent injury) upon another human being whether a criminal or not, and so Aquinas's treatment of the death penalty is in direct contradiction with his moral teaching as a whole. Whereas others have argued (see Long's *Teleological Grammar,* 58–62) that Aquinas is quite consistent to allow for the intentional killing of criminals by agents of the state, it remains mysterious why he relies upon the strange argument that humans who commit terrible crimes are actually less than human. Instead of arguing for the subhumanity of violent criminals who are no longer deserving of charity, why not reiterate the argument that putting criminals to death need not be motivated by "hatred of the sinners, but out of the love of charity, by which [the judge] prefers the public good to the life of the individual"? (*ST,* II-II, 25.6 ad 2).

something like society's moral stability is at stake when Aquinas answers an objection in the *Prima Secundae* that has specifically to do with punishment's medicinal function. The question at hand is whether punishment is due even after the "stain of sin" has been removed from the criminal. In other words, even after the criminal's inordinate will has been corrected, does punishment still need to be inflicted? According to the objection, no, because, since punishment is a kind of "medicine," the punishment of a criminal already restored to righteousness would be redundant. Aquinas responds by saying that, even after the sin of sin is removed,

> [p]unishment is still requisite in order that the other powers of the soul may be healed, since they were disordered by the sin committed, so that, to wit, the disorder may be remedied by the contrary of what caused it. Moreover punishment is requisite to restore the equality of justice, *and to remove the scandal given to others, so that those who were scandalized at the sin may be edified by the punishment.*[52]

Aquinas's appeal here to the "scandal" of the sin or crime means much more than simply the emotional shock it may cause to onlookers. In Aquinas's understanding scandal refers specifically to the moral or spiritual harm to someone that may result from another's actions. Whether causing someone else to sin was part of the sinner's intention or not, a person may be guilty of scandal if his actions are imitated by others who follow his example. For example, observing that an older and respected relative acquires money from regularly entering the homes of the elderly and robbing them, an impressionable young man may be led to follow this sort of behavior. Though his implicit knowledge of the natural law *(synderesis)* speaks out against this kind of crime, the youngster's weakness and lack of experience in applying the moral law to specific situations causes him to fall in the same way and, if he persists, may result in his complete undoing.[53] If his old-

52. *ST,* I-II, 87.6 ad 3 (emphasis is my own).

53. According to Aquinas, scandal presupposes some degree of imperfection on the part of the one scandalized (*ST,* II-II, 43.5).

er relative is apprehended, however, the younger man's character may be salvaged in more than one way. To be sure, he may avoid committing robbery simply because he fears the punishment. But he may also be reminded by the punishment of a higher truth, namely, that his older relative's actions are not worthy of imitation *in their own right.* The punishment, in other words, expresses and reaffirms the political community's indignation at the crime committed and solders that commitment in the minds of potential criminals whose moral future still lay undetermined. Such an example would fit well with Aquinas's view of political society as a training ground for the moral life, and of his view that punishment itself can assist the state's ability to facilitate virtue, not just through "force and fear,"[54] but by giving expression to the very same moral law that undergirds civil society and in defiance of which the criminal acts. This expressive function hinted at by Aquinas's notion of medicinal punishment has been insisted upon by punishment theorists in modern times. The following passage from Joel Feinberg's well-known essay, "The Expressive Function of Punishment," helps us understand what Aquinas is getting at, both in his argument for capital punishment and in his mention of removing scandal as one of punishment's medicinal capabilities.

> Both penalties and punishment are authoritative deprivations for failures; but, apart from these common features, penalties have a miscellaneous character, whereas punishments have an important additional characteristic in common. That characteristic, or specific difference . . . is a certain expressive function: punishment is a conventional device for the expression of attitudes of resentment and indignation, and of judgments of disapproval and reprobation, on the part either of the punishing authority himself or of those "in whose name" the punishment is inflicted. Punishment, in short, has a symbolic significance largely missing from other kinds of penalties.[55]

54. *ST,* I-II, 95.1.

55. Feinberg, "The Expressive Function of Punishment," in *Doing and Deserving* (Princeton, N.J.: Princeton University Press, 1970), 97–98.

Whether we interpret Aquinas's defense of capital punishment as primarily an appeal to the physical protection of society, the moral protection of society, or both, one striking fact remains: when it comes to justifying the death penalty, Aquinas leaves out any reference to retribution or the need to restore the equality of justice. In light of his emphasis upon retribution elsewhere[56] (and especially in light of his claims that punishment, considered "under the aspect of punishment," is essentially retributive),[57] this absence is especially glaring. On the basis of Aquinas's punitive theory we have seen thus far, one could easily imagine an argument for the death penalty that is entirely different from the one we have seen. It is "praiseworthy and advantageous" to put certain criminals to death, Aquinas might have said, because some crimes are so grave that the equality of justice cannot be restored without killing those who perpetrate them. In other words, some criminals simply deserve to be killed notwithstanding any useful consequences or protection their deaths might bring about. To be sure, all punishments (whether or not they inflict death) have the potential to protect the innocent from harmful criminals. They may do so by rehabilitating the criminal to a point where he is no longer dangerous, by frightening the criminal from committing future crimes, by frightening others through general deterrence, or by reaffirming the moral law against which the criminal acted. For a philosopher like Aquinas who takes retribution seriously, however, are not such consequences of punishment somewhat beside the point? Should he not at least mention the importance of rehabilitation, protection, and deterrence only once it is guaranteed that the punishment is just? Simply put, if Aquinas affirms that punishment is essentially retributive when considered "under the aspect of punishment," why does his justification for capital punishment make no mention of retribution? To what extent is Aquinas really a retributivist?

56. Especially in *ST,* I-II, 87.1.

57. *ST,* II-II, 108, 4.

Unfortunately, Aquinas does not provide an explanation for the conspicuous absence of retribution in his defense of capital punishment. As to why his account of the death penalty differs so markedly from his theory of punishment in general is, therefore, left to us to speculate. In this regard, we may find at least a partial explanation by looking to Aquinas's understanding of retribution itself. As we observed in chapter four, the essence of retribution consists in reestablishing the equality of justice by inflicting a punitive evil upon a criminal against his will. The reason for this, Aquinas explained, is that the crime that deserves punishment consisted precisely in the voluntary transgression of a criminal who "overindulged" his will at the expense of the common good. This is substantially different from other forms of retributivism that result in a stricter adherence to the equality of justice. For example, Kant argues that the only legitimate reason for punishing a criminal is "because he has committed a crime."[58] By this he means, among other things, that only the criminal's external action should be considered in matters of political justice.[59] By remaining relatively indifferent to the criminal's "interior act," Kant deliberately ignores the diversity of psychological factors from which criminal behavior is carried out. This is why he famously relies on a strict application of the *lex talionis* to determine which kinds of punishments should be inflicted. As he says, "any undeserved evil that you inflict on someone else among the people is one that you inflict upon yourself. If you vilify him, you vilify yourself; if you steal from him, you steal from yourself. Only the Law of Retribution *(jus talionis)* can determine the kind and degree of punishment."[60] Alternatively, since Aquinas understands retribution to be a repression of the criminal's voluntary

58. Immanuel Kant, *Metaphysics of Morals,* trans. Mary Gregor (Cambridge: Cambridge University Press, 1996), 6.331.

59. Ibid., 6.231 (For a clear discussion of this aspect of Kant's legal thought, see Ernest Weinrib, "Law as Idea of Reason," in *Essays on Kant's Political Philosophy,* ed. Howard Williams [Cardiff: University of Wales Press, 1992], 25–26).

60. Ibid., 6.332.

"overindulgence," determining so far as possible the degree of willfulness in the criminal's interior act becomes of paramount importance. Following Aquinas's principles, a crime committed less voluntarily (on account of ignorance, passion, or some other mitigating factor) would constitute a lesser transgression of the law and would require, in turn, a lesser punishment. This aspect of Aquinas's penology could be seen as both an advantage and a disadvantage. On the one hand, it allows for much greater precision in determining the proper degree of punishment necessary to restore the equality of justice. On the other hand, it requires those responsible for sentencing to understand a criminal's *mens rea* much more thoroughly than even Aquinas would himself admit is possible for human beings. As he explains in arguing for human law's limitations (and the resulting need for divine law), "man is not competent to judge of interior movements, that are hidden, but only of exterior acts which appear."[61] One explanation for Aquinas's lack of interest in retribution regarding capital punishment may be the simple fact that the precise amount of punishment necessary to restore justice is never entirely knowable. The most human authorities can hope for, Aquinas might say, is approximating what justice requires in accordance with the constraints of their limited human condition. This is not to say, of course, that the equality of justice is ultimately abandoned by Aquinas as a motive for punishment. Perhaps when it comes to inflicting a punishment as severe and as final as death, however, the uncertain standard of what justice requires should give way to the more certain standards of what immanently threatens the welfare of innocent citizens.

If we examine another important aspect of Aquinas's penology, we find an additional reason to suspect that retribution is relegated to a less important motive, not only for capital punishment, but for all punishments inflicted in the political order. In the *Summa Theologiae,* Aquinas considers the question of whether aveng-

61. *ST,* I-II, 91.4.

ing crime should "be wrought by means of punishments customary among men." Ultimately answering in the affirmative, he first considers an objection that argues that all crimes consisting of mortal sins should be punished with death. The argument is very straightforward. Since mortal sins are those actions punished by God with spiritual death, and since human justice should imitate divine justice, all such sins should be punished by human authorities with temporal (or bodily) death. In his reply, Aquinas does not take issue with the general principle that human authorities should imitate divine justice. He does, however, remind us that punishments in political society should have a somewhat different orientation than the punishments of God.

> All who sin mortally are deserving of eternal death, as regards future retribution, which is accordance with the truth of divine judgment. But the punishments of this life are more of a medicinal character; wherefore the punishment of death is inflicted on those sins alone which conduce to the grave undoing [*pernicies*] of others.[62]

We have already seen that punishment *can be* medicinal. What we now learn is that the punishments "of this life," which undoubtedly includes those inflicted by political authority, are *more* medicinal than retributive. The fact that human punishments are "more of a medicinal character" does not mean, of course, that they are exclusively medicinal. If they were, the equality of justice would be entirely beside the point of human punishments (which Aquinas obviously does not hold). It also does not mean that divine punishments are exclusively retributive. As Aquinas argues more than once, divine punishments are sometimes inflicted upon man "for the sake of his soul's health and the glory of God."[63] Such is Aquinas's explanation for the punishment of the blind man in chapter nine of John's Gospel, who was punished neither for his own sin nor the sins of his parents, but that "the works of God may be manifested, and from them that God be known."[64] We must take

62. *ST,* II-II, 108.3 ad 2.
63. *ST,* I-II, 87.7.
64. Thomas Aquinas, *Commentary on the Gospel of St. John,* vol. 2, trans. James A.

this remark to mean just what it says, namely, that human punishments are *more* medicinal than retributive, and should therefore be *primarily* designed to restore criminals back to willfully law-abiding citizens (just as medicines restore sick people to health), protecting society, and deterring other potential criminals, since "the punishment inflicted according to human laws is not always intended as a medicine for the one who is punished, but sometimes only for others . . . that at least they may be deterred from crime through fear of punishment."[65]

But why are human punishments more medicinal? Looking back upon Aquinas's argument for the debt of punishment (upon which the entire institution of punishment's legitimacy depends), he seemed to say that the punishments of political society are independent of those inflicted by God. The reason for this was that a particular sin may simultaneously offend the order of reason, the political order, and the order of divine law. Hence, "man can be punished with a threefold punishment corresponding to the three orders to which the human will is subject."[66] Following this line of argument, the fact that someone may be punished by God (whether in this life or the next) for committing injustice would not seem to absolve or mitigate the debt of punishment owed to him by the political community. Aquinas takes up this issue even more directly in the *Summa Contra Gentiles,* where the question arises as to whether human beings are entitled to punish evildoers at all. In the course of his answer, Aquinas explains why political authorities are in fact entitled to punish. At the same time, however, he gives us reason to wonder just how independent the human order of justice is.

Since some people pay little attention to the punishments inflicted by God, because they are devoted to the objects of sense and care only

---

Weisheipl, O.P., S.T.M., and Fabian R. Larcher, O.P. (Petersham, Mass.: St. Bede's Publications, 1998), 1301.

65. *ST,* I-II, 87.3 ad 2; cf. *ST,* I-II, 87.8 ad 2.

66. *ST,* I-II, 87.1.

for the things that are seen, it has been ordered accordingly by divine providence that there be men in various countries whose duty it is to compel these people, by means of sensible and present punishments, to respect justice.[67]

Elaborating upon the authority from which human punishments are derived, Aquinas continues.

The men who are put in positions over other men are like executors of divine providence; indeed God through the order of His providence directs lower beings by means of higher ones. . . . But no one sins by the fact that he follows the order of divine providence. Now, this order of divine providence requires the good to be rewarded and the evil to be punished. . . . Therefore, men who are in authority over others do no wrong when they reward the good and punish the evil.[68]

From the above passages we are given to understand that the "order of human law" is embraced by what Aquinas now calls the "order of divine providence." Just as God himself is the author of punishments in the "order of divine law," human authorities are entitled to inflict punishments in political society only inasmuch as they are "executors of divine providence." To say that the order of human law is independent from the order of divine law does not mean that it is independent of the broader and more universal order of divine providence to which all created things are subject.[69] Upon reflection, this teaching is perfectly consistent with the foundation of Aquinas's natural law theory seen earlier. Far from enjoying independence from divine providence, human affairs are embraced by the eternal law, which Aquinas understands as nothing other than "the very idea of the government of things in God the ruler of the universe."[70] In a way, then, the punishments of political society still originate in God "at whose behest" and according to whose providence they are carried out by legitimate human authorities.[71] This may explain, therefore, why Aquinas does not consider it the primary responsibility of

67. *SCG,* III, 146.1.
68. *SCG,* III, 146.2.
69. *ST,* Ia. 22.2.
70. *ST,* I-II, 91.1.
71. *ST,* II-II, 64.6 ad 1.

human law to punish with a view to "future retribution." Although a crime that goes unpunished results in a real injustice, humans may take comfort in the inevitable retribution that God will render to everyone for their violations of human and divine law alike. For this reason, Aquinas can emphasize the validity of retribution in matters of criminal punishment without insisting upon its centrality. Far more central, it seems, is the stability, order, and moral virtue of political society that would be compromised without human punishments on account of those who "pay little attention to the punishments inflicted by God." This unexpected shift of emphasis explains why Aquinas, at times, allows for the remission of punishment by those possessing "full authority in the commonwealth" and exercising "discretion," and at other times admits that "a lesser fault is [sometimes] punished with a graver punishment . . . in order that a great danger be avoided."[72] Again, this does not mean that Aquinas would allow travesties of justice to occur for the sake of rehabilitation or deterrence. The equality of justice remains a real good worth protecting. In assigning it to a secondary place in the temporal order, however, Aquinas explains his apparent tolerance for injustice by reminding us that "the punishments in the present life are used as medicines."[73] Considering the additional (and often competing) "medicinal" goals of punishment, the limitations of the human condition, and the larger order of divine providence of which human society is only a part, Aquinas can only recommend a retributive theory of punishment that considerably understates the necessity of retribution.

72. *ST,* II-II, 67.4 (corpus and ad 1).

73. Thomas Aquinas, *On Evil,* trans. Jean T. Oesterle (South Bend, Ind.: University of Notre Dame Press, 1995), 2.10 ad 4.

6

CAPITAL PUNISHMENT, *EVANGELIUM VITAE*, AND THE THOMISTIC THEORY OF PUNISHMENT

The purpose of the foregoing chapters has been to demonstrate the philosophical pitfalls of contemporary utilitarian and retributivist theories of punishment and to present accurately Thomas Aquinas's theory of punishment as a legitimate alternative. Readers of Aquinas coming from the Catholic tradition will also find useful some discussion of what this presentation of Aquinas's teaching means for his compatibility (or lack thereof) with the contemporary Catholic Church's position on the death penalty, the most recent statement of which is found in Pope John Paul II's encyclical letter, *Evangelium Vitae (The Gospel of Life).*

Evangelium Vitae (hereafter *EV),* of course, is far from containing a thematic discussion of capital punishment. The overwhelming emphasis of the document is, rather, upon other evils of contemporary society such as abortion, euthanasia, physician-assisted suicide, and medical technologies of various kinds that imperil human embryos. In the third and most forthright chapter, however, John Paul II spends two sections explicitly devoted to the death penalty, and says some things that many have taken to be an assertion that capital punishment is intrinsically wrong, thus placing it in the same moral category as the other evils mentioned and condemned throughout the document.

After reasserting the importance of the Fifth Commandment, the pope acknowledges that the prohibition against killing does not forbid every action that happens to result in a person's death. Following upon a long-standing principle of Catholic moral thought, he states that actions may sometimes be taken that are lethal to some people while necessary for defending oneself or others. Quoting the *Catechism of the Catholic Church* (hereafter CCC) John Paul II writes that "'legitimate defense can be not only a right but a grave duty for someone responsible for another's life, the common good of the family or of the state.' Unfortunately it happens that the need to render the aggressor incapable of causing harm sometimes involves taking his life. In this case the fatal outcome is attributable to the aggressor whose action brought it about, even though he may not be morally responsible because of a lack of the use of reason."[1] Interestingly, this quotation ends with a reference to Aquinas's discussion, not of capital punishment, but of self-defense. In the article of the *Summa Theologiae* cited by the pope, Aquinas, too, explains that private citizens, so long as they do not use "more than necessary violence," may inflict a lethal blow upon an aggressor in order to preserve their own lives (or, presumably, the lives of those in their care).[2] As we observed in chapter five,[3] Aquinas continues to argue that the death of the aggressor must be beside the intention of the private defender. In other words, the inflictor of death is not *killing in order to save his own life,* but is rather subduing or rendering harmless the assailant in order to save his own life, which has the foreseen but unintended consequence of killing the aggressor. As Aquinas continues, however, the same moral restraints do not exist in the case of capital punishment, where those with "public authority acting for the common good" may directly intend the death of criminals by killing them.

This brings us to the primary point of contention for interpreters of *EV* with respect to capital punishment. Whereas Aqui-

1. *Evangelium Vitae,* Vatican Translation, sec. 55.

2. *ST,* II-II, 64.7.

3. See note 46 of that chapter.

nas hastens to distinguish between capital punishment and private defense, John Paul II proceeds with language that appears to conflate the two. After explaining the principle of legitimate self-defense, the pope immediately continues to say that "*this* is the context in which to place the problem of the death penalty."[4] It is not clear whether John Paul II is explicitly denying the Thomistic position by saying that capital punishment's only defensibility is under the umbrella of legitimate defense, but the paragraph that follows includes a statement as to the purpose of punishment in general with which Aquinas's agreement would be, at best, mixed.

> The primary purpose of the punishment which society inflicts is "to redress the disorder caused by the offence." Public authority must redress the violation of personal and social rights by imposing on the offender an adequate punishment for the crime, as a condition for the offender to regain the exercise of his or her freedom. In this way authority also fulfils the purpose of defending public order and ensuring people's safety, while at the same time offering the offender an incentive and help to change his or her behavior and be rehabilitated.[5]

Surely, Aquinas would agree that punishment must "redress the disorder caused by the crime." Surely, he would agree that the punishment imposed must be "adequate for the crime." Though he would likely agree that most punishments be imposed as a necessary condition for reentering society, he would be sure to acknowledge two exceptions, namely, permanent exile and death.[6] Likewise, whereas Aquinas would also agree that punishment in the political order is primarily medicinal or rehabilitative, and would thus agree that most punishments should offer criminals the "incentive and help" they need to change their ways, he would nonetheless remind us that punishment's medicinal value may also be understood in terms of deterrence and "not only for the one who is punished."[7] The main point is this: If John Paul II's above statement is meant as an all-embracing delineation as to the limits and

4. *EV,* sec. 56 (emphasis is my own).

5. Ibid.

6. See *ST,* II-II, 108.3.

7. *ST,* I-II, 87.3 ad 2.

purposes of punishment in general, his words would seem to exclude the possibility of the death penalty altogether, thus bringing him into direct opposition with Aquinas. The claim that the death penalty can be a necessary condition for reentering society is obviously absurd (though it may not be as absurd to suggest that the death penalty is rehabilitative). If the above statement was written not as a definitive statement regarding the nature of punishment, Aquinas may agree on the condition that the necessary qualifications are made which would make room for the death penalty, but it is difficult not to notice that such qualifications are conspicuous in *EV* by their absence.

The pope's remarks as to the purposes of punishment are significant, not only for determining their consistency with the doctrine of Aquinas, but for understanding the remaining paragraphs of the same section where the question of the death penalty is directly taken up. As John Paul II concludes:

> It is clear that, for these purposes to be achieved, the nature and extent of the punishment must be carefully evaluated and decided upon, and ought not go to the extreme of executing the offender except in cases of absolute necessity: in other words, when it would not be possible otherwise to defend society. Today however, as a result of steady improvements in the organization of the penal system, such cases are very rare, if not practically non-existent. In any event, the principle set forth in the new Catechism of the Catholic Church remains valid: "If bloodless means are sufficient to defend human lives against an aggressor and to protect public order and the safety of persons, public authority must limit itself to such means, because they better correspond to the concrete conditions of the common good and are more in conformity to the dignity of the human person."[8]

As thoughtful commentators have pointed out, these words are very suggestive. There almost appears to be a deliberate disconnect between this final statement regarding the death penalty and the previous statement regarding the institution of punishment

8. *EV,* sec. 56.

as a whole. One might ask, if the purpose of punishment is to redress the disorder caused by the crime, is it not possible that a particular punishment may be able to redress the disorder caused by the crime but not necessary to protect society and "defend human lives" from the dangerous criminal? Might not the death penalty as inflicted in modern democratic states (equipped with modern incarceration facilities) be an example of such a punishment? Since self-defense is only one of many functions of punishment, and since the death penalty is only justified in terms of self-defense, it might seem as though the pope is (albeit subtly) suggesting that capital punishment is not morally defensible *as punishment.* This difficulty has led some scholars to argue that the pope's intention is to convey something directly at odds with Aquinas, namely, that the only terms on which capital punishment may be defended are those of self-defense. In other words, the rare (if not "nonexistent") conditions under which the death penalty may be inflicted do not constitute examples of the legitimate infliction of death, but are rather examples of *self-defense writ large.* What's more, these same scholars have argued that the most faithful reading of *EV* includes the proposition that the deliberate killing of another human being is morally forbidden regardless of whether the agent of death holds public authority acting on behalf of the common good and regardless of whether the criminal is guilty of a capital offense. On this reading, in other words, states may execute persons only under conditions where the criminal's death is a foreseen but unintended consequence with moral equivalence to the situation of a private individual defending his own life against an aggressor.

By far the most thorough and articulate exponent of this interpretation of *EV* is E. Christian Brugger. In a recent statement on the issue, Brugger lists "eight indicators" suggesting that *EV* advances the new doctrine that capital punishment is only justifiable as self-defense.[9] These indicators are taken, not directly from the

9. See E. Christian Brugger, "Rejecting the Death Penalty: Continuity and Change in the Tradition," *Heythrop Journal* 49 (2008): 388–404.

text of *EV,* but from the more recently republished *CCC* in accordance with which most Catholic theologians would agree any papal encyclical should be interpreted. Brugger's eight indicators are the following: (1) Capital punishment is treated in the *CCC* under a subsection (2267) entitled "legitimate defense," rather than one entitled "punishment." (2) The *CCC* explicitly denies (2263) that anything describable as legitimate defense is an "exception" to the Fifth Commandment's prohibition against killing, a significant, and undoubtedly conscious, change from the 1566 *Roman Catechism* which treated capital punishment as just that, an "exception." (3) The text of the *CCC* uses Aquinas's double-effect reasoning in its account of legitimate defense, even referencing (like *EV*) Aquinas's account of self-defense, but never Aquinas's account of capital punishment. (4) The 1997 edition of the *CCC* includes a change from a prior 1992 French edition which included the discussion of capital punishment in the previous section (2266), where punishment's more retributive function is expressed (just as in *EV*) as that which "redresses the disorder caused by the offense." In the 1997 edition, however, capital punishment receives its own section (2267), thus again indicating a tendency not to justify it as punishment. (5) The 1997 *CCC* refers to those put to death by the state as "aggressors," rather than "the condemned" or "the guilty," more in keeping with legitimate defense/double-effect reasoning. (6) The *CCC* states that capital punishment ought not to be used when the state has alternative means of "rendering [the criminal] incapable of doing harm," which, again, is traditional language used for explaining legitimate private defense, not punishment. (7) The *CCC* states that capital punishment may only be inflicted in cases of "absolute necessity," which again indicates situations where an aggressor is killed in an act of self-defense rather than in cases where an incarcerated criminal is rendered his just deserts. Whereas inflicting death may very well be absolutely necessary *as self-defense,* Brugger observes, it is never absolutely necessary *as punishment.* (8) The 1997 edition of the *CCC* removes a reference to capital punishment that appeared in the 1992 edition. Whereas the 1992 edition stated the following: "the Church has acknowledged as well founded the right and duty of legitimate authority to punish malefactors by means of penalties commensurate with the gravity of the crime, *not excluding, in cases of extreme gravity, the death penalty*"; the 1997 edition simply states that "legitimate public authority has the right and duty to inflict punishment proportionate to the gravity of the offense," thus relegating, as we have seen, the treatment of capital punishment to the following section that relies more upon the language of self-defense.[10]

To be sure, Brugger's indicators are suggestive, but as he himself admits, not conclusive. They are, after all, only indicators. For example, the fact that the *CCC* denies that legitimate defense is an "exception" to the Fifth Commandment tells us very little about the morality of capital punishment, and just because capital punishment is included in a section entitled "legitimate defense" does not necessarily mean that it may only be justified in the same way as the self-defense of a private individual. What Brugger admits is retributive language concerning punishment in general is also contained in the legitimate defense section. True, the 1566 *Roman Catechism* states that capital punishment is an exception to the Fifth Commandment whereas the 1997 *CCC* does not. But the Church could still be denying that capital punishment is an exception to the Fifth Commandment without going so far as to say that it may only be justified as self-defense writ large. Perhaps this reflects a development, for example, not in the way the Church understands the death penalty, but in the way it understands what constitutes an exception to a divine commandment. I do not really wish, however, to dwell upon Brugger's indicators. The fact remains that the Church, both in the 1997 *CCC* and in *EV*, could have simply stated that the death penalty is only justifiable as indirect killing, but has obviously stopped short of doing so. One indicator implying the opposite of Brugger's conclusion is that *EV* itself, in the section

10. Ibid., 390–92.

following the discussion of capital punishment, makes the claim that the Fifth Commandment "has absolute value when it refers to the *innocent person.*"[11] Later in that section, likewise, John Paul II emphatically states that "*the direct and voluntary killing of an innocent human being is always gravely immoral.*" If capital punishment is only to be justified in terms of self-defense, there would be no reason for the pope to include the word "innocent" in this definitive statement. If justifiable instances of the death penalty are only *indirect,* he may have simply stated that it is always wrong *directly* to kill another human being, period. As Brugger himself argues, in order to make explicit a new teaching that capital punishment is only justifiable as self-defense, the Church would have to "explicitly reject all properly retributive killing by political authority as inconsistent with the inviolable good of the human person."[12] If this were to happen, the teaching of the Church would surely become irreconcilable with the teaching of Aquinas. As of yet, however, no such statement has been made.

Just as Christian Brugger has attempted to bring the teaching of *EV* into conflict with that of Aquinas, others have argued that Aquinas's theory of punishment, and capital punishment in particular, should be interpreted as perfectly consistent with *EV.* The most thorough argument to this effect remains that of Steven Long. In a well-known article from 1999, Long advances the thesis that the text of *EV* must be read in the context of the wider theological tradition that includes the doctrine of Aquinas (Long points out that only two patristic theologians, Tertullian and Lactantius, have opposed the death penalty unequivocally).[13] As Long admits, *EV* and the doctrine of Aquinas do seem to be at odds if we limit ourselves only to the text of the document. More specifically, the text of *EV* alone would have us believe that capital punishment should only be inflicted when the "physical pro-

11. *EV,* sec. 57.
12. "Rejecting the Death Penalty: Continuity and Change in the Tradition," 395.
13. "*Evangelium Vitae,* St. Thomas Aquinas, and the Death Penalty," 513.

tection of society" cannot otherwise be protected, or when the very life of the criminal poses a "clear and present danger" to those around him.[14] Read along with the tradition, however, punishment's necessity to "defend society" should be understood as having a much wider meaning. It is not only the physical protection of society, Long claims, but also the moral protection of society that the encyclical allows for capital punishment to be inflicted. As Long sees it, to read the encyclical as merely allowing for capital punishment in cases of physical danger is to presuppose a "reductionist" understanding of political society.[15] By this I take him to mean an understanding of political society characteristic of those thinkers examined in chapters one and two of this study, namely, those who view political society as nothing more than a "cooperative venture" between individuals that makes the pursuit of individual goals more efficient. If one presupposes, however, a view of political society identified by Aquinas's fuller and richer understanding of the common good (seen in chapters three and five of this study) a new meaning of *EV* opens up more consistent with the Catholic tradition.

Long's account of Aquinas's theory of punishment is, for the most part, unproblematic. He acknowledges that, for Aquinas, punishment may have a multiplicity of legitimate goals, including deterrence, rehabilitation, protection, and retribution. He also acknowledges that, for Aquinas, the punishments rendered by political authority are primarily "medicinal." By far, however, Long most forcefully emphasizes Aquinas's view that punishment is necessary to "manifest a transcendent order of justice." With this frequently used expression, Long has in mind the primarily medicinal function of expressing society's disapproval of the crime committed and reaffirming society's commitment to justice. As he puts it, "social recognition of the reign of justice is good not merely for deterrent reasons, but because it purifies society, lifts

14. Ibid., 517.
15. Ibid., 518.

the social conscience higher, and directs the mind to final justice. It bathes the wound," Long continues, "suffered by society in that divine justice which all right social order participate."[16] Interestingly, Long emphasizes the medicinal *manifestation* of a transcendent order of justice far more than the retributive *vindication* of justice (perhaps even more than Aquinas does), but his general interpretation of Aquinas is fundamentally in keeping with the claim that the punishments of this life are primarily medicinal and with the noninstrumental conception of the common good held by Aquinas and from which, as we have seen, his theory of punishment emerges. Perhaps most importantly, Long acknowledges that, for Aquinas, political authorities derive their authority from God just as human laws are derived from the eternal law. As a result, criminals may be directly put to death by such authorities.

The more controversial aspect of Long's argument is not his interpretation of Aquinas, but rather his interpretation of *EV*. As he himself admits, the text of *EV* alone would have us believe that capital punishment is only justifiable when it is necessary for the physical protection of society. When one reads *EV* in light of Aquinas, however, capital punishment's ability to "defend society" should be understood as more than defending people's lives, liberty, and physical welfare, but also as protecting the moral and spiritual welfare of citizens which punishment, Aquinas believes, can and must promote. Therefore, when John Paul II says that capital punishment ought not be inflicted unless it is necessary to "defend society," this does not necessarily rule out cases when the continued life of a criminal poses no physical danger. If society is perfectly capable of defending itself from a serial killer through permanent incarceration without parole, for example, inflicting the death penalty, on Long's reading of *EV*, may still be necessary to "defend society" with respect to its moral well-being.

Why, then, according to Long, does John Paul II state that inflicting the death penalty is almost never appropriate? For Long,

16. Ibid., 523.

again, the answer has to do with the moral rather than the physical protection of society. Acknowledging that such a rationale is not explicitly made in *EV*, Long speculates that the pope is warning us against the use of the death penalty, not because it is unjust as a punishment, but because, given the disregard modern states have for human life on the whole and the moral confusion associated with the "culture of death," the moral efficacy of capital punishment is primarily lost upon those who, under different social conditions, would stand to benefit from the "manifestation of the transcendent order of justice." As Long argues, "*a more plausible reading* is that, in light of the culture of death, the encyclical stresses that it is better for contemporary societies to avoid the use of the death penalty . . . [which is] especially pertinent inasmuch as contemporary secular societies tend to lack the basis for imposing the death penalty in a virtuous fashion, and no longer embody those moral norms by reference to which such penalty is morally intelligible."[17]

How plausible is Long's interpretation? It is, to be sure, difficult to find fault with the claim that papal encyclicals (and other such documents) should be interpreted in light of the Catholic tradition, and I see no reason not to include, for the purposes of interpreting modern magisterial documents, that tradition's most celebrated theologians (even if their writings are not part of the ordinary Magisterium of the Church represented by ecumenical councils and other official pronouncements on matters of faith and morals). Long's worry that reading *EV* at face value brings the document into conflict with the theological tradition of the Church is, indeed, quite legitimate. The problem for Long's interpretation, however, is that reading *EV* as he does leads to an interpretation of John Paul II's language that is not only improbable, but which is actually in conflict with itself. For criticism of Long's position we may, once again, turn to E. Christian Brugger.[18]

17. Ibid., 546–47.

18. See "Catholic Moral Teaching and the Problem of Capital Punishment," in

As Brugger explains, Long seems to begin with the premise that whatever is said in a papal encyclical must be interpreted as consistent with the consensus of the Catholic intellectual tradition despite any appearances to the contrary. Now Long's method of interpretation may be valid with respect to those documents (such as the judgment of ecumenical councils) of equal or greater magisterial authority, but it can hardly be used to ensure that all judgments on faith and morals be consistent with the teaching of Aquinas. In a way, Long's hermeneutic eliminates the possibility of debate from the outset, since the *very claim* Brugger (and others) are making is that *EV* is teaching something new. Again, if the novelty of *EV* brings it into conflict with another equally authoritative document of the Church, it may be argued that one can stretch the apparent meaning of the text in order to preserve the coherence of the tradition, but the same cannot be said for ensuring the coherence between *EV* and Aquinas. Hence, Long begins with a "methodological error" captured in the following passage of Brugger's criticism:

> The meaning of an ecclesiastical statement or document is constituted in the first place by the intention(s) of the authors. This is why it is possible to ask to what degree a particular magisterial assertion corresponds to or departs from the tradition *to which it contributes.*[19]

That Pope John Paul II intended the "defense of society" to include the "manifestation of a transcendent order of justice" is highly unlikely.[20] The reason for this stems from EV's claim, not just that capital punishment may only be administered in cases

The Catholic Citizen: Debating the Issues of Justice, ed. Kenneth D. Whitehead (South Bend, Ind.: St. Augustine's Press, 2004), 129–38.

19. Ibid., 130.

20. Perhaps Long is suggesting that, in interpretation, coherence with the Church's intellectual tradition should trump even the author's actual original intention (rather than just the appearance of that intention). If so, his methodology would strangely resemble Justice William Brennan's concept of the evolving constitution according to which original intent may be relegated to something of secondary importance.

of "absolute necessity," but also and especially in the claim that such cases of absolute necessity are "very rare, if not practically non-existent." Why, we must ask, if the defending of society included the manifestation of a transcendent order of justice would the need for capital punishment be so rare? On Long's account, the answer to this question is *prudential* rather than *doctrinal.*[21] In other words, capital punishment should be restricted if not eliminated because of the moral confusion associated with the culture of death and the inability of modern states to administer it virtuously. True though this observation may be, however, it does not exactly answer the question. Because of the current moral confusion of modern society, one might argue, contemporary states are *all the more* in need of the manifestation of a transcendent order of justice. As Long himself argues, the death penalty manifests the order of justice far more effectively than "a life sentence in an air-conditioned facility with cable TV."[22] The death penalty, on Aquinas's analysis, would remain as necessary to manifest (or, even more so, to vindicate) justice as it ever was regardless of whether all of those to whom it is manifested have the appropriate response. Hence, if the "defense of society" is to be interpreted with the full moral meaning that Long attributes to it, the claim that the death penalty is almost never necessary would be patently false. As Brugger argues, "the text [of *EV*] does not state or imply that it would be merely 'better' to avoid inflicting death; it states that occasions warranting the death penalty 'are very rare, if not practically non-existent.'"[23] Moreover, *EV* attributes the rarity of cases where capital punishment is necessary to "improvements in the organization of the penal system." On Long's reading, however, the rarity of such occasions would derive, not from an improved penal system, but from the culture of death itself.

If Long's emphatically Thomistic reading of *EV* does not stand

21. "*Evangelium Vitae,* St. Thomas Aquinas, and the Death Penalty," 539.
22. Ibid., 545.
23. "Catholic Moral Teaching and the Problem of Capital Punishment," 133.

under heavy scrutiny, therefore, must we conclude that *EV* contradicts the teaching of Aquinas? The answer to this question, I believe, is no. One must remember that to reject Long's Thomistic reading of *EV* is not necessarily to accept Brugger's interpretation according to which *EV* eliminates the possibility of any direct killing by agents of the state. What I would like to recommend, therefore, is a reading of *EV* that maintains a coherence with Aquinas's theory of punishment while not stretching the language of the document beyond plausibility. As we have seen, Aquinas understands punishment to have several purposes, and the purpose of punishment most central to its nature is retribution, the reestablishment of the equality of justice, or what *EV* calls the redress of the disorder caused by the crime.[24] As we have also seen, however, the punishments of "this life" are more of a medicinal character and this seems to be especially true in the case of capital punishment, since never once does Aquinas mention retribution as a justification for this ultimate temporal penalty. Though Aquinas does not give us any clear indications as to why he does not refer to retribution in his discussion of capital punishment itself, we observed in chapter five that there may be several reasons for the omission. First, because the vindication of justice, in Aquinas's view, consists in a repression of the criminal's will sufficient to counteract the willful crime, knowing the exact amount of retribution due to the criminal requires knowing that criminal's exact degree of willfulness. As Aquinas himself admits, however, this is never fully possible for human judges, for "*man* is not competent to judge of interior movements, that are hidden, but only of exterior acts which appear."[25] Second, and probably more importantly, Aquinas believes that retribution is something that will ultimately be achieved with perfection by divine justice. Although exacting the debt of punishment is certainly not irrelevant for human authorities, it would make sense that imposing the most severe

24. *ST,* II-II, 108.4.
25. *ST,* I-II, 91.4.

and final human penalty would be done with extreme caution. Not only is it good to err on the side of leniency, since "it is better to *err* frequently through thinking well of a *wicked man*, than to *err* less frequently through having an *evil* opinion of a *good man*,"[26] but even when a guilty criminal receives less than deserved we may be nonetheless confident that justice will be served under the all-embracing hand of divine providence from which the human authority to punish derives its legitimacy in the first place. It therefore makes perfect sense that Aquinas would mention only those medicinal functions of punishment in discussing the penalty of death, since these are the factors most on the minds of prudent judges.

If this is so, what would Aquinas have to say about a situation, such as our own, where society could be protected from dangerous criminals through "bloodless means?" Before such times the death penalty was far more defensible as judges would rightly consider four factors: (1) the physical safety of innocent citizens is jeopardized by the continued temporal life of the criminal, (2) the infliction of death may very well deter others, (3) the moral fabric of society would be strengthened by inflicting death upon the criminal, and (4) the criminal very well may deserve death. Nowadays, however, (1) is quite possibly eliminated due to "steady improvements in the organization of the penal system." (2) is highly debatable due to the fact that executions are no longer public and that Western democracies (the same ones with improved penal systems) are much larger than the small societies that predominated in thirteenth-century Europe and in which the criminal was more likely personally known to others. And (3) is greatly diminished by the fact that the moral fabric of society is no longer in a position to benefit from the "manifestation of a transcendent order of justice" that the death penalty provides. Since modern democracies (and their citizens) no longer understand themselves as participants in divine providence, Long is probably quite right to say

26. *ST,* II-II, 60.4.

that these states "lack the basis for imposing the death penalty in a virtuous fashion." What modern judges and legislators are left with, therefore, is the infliction of death for purely retributive reasons, something that was always accompanied in Aquinas's time by other compelling "medicinal" considerations. On perfectly Thomistic grounds, therefore, one might truthfully say that the imposition of the death penalty is no longer justified precisely because of the fact that society may be *physically* protected or defended by other means. Saying so does not commit Pope John Paul II to the view that retribution is an illicit motive for punishment, but only perhaps to the prudential view, shared by Aquinas, that retribution *alone* is not a sufficient motive for the punishment *of death.* Nor does this position commit the pope to the view that inflicting death is inherently wrong even by those with public authority. He might very well agree with Aquinas that public officials *do* have the right to inflict death but that such a right is better not exercised when retribution is the only foreseeable good from such a penalty. We certainly need not worry, on my view, that by interpreting the "defense of society" phrase in *EV* as the physical protection of society we are committing the pope to an instrumental view of the common good including nothing but the mutual material benefit of individuals. Nor do we need to read more into the encyclical than the text warrants by surmising that the pope is relegating proper uses of capital punishment to cases of self-defense writ large.

To see the text of *EV* as consistent with Aquinas's teaching, one final hurdle remains. Without a doubt the central message of *EV* is that all human beings, from the first instance of their existence in the womb, possess an inviolable dignity that may not be taken away. Contrary to the strong utilitarian influences in contemporary culture, therefore, the pope asserts that human beings are valuable, not for their usefulness to society or the degree of physical pleasure they can enjoy, but simply by virtue of the fact that they are human. Human dignity, moreover, is not contingent upon a person's moral vicissitude. Using the story of Cain and Abel as his point of departure, John Paul II specifically emphasizes that even the worst criminals retain a dignity that must be respected.

> And yet God, who is always merciful even when he punishes, "put a mark on Cain, lest any who came upon him should kill him" (Gen 4:15). He thus gave him a distinctive sign, not to condemn him to the hatred of others, but to protect and defend him from those wishing to kill him, even out of a desire to avenge Abel's death. *Not even a murderer loses his personal dignity,* and God himself pledges to guarantee this.[27]

This passage is important because a similar issue arises in Aquinas's discussion of capital punishment. As one of the objections to Aquinas's position states, capital punishment is wrong because of the requirement to have charity for every human being. Since killing a man appears to be incompatible with such charity, and since one may never do evil so that good may come, the death penalty cannot be justified. Aquinas's response, already quoted in the previous chapter, brings up the subject of human dignity.

> By *sinning man* departs from the order of *reason*, and consequently falls away from the dignity of his manhood, in so far as he is *naturally* free, and *exists* for himself, and he falls in a way into the slavish state of the beasts, by being disposed of according as he is useful to others. This is expressed in *Psalm 48:21*: "Man, when he was in *honor*, did not understand; he hath been compared to senseless beasts, and made like to them," and *Proverbs 11:29*: "The fool shall serve the wise." Hence, although it be *evil* in itself to kill a man so long as he preserve his dignity, yet it may be *good* to kill a man who has *sinned*, even as it is to kill a beast. For a bad *man* is worse than a beast, and is more harmful, as the *Philosopher* states (Polit. i, 1 and Ethic. vii, 6).[28]

To be sure, this passage is difficult to reconcile with the position of *EV*. Understood properly, however, one need not arrive at the conclusion that Aquinas is saying something contradictory to the words of John Paul II. Let us begin by examining the objec-

27. *EV*, sec. 9.

28. *ST*, II-II, 64.2 (the phrase "in a way" [*quodammodo*] does not appear in the Christian Classics edition. It is, however, essential for understanding Aquinas's meaning).

tion to which the above quotation is the response. As the objection states, "it is not lawful, for any *good* end whatever, to do that which is *evil* in itself. . . . Now to kill a man is *evil* in itself, since we are bound to have *charity* towards all *men*. . . . Therefore it is nowise lawful to kill a man who has *sinned*." Paraphrasing Aquinas, we might break the argument down into the following structure:

Premise 1	One may never do that which is evil for the sake of achieving good consequences.
Premise 2	We are bound to have charity for all human beings.
Implicit Premise A	To act in a way that is inconsistent with charity is evil in itself.
Implicit Premise B	To kill a human being (even a sinner) is inconsistent with charity.
Premise 3	To kill a human being (even a sinner) is evil in itself.
Conclusion	One may never kill another human being.

Wherein lies Aquinas's objection to this argument? It is certainly not in Premise 1. As we observed in chapter three, Aquinas understands certain kinds of actions (e.g., lying) to be unlawful regardless of the good consequences it promotes or the bad consequences it hinders. It is also impossible to see that Aquinas is taking issue with Premise 2. Earlier in the *Summa Theologiae,* Aquinas explained that we are bound to have charity for all humans and emphasized this fact especially with respect to "sinners."[29] While taking special care to say that sinners must not be loved *as sinners,* not that is, with respect to their *guilt,* Aquinas asserts that they must be loved with respect to their *nature.* Since it is by virtue of a person's rational nature that he or she is created in the image of God,[30] and since all human beings *as human*

29. *ST,* II-II, 25.6.
30. See *ST,* I-II, Prologue.

possess a rational nature, Aquinas's position is coextensive with that of Pope John Paul II regarding those to whom charity is due.[31] As Aquinas explains, "sinners do not cease to be human beings, because sin does not do away with nature. Therefore, sinners are to be loved with charity."[32] Looking at Implicit Premise A, we may again see that Aquinas is in perfect agreement. Indeed, the very definition of mortal sin for Aquinas is that which turns the agent away from charity.[33] Moreover, Aquinas identifies several kinds of sins as mortal precisely because they are incompatible with the charity we are bound to have, not only for God, but for all human beings. Among these are envy,[34] theft,[35] cursing,[36] and anger.[37]

Aquinas's problem with the above argument enters in with Implicit Premise B, and we can begin to understand the issue at hand by looking to Aquinas's *respondeo* earlier in the article. In executing a criminal, the agent of the state may very well intend the criminal's death, but his action is nevertheless motivated, not out of hatred for the criminal, but out of a love for the common good. The only thing hated, properly speaking, is the criminal's sin, which the punishment is intended to repress. Aquinas's words are revealing:

> When, however, they fall into very great *wickedness*, and become incurable, we ought no longer to show [sinner's] friendliness. It is for this reason that both Divine and *human* laws command such like sinners to be put to death, because there is greater likelihood of their harming others than of their mending their ways. Nevertheless the judge puts this into effect, not out of *hatred* for the sinners, but out of the love of *charity*, by reason of which he prefers the public *good* to the life of the *individual*. Moreover the death inflicted by the judge profits the sinner, if he be *converted*, unto the expiation of his crime; and, if he be not

31. An exception to this may be Aquinas's understanding of human life *in utero*. Whereas Aquinas believed that the rational soul is infused after conception, the Catholic Church's teaching on this question remains somewhat more open.

32. *ST,* II-II, 25.6 (sed contra).

33. *ST,* I-II, 72.5.

34. *ST,* II-II, 36.3.

35. *ST,* II-II, 66.6.

36. *ST,* II-II, 76.3.

37. *ST,* II-II, 158.3 (the sin of anger as opposed to the passion of anger).

converted, it profits so as to put an end to the *sin*, because the sinner is thus deprived of the power to *sin* any more.[38]

Not only is the judge's decision to execute the criminal not a sin against charity; it may even be partially motivated by charity *for the criminal himself.* To read the passage where Aquinas compares criminals with beasts, therefore, one must be careful not to take his analogy too far. He certainly does not mean that serious criminals are no longer human. He certainly does not mean that serious criminals should no longer be shown charity. He does not even appear to mean that such criminals lose their human dignity. What he says is that *by sinning* a criminal "falls away" *(decedit)* from his dignity. In a way, one might argue that it is precisely the sinner's dignity that makes his sin possible in the first place, since the sin committed "departs from the order of reason" and it is precisely that order of reason, as we have seen, that bestows dignity upon persons, thus making them worthy of charity. Though Aquinas says that serious criminals fall into the slavish state of beasts, therefore, one should read his words in the context of his broader understanding of charity and the dignity of the human person. At the very least, we may observe that the analogy between sinners and beasts is understood by Aquinas as having limits, as evidenced by his insertion of the phrase "in a way" *(quodammodo).*[39] Rather than arguing that a serious sinner has sunk to the level of a dog, deserves to be shown no charity, and may be killed, therefore, Aquinas is saying that the sinner, though resembling a dog, retains his dignity and may be killed in spite of this fact for the sake of, and out of love for, the common good. The concept of the common good, therefore, is essential. What it reveals is that Aquinas is far from making the bald

38. *ST,* II-II, 25.6 (ad 2). This passage also is cited in a excellent article by Fr. Lawrence Dewan that arrives at the same conclusion regarding Aquinas's view of human dignity; see "Thomas Aquinas, Gerard Bradley, and the Death Penalty: Some Observations," *Gregorianum* 82, no. 1 (2001): 149–65.

39. See Dewan, "Thomas Aquinas, Gerard Bradley, and the Death Penalty," 159.

utilitarian claim that one person may be killed for the benefit of the many. If this was truly his position, he would not argue, in article six of the same question, that it is always wrong to kill the innocent (as a Christian Aquinas would have been well aware of the Pharisaic motto preferring the death of one to the demise of many). What he does argue, though, is that even though it is evil to kill a human being considered simply as an individual because of the rational nature every human possesses, such killing "becomes lawful in relation to the common good."[40]

To sum up, the doctrine of Aquinas on the death penalty and that of *EV* are certainly not identical. To see them as contradictory, however, one must come to one of the following conclusions: first, that John Paul II intended to convey that no one, not even an agent of the state, may ever directly inflict death upon another human being for any reason and under any circumstances; second, that Aquinas believed that the death penalty could be morally inflicted for retributive reasons alone; third, that Aquinas held an understanding of human dignity incompatible with that advanced in *EV*. Whereas one may point to evidence supporting the first of these, it remains that no such evidence is conclusive. As for the second and third claims, I hope the foregoing discussion has convincingly shown that these are simply false.

40. *ST,* II-II, 64.6.

Conclusion

THOMAS AQUINAS AND MODERN THEORIES OF PUNISHMENT

The foregoing presentation of Aquinas's thought has been intended to suggest that the thirteenth-century theologian and philosopher might have something to contribute to the contemporary debate over the justification of legal punishment. To sum up the essential points necessary to confirm this thesis, we may now compare Aquinas's penology with those presented in the first two chapters. We may begin by comparing Aquinas's theory of punishment with the utilitarian approach of Jeremy Bentham. As we recall from chapter one, the central thesis of Bentham's penology is that punishment is evil by definition and must therefore be justified by some good consequence sufficient to outweigh the evil suffered by the criminal. Moreover, retribution is a fundamentally irrational motive for punishing because (aside from any minimal amount of satisfaction disgruntled victims might feel by seeing criminals suffer) it cannot be connected with any ostensible good or benefit to society. Punishment as retribution is nothing more than the useless glorying in the harm of another person, and is always opposed to the principle of utility that must govern all of man's individual and collective actions.

We might initially observe that Aquinas actually shares a few of Bentham's premises. Like Bentham, Aquinas also agrees that punishment is inherently evil. As we saw in chapter four, the evil that pertains to the rational creature is exhaustively divided into the *malum culpae* and the *malum poenae.* Though punishment is less evil than fault, Aquinas is consistent in affirming that punishment, by its very nature, *harms* the one suffering it in some significant way. This is precisely why, moreover, Aquinas teaches that punishment may never be inflicted for its own sake. In other words, punishment may never be imposed simply as an infliction of harm upon a criminal. If punishment is, as Aquinas explains in the *Secunda Secundae,* "directed chiefly to the evil of the person on whom [it is inflicted]," it is "altogether unlawful." As he continues to explain, "to take pleasure in another's evil belongs to hatred, which is contrary to the charity whereby we are bound to love all men. Nor is it an excuse," Aquinas continues, "that [the punisher] intends the evil of one who has unjustly inflicted evil on him, as neither is a man excused for hating one that hates him: for a man may not sin against another just because the latter has already sinned against him, since this is to be overcome by evil, which was forbidden by the Apostle, who says: *Be not overcome by evil, but overcome evil by good.*"[1] When discussing the subject of charity earlier on, Aquinas had this to say: "In the infliction of punishment it is not the punishment itself that is the end in view, but its medicinal properties in checking sin; wherefore, punishment partakes of the nature of justice, in so far as it checks sin."[2]

Aquinas, though a kind of retributivist, *agrees* with Bentham's position that punishment must serve a further good and that it may not be inflicted for its own sake. Where Aquinas and Bentham disagree is on which *kinds* of goods those inflicting punishment are permitted to seek and which kinds of goods to emphasize. To be sure, Aquinas (far more than Kant) understands deterrence as a legitimate goal of legal authorities (not, as Kant would restrict it, as a merely incidental side effect for which one

1. *ST,* II-II, 108.1.
2. *ST,* II-II, 43.7 ad 1.

may hope). As he argues, "[punishments] are not always intended as medicines for the one who is punished: thus . . . according to Proverbs 'the wicked man being scourged, the fool shall be wiser.'"[3] But although Aquinas acknowledges that punishment may be effective in frightening "fools" from committing crimes, he also holds out a hope that transcends anything that utilitarian principles would allow Bentham to suggest. In addition to teaching us that crime does not serve even our own immediate self-interest, punishment can direct us toward living justly as something good in and of itself. As we observed in chapter five, Aquinas's discussion of law proposes that punitive sanctions do not only motivate through "force and fear," but that criminals may further "be brought to do willingly what hitherto they did from fear, and thus become *virtuous*."[4] To a philosopher such as Bentham harboring a fundamentally hedonistic and individualist conception of human nature, Aquinas's claim would be truly perplexing. Since Aquinas defends a position according to which human beings are naturally political animals, however, his fuller conception of rehabilitation becomes much more plausible. For Aquinas, rehabilitation means far more than what it means for Bentham, namely, the realization that a criminal act is not worth the risk. It means, rather, a recommitment to a political good that is truly common, something that is not merely reducible to a means for the realization of one's own interests, but the pursuit of which nonetheless perfects the individual as a person living within society.

We may observe something similar in comparing Aquinas and Bentham on the question of retribution. In responding to Bentham's suggestion that retribution constitutes a useless reveling in the harm of another person, Aquinas would respond by saying that retribution serves the further purpose of justice. Although Aquinas consistently holds that "the punishments of this life are more of a medicinal character,"[5] reestablishing the equality of justice remains an essential good that punishment achieves. As we

3. *ST,* I-II, 87.3 ad 2.

4. *ST,* I-II, 95.1.

5. *ST,* II-II, 108.3 ad 2.

have seen, when the very same common good to which humans have a natural inclination is encroached upon by one of society's members, it is natural and good, Aquinas argues, for society as a whole to repress the criminal's will by inflicting something harmful. Again, the infliction of harm is not an end in itself, but is rather a means of realizing a state of affairs that is naturally desired by human beings. Because this desire, Aquinas thinks, is something emanating from human nature itself (rather than from a perversion of human nature), it may be understood as a *real good* worthy of lawgivers' serious attention (along with punishment's medicinal properties) and as something without which political society would be seriously lacking. What distinguishes Aquinas's teaching from that of utilitarianism, therefore, is not a denial that the law must promote the happiness of its subjects, but rather his understanding of the multifaceted human good in which that happiness consists and which is not reducible to the greatest pleasure for the greatest number. For Aquinas, in other words, promoting the common good does not simply amount to satisfying the desires of as many people as possible or minimizing their pain, but also in promoting what those desires *should* be, which includes justice and virtue in addition to peace and security. Aquinas's theory of punishment, therefore, is no less "forward-facing" than that of utilitarianism. To be sure, restoring the equality of justice through punishment requires that punishments be anchored in the past offense of the criminal being punished. But this does not mean for a moment that retribution is purposeless or merely a disguise for irrational vengeance. Though punishment must make reference to the crime committed, the retributive goal of punishment to reestablish the equality of justice remains something to be accomplished as a *consequence* of punishment in the future.

Perhaps the foregoing points would be made by any retributivist in defending his position against utilitarianism. One could even imagine Kant defending his penology along similar lines. As we argued in chapter four, however, Aquinas's theory of punishment presents a superior alterative to utilitarianism than what Kant provides, and this for three reasons. First, and most fundamentally, the connection between punishment and natural law in Aquinas's thought means that retribution ought to be pursued (not necessarily at all costs) as something that is part of the human good, a good that is primarily revealed to us through our natural inclinations. For Kant, one might say, retribution is *required* but not necessarily good. In other words, as a categorical imperative retribution is something that pure reason concludes ought to be rendered, but which does not have any connection (as no moral good has) with how human beings are naturally constituted. Particularly in light of the fact that Kant never explains how pure reason even arrives at the conclusion that punishment is morally required (as, e.g., he explains how pure reason arrives as the prohibition against lying), Aquinas's basis for retribution is on surer footing than its Kantian counterpart. Second, as we observed in chapter four, Aquinas avoids the implausible conclusions of the infamous *lex talionis* upon which Kant insists. On Aquinas's analysis, the equality of justice is reestablished by imposing something against the criminal's will that represses his inordinate criminal act. What matters, then, is not the *kind* of crime committed, but the *degree* to which the criminal's will encroached upon the common good in the commission of the crime. Hence, Aquinas need not cleave to the strange and inapplicable version of poetic justice that the *lex talionis* requires. Finally, one might add that Aquinas's rationale for retribution provides a basis for mercy for which Kant simply cannot account. This is because, under Kantian principles, any deviation from what the criminal's external act deserves constitutes a violation of justice. Kant leaves little or no room to adjust the penalty for those who committed crimes from psychological motives that might constitute mitigating circumstances that would warrant a more lenient sentence. The law, therefore, must have it that all murderers suffer the death penalty and authorities must always see to it that the law is followed.

On the other hand, Aquinas's understanding of punishment does provide a way to conceive of mercy and to defend it as praiseworthy. If the goal of punishment is to redress the inequality caused by the overindulgence of the criminal will, the focus must be on that inordinate act of willing rather than upon the external action on which Kant focuses. Some crimes, however, are committed less voluntarily than others, and thus involve less of an overindulgence of the will. Under this principle, therefore, the law can impose more lenient penalties for crimes committed less voluntarily (and therefore less culpably). Even though such crimes may have caused great harm, their punishments need not be as severe or (what amounts to the same thing) as "contrary to the will" of the ones who commit them. This does not mean that the criminal is freed from making reparation in accordance with the damage done through his criminal behavior (even though the debt of punishment is reduced, commutative justice still requires him to pay restitution for damages). It does mean, however, that the law may consider morally relevant psychological information that Kant forbids it to consider. As Aquinas explains, sometimes a culpable action is less culpable "through having something connected with it that is against the sinner's will, [in which case] it may, in this respect, call for mercy."[6] Whether a criminal's culpability is reduced through ignorance, passion, or something else, the law should mercifully recognize the reduced volition of the criminal in question and respond with lesser punishments. But this can only be achieved if one adheres to Thomistic (rather than Kantian) principles, understanding punishment as necessary to redress the criminal's inordinate will rather than simply to match his crime.[7]

Finally, Aquinas's explanation of retribution is also immune to those irresolvable problems with the more contemporary unfair advantage theory discussed in chapter two. Though certainly

6. *ST,* II-II, 30.1 ad 1.

7. This last point regarding mercy is, nearly verbatim, taken from my own "Two Theories of Retributive Punishment: Immanuel Kant and Thomas Aquinas," 335.

modern retributivism's "best foot forward," the unfair advantage theory cannot, in the end, explain the concept most central to its teaching, namely, how a criminal act constitutes an advantage over society than must be cancelled out by the disadvantage of punishment for the sake of fairness. As the promoters of this theory recognize, the advantage to be removed cannot be understood as any material advantages of the crime (such as the monetary benefit of an act of robbery). The advantage, rather, is the excess freedom enjoyed in the commission of the crime itself. As we observed, such an explanation of punishment emanates from a very specific contractarian view of the state, namely, that all citizens enter political life for the sake of maximizing their individual ratio of benefits and burdens. Actions that they might otherwise like to perform (such as theft or murder) are refrained from in society in order to enjoy the peace and security that society provides. This is precisely why, we will recall, crimes must be punished according to the unfair advantage theory. Those who enjoy society's benefits while renouncing the burdens of citizenship do not only owe compensation to their immediate victims; they also deserve to have the "excess freedom" they gained be erased through the imposition of something disadvantageous, that is, punishment. Aside from the arguably fiendish understanding of murderous and similar actions as advantageous to the one performing them, the defenders of the unfair advantage theory have never been able to explain exactly how the commission of crime *itself* constitutes an advantage. As we observed one helpful critic put it in chapter two, the unfair advantage theory has simply "reified the criminal's act of law-violation, misleadingly labeled it" "'freedom,'" and treated it as the "'unfair advantage'" to be taken away."[8]

As we saw in chapter five, Aquinas's theory of punishment is not subject to these same pitfalls because, contrary to the interpretation of John Finnis, Aquinas holds neither to an unfair advantage theory of punishment nor to the understanding of political society

8. David Dolinko, "Some Thoughts about Retributivism," 548.

that underlies it. Though he does speak of punishment in terms of repressing the criminals overindulgent will, Aquinas never implies that such an indulgence is "beneficial" or "advantageous" in any way to the criminal. Aside from any material benefits of crime, the unjust act itself is, on Aquinas's analysis, profoundly disadvantageous to the one performing it. This is in large part due to the fact that harming the common good is something that contravenes one of humanity's most fundamental inclinations, namely, to live as a part of political society. Contrary to the modern conception of society as a mutually beneficial venture justified by the fact that individuals pursue their own interests more effectively, Aquinas maintains the classical teaching (though duly modified to accommodate Christian revelation) that man is a naturally political animal and that the common good is a "greater and more divine" good worthy for its own sake of individual pursuit, rather than an artifice of human making devised from a cost-benefit analysis.

Nowadays, Aquinas's theory of punishment is both compelling and difficult to accept for precisely the same reasons. Because his theory of morality, law, and the common good are so different from those underlying modern utilitarian and retributivist thought, Aquinas's theory of punishment avoids many, if not all, of the problems those theories have encountered. On the other hand, to accept Aquinas's theory of punishment without removing it from its proper philosophical context requires a reconsideration of moral and political theories, such as natural law and the political dimension of human nature, that by many have long since been considered discredited. It has, of course, been well beyond the scope of this study to defend Aquinas's moral and political teachings as a whole against the modern criticism of the past half-century. At most, what I have hoped to illustrate is that the ultimate rationale and justification for legal punishment may not be as elusive as the modern debate suggests, so long as one is willing to look beyond the moral, political, and punitive theories that have dominated that debate.

Selected Bibliography

Acton, H. B. *The Philosophy of Punishment.* London: Macmillan, 1969.

Aquinas, St. Thomas. *Commentary on Aristotle's Politics.* Translated by Richard Regan. Indianapolis, Ind.: Hackett, 2007.

———. *On Law, Morality, and Politics.* Translated by Richard Regan. Indianapolis, Ind.: Hackett, 2002.

———. *Aquinas: Political Writings.* Translated by R. W. Dyson. Cambridge: Cambridge University Press, 2002.

———. *Commentary on the Gospel of St. John.* Vol 2. Translated by James A. Weisheipl, O.P., S.T.M., and Fabian R. Larcher, O.P. Petersham, Mass.: St. Bede's Publications, 1998.

———. *On Evil.* Translated by John Oesterle. South Bend, Ind.: University of Notre Dame Press, 1995.

———. *Commentary on Aristotle's* Nicomachean Ethics. Translated by C. I. Litzinger, O. P. South Bend, Ind.: Dumb Ox Books, 1993.

———. *Literal Exposition on Job.* Translated by Anthony Damico and Martin Yaffe. Atlanta, Ga.: Scholars Press, 1989.

———. *Opera Omnia.* Iussu impensaque Leonis XIII P.M. edita. Rome: ex typographia polyglotta et al., 1882–1989.

———. *On Kingship* (to the King of Cyprus). Translated by Gerald B. Phelan. Toronto: Pontifical Institute of Medieval Studies, 1982.

———. *Summa Theologiae.* Translated by the Fathers of the English Dominican Province. Westminster, Md.: Christian Classics, 1981.

———. *Summa Contra Gentiles.* South Bend, Ind.: University of Notre Dame Press, 1975.

Aristotle. *The Politics.* Translated by Carnes Lord. Chicago: University of Chicago Press: 1984.

———. *The Nicomachean Ethics.* Translated by Martin Ostwald. New York: Macmillan, 1962.

Augustine of Hippo, St. *On Free Choice of the Will.* In *Augustine: Earlier Writings,* ed. J. H. S. Burleigh (Philadelphia: Westminster Press, 1952).

Benn, S. I. "An Approach to the Problems of Punishment." *Philosophy* 33 (1958): 325–41.

Bentham, Jeremy. *Introduction to the Principles of Moral and Legislation.* London: Athlone Press, 1970.

Berns, Walter. *For Capital Punishment: Crime and the Morality of the Death Penalty.* Lanham, Md.: University Press of America, 1991.

Bradley, F. H. *Ethical Studies.* Oxford: Oxford University Press, 1876.

Bradley, Gerard. "No Intentional Killing Whatsoever: The Case of Capital Punishment." In *Natural Law and Moral Inquiry: Ethics, Metaphysics, and Politics in the Work of Germain Grisez,* ed. Robert George (Washington, D.C.: Georgetown University Press, 1998), 155–73.

Brugger, E. Christian. "Rejecting the Death Penalty: Continuity and Change in the Tradition." *Heythrop Journal* 49 (2008): 388–404.

———. "Catholic Moral Teaching and the Problem of Capital Punishment." In *The Catholic Citizen: Debating the Issues of Justice,* ed. Kenneth D. Whitehead (South Bend, Ind.: St. Augustine's Press, 2004), 129–38.

Burgh, Richard. "Do the Guilty Deserve Punishment?" *Journal of Philosophy* 79, no. 4 (1982), 193–210.

Byrd, B. Sharon. "Kant's Theory of Punishment: Deterrence in Its Threat, Retribution in Its Execution." *Law and Philosophy* 8 (1989): 151–200.

Corlett, J. Angelo. "Foundations of a Kantian Theory of Punishment." *Southern Journal of Philosophy* 31 (1993): 263–83.

Cottingham, J., "Varieties of Retribution." *Philosophical Quarterly* 29 (1979), 238–246.

Crofts, Richard. "The Common Good in the Political Theory of Thomas Aquinas." *The Thomist* 37 (1973): 155–73.

Dagger, Richard. "Playing Fair with Punishment." *Ethics* 103, no. 3 (1993): 473–88.

Davis, M. *To Make the Punishment Fit the Crime.* Boulder, Colo.: Westview Press, 1992.

———. "The Relative Independence of Punishment Theory." *Law and Philosophy* 7 (1989): 321–50.

Dengan, Daniel A. "Two Models of Positive Law in Aquinas: A Study of the Relationship of Positive and Natural Law." *The Thomist* 46 (1982): 1–32.

Dewan, Lawrence. "Thomas Aquinas, Gerard Bradley, and the Death Penalty: Some Observations." *Gregorianum* 82, no. 1 (2001): 149–65.

———. "St. Thomas, John Finnis, and the Political Good," *The Thomist* 64, no. 3 (2000): 337–74.

Di Blasi, Fulvio. *God and the Natural Law: A Rereading of Thomas Aquinas.* South Bend, Ind.: St. Augustine's Press, 2006.

Dolinko, David. "Some Thoughts about Retributivism." *Ethics* 101, no. 3 (1991): 537–59.

Dougherty, Jude P. 1987. "Aquinas on Punishment." In *Studi Tomistici* (Proceedings from the Fourth Symposium on St. Thomas Aquinas' Philosophy) 30, ed. L. J. Elders, S. V. D., and K. Hedwig (Vatican City: Pontificia Accademia di S. Tommaso e di Religione Cattolica, 1987), 161–70.

Duff, Antony, "Legal Punishment." In *The Stanford Encyclopedia of Philosophy* (2008). Available online at *http://plato.stanford.edu/entries/legal-punishment/.*

Duff, Antony, with D. Garland. *A Reader on Punishment.* Oxford: Oxford University Press, 1994.

Dulles, Avery Cardinal. "Catholicism and Capital Punishment." *First Things* 112 (April 2001): 30–35.

Eschmann, I. T. "St. Thomas Aquinas on the Two Powers." *Mediaeval Studies* 20 (1958): 177–205.

———. "Studies on the Notion of Society in St. Thomas Aquinas, Part I." *Mediaeval Studies* 8 (1946): 1–42.

———. "A Thomistic Glossary on the Principle of the Preeminence of a Common Good." *Mediaeval Studies* 5 (1943): 123–66.

Falls, Margaret. "Retribution, Reciprocity, and Respect for Persons." *Law and Philosophy* 6, no. 1 (1987): 25–51.

Feinberg, Joel. "The Expressive Function of Punishment." In *Doing and Deserving* (Princeton, N.J.: Princeton University Press, 1970), 95–118.

Fingarette, Herbert. "Punishment and Suffering." *Proceedings and Addresses of the American Philosophical Association* 50 (1977): 499–525.

Finnis, J. *Aquinas: Moral, Political and Legal Theory.* Oxford: Oxford University Press, 1998.

———. *Natural Law and Natural Rights.* Oxford: Clarendon Press, 1980.

Fortin, Ernest. "Thomas Aquinas." In *The History of Political Philosophy,* eds. Leo Strauss and Joseph Cropsey (Chicago: University of Chicago Press, 1987), 248–75.

Fleischaker, Samuel. "Kant's Theory of Punishment." In *Essays on Kant's Political Philosophy,* ed. Howard Williams (Cardiff: University of Wales Press, 1992), 191–212.

Friel, George Quentin. *Punishment in the Philosophy of Saint Thomas Aquinas and among Some Primitive Peoples.* Washington, D.C.: The Catholic University of America Press, 1939.

Froelich, Gregory. "Ultimate End and Common Good." *The Thomist* 57 (1993): 609–19.

———. "The Equivocal Status of 'Bonum Commune.'" *New Scholasticism* 63 (1989): 38–57.

Foucault, Michel. *Discipline and Punish: The Birth of the Prison.* New York: Vintage Books, 1995.

Fuller, Timothy. "Jeremy Bentham and James Mill." In *The History of Political Philosophy,* 3rd ed., ed. Leo Strauss and Joseph Cropsey (Chicago: University of Chicago Press, 1987).

Gilby, Thomas. *The Political Thought of Thomas Aquinas.* Chicago: University of Chicago Press, 1958.

Grégoire, Stéphanie. "Punishment: Aquinas and the Classic Debate." *Angelicum* 86 (2009): 375–98.

Grisez, Germain. "The First Principle of Practical Reason: A Commentary on the *Summa Theologiae,* 1–2, Question 94, Article 2." *Natural Law Forum* 10 (1965): 168–201.

Hampton, J. "The Moral Education Theory of Punishment." *Philosophy and Public Affairs* 13 (1984): 208–38.

Hart, H. L. A. *Punishment and Responsibility.* Oxford: Oxford University Press, 1968.

Hassner, Pierre. "Immanuel Kant." In *History of Political Philosophy,* 3rd ed., ed. Leo Strauss and Joseph Cropsey (Chicago: University of Chicago Press, 1987).

Hebert, Gary. "Immanuel Kant: Punishment and the Preconditions of Moral Existence." *Interpretation* 23 (1995): 61–75.

Hittinger, F. Russell. *The First Grace: Rediscovering the Natural Law in a Post-Christian World.* Wilmington, Del. : ISI Books, 2003.

———. *A Critique of the New Natural Law Theory.* South Bend, Ind.: University of Notre Dame Press, 1987.

Hobbes, Thomas. *Leviathan.* Indianapolis, Ind.: Hackett, 1994.

Honderich, T. *Punishment: The Supposed Justifications Revisited.* London: Pluto, 2005.

John Paul II, Pope. *Evangelium Vitae,* Vatican translation (1994) , available online at *http://www.vatican.va/holy_father/john_paul_ii/encyclicals/documents/hf_jp-ii_enc_25031995_evangelium-vitae_en.html.*

Kant, Immanuel. *Groundwork for the Metaphysics of Morals.* Translated by James Ellington. Indianapolis, Ind.: Hackett, 1993.

———. *The Metaphysics of Morals.* Translated by Mary Gregor. Cambridge: Cambridge University Press, 1996.

Kempsall, M. S. *The Common Good in Late Medieval Political Thought.* Oxford: Oxford University Press, 1999.

Keys, Mary. *Aquinas, Aristotle and the Promise of the Common Good.* Cambridge: Cambridge University Press, 2006.

Koritansky, Peter. "Thomas Aquinas: Political Philosophy" In *The Internet Encyclopedia of Philosophy,* 2007, available online at *http://www.iep.utm.edu/a/aqui-pol.htm.*

———. "Two Theories of Retributive Punishment: Immanuel Kant and Thomas Aquinas." *History of Philosophy Quarterly* 22, no. 4 (October 2005): 319–38.

Lacey, Nicola. *State Punishment: Political Principles and Community Values.* London: Routledge, 1994.

Lisska, Anthony. *Aquinas's Theory of Natural Law: An Analytic Reconstruction.* Oxford: Oxford University Press, 1996.

Lewis, C. S. "The Humanitarian Theory of Punishment." In *God in the Dock,* ed. Walter Hooper (Grand Rapids, Mich.: William B. Eerdman, 1970).

Locke, John. *Second Treatise of Civil Government.* Edited by C. B. MacPherson. Indianapolis, Ind.: Hackett, 1980.

Long, Stephen A. *The Teleological Grammar of the Moral Act.* Naples, Fla.: Sapientia Press, 2007.

———. "*Evangelium Vitae* and the Death Penalty." In *The Catholic Citizen: Debating the Issues of Justice,* ed. Kenneth D. Whitehead (South Bend, Ind.: St. Augustine's Press, 2004), 105–22.

———. "*Evangelium Vitae,* St. Thomas Aquinas, and the Death Penalty" *The Thomist* 63 (1999): 511–52.

Lyons, William. "Deterrent Theory and Punishment of the Innocent." *Ethics* 84 (1974): 346–48.

Maritain, Jacques. *St. Thomas and the Problem of Evil.* Milwaukee, Wis.: Marquette University Press, 1942.

Martinez, Marie Louise. "Distributive Justice According to St. Thomas." *Modern Schoolman* 24 (1947): 208–23.

McCloskey, H. J. "Utilitarian and Retributive Punishment." *Journal of Philosophy* 64, no. 3 (1967), 91–110.

———. "A Non-Utilitarian Approach to Punishment." *Inquiry* 8 (1965): 249–63.

McGrath, Oswin. "St. Thomas' Theory of Original Sin." *The Thomist* 16 (1953): 161–89.

McInerny, Ralph. *Ethica Thomistica.* Washington, D.C.: The Catholic University of America Press, 1982.

———. "The Principles of Natural Law." *American Journal of Jurisprudence* 25 (1980): 1–15.

Morison, John. "Hart's Excuses: Problems with a Compromise Theory of Punishment." In *The Jurisprudence of Orthodoxy: Queen's University Essays on H. L. A. Hart,* ed. Philip Leith and Peter Ingram (London: Routledge, 1988), 117–146.

Morris, Herbert. "A Paternalistic Theory of Punishment." *American Philosophical Quarterly* 18 (1981): 263–71.

———. "Persons and Punishment." *The Monist* 52 (1968): 475–501.

Murphy, Jeffrie. *Getting Even: Forgiveness and Its Limits.* Oxford: Oxford University Press, 2003.

———. "Moral Epistemology, the Retributive Emotions, and the 'Clumsy Moral Philosophy' of Jesus Christ." In *The Passions of Law,* ed. S. Bandes (New York: New York University Press, 1999), 149–67.

———. Review of George Sher's *Desert. Philosophical Review* 99, no. 2 (1990), 280–83.

———. "Does Kant Have a Theory of Punishment?" *Columbia Law Review* 87 (1987): 509–32.

———. "Retributivism, Moral Education and the Liberal State." *Criminal Justice Ethics* 4 (1985): 3–11.

———. "Marxism and Retribution." *Philosophy and Public Affairs* 2, no. 3 (1973): 217–43.

———. "Kant's Theory of Criminal Punishment." In *Proceedings from the Third International Kant Congress* (Dordrecht, Holland: D. Reidel, 1972), 69–97.

Murphey, Jeffrie, and Jean Hampton. *Forgiveness and Mercy.* Cambridge: Cambridge University Press, 1988.

Nietzsche, Friedrich. *Genealogy of Morals.* Translated by Walter Kaufmann and R. J. Hollingdale. New York: Vintage Books, 1989.

Nemeth, Charles. *Aquinas in the Courtroom: Lawyers, Judges, and Judicial Conduct.* Westport, Conn.: Praeger, 2001.

Novak, Michael. "Aquinas and the Heretics." *First Things* 58 (December 1995): 33–38.

Pakaluk, Michael. "Is the Common Good of Political Society Limited and Instrumental?" *Review of Metaphysics* 55 (2001): 57–94.

Philips, M., "The Justification of Punishment and the Justification of Political Authority." *Law and Philosophy* 5 (1986).

Primoratz, Igor. *Justifying Legal Punishment.* Atlantic Highlands, N.J.: Humanities Press International, 1999.

———. "Punishment as Language." *Philosophy* 64 (1989): 187–205.

Porter, Jean. *Nature as Reason: A Thomistic Theory of the Natural Law.* Grand Rapids, Mich.: W. B. Eerdmans, 2004.

———."Reason, Nature, and the End of Human Life: A Consideration of John Finnis' *Aquinas.*" *Journal of Religion* 80, no. 3 (July 2000): 476–84.

Rawls, John. "Two Concepts of Rules" In *The Philosophy of Punishment,* ed. H. B. Acton (London: Macmillan, 1969), 105–14.

Sadursky, Wojciech. "Distributive Justice and the Theory of Punishment." *Oxford Journal of Legal Studies* 5, no. 1 (1985), 47–59.

Schaefer-Landau, Russ. "The Failure of Retributivism." *Philosophical Studies* 82 (1996): 289–316.

Schedler, George. "Anselm and Aquinas on the Fall of Satan: A Case Study of Retributive Punishment." *Proceedings of the American Catholic Philosophical Association* 56 (1982): 61–69.

Scheid, D. "Constructing a Theory of Punishment, Desert, and the Distribution of Punishments." *Canadian Journal of Law and Jurisprudence* 10 (1997): 441–506.

———. "Davis, Unfair Advantage Theory and Criminal Desert." *Law and Philosophy* 14 (1995): 375–409.

———. "Davis and the Unfair-Advantage Theory of Punishment: A Critique." *Philosophical Topics* 18 (1990): 143–70.

———. "Kant's Retributivism." *Ethics* 93 (1983): 262–82.

Sher, George. *Desert.* Princeton, N.J.: Princeton University Press, 1987.

Simon, Yves. *A General Theory of Authority*. South Bend, Ind.: University of Notre Dame Press, 1980.

Smart, J. J. C., and Bernard Williams. *Utilitarianism: For and Against.* Cambridge: Cambridge University Press, 2007.

Solomon, Robert. "Justice v. Vengeance: On Law and the Satisfaction of Emotion." In *The Passions of Law,* ed. Susan Bandes (New York: New York University Press, 1999), 123–48.

Sprigge, T. L. S. "A Utilitarian Reply to Dr. McCloskey's 'A Non-Utilitarian Approach to Punishment.'" *Inquiry* 8 (1965): 264–91.

Stearns, J. Brenton. "Bentham on Public and Private Ethics." *Canadian Journal of Philosophy* 5 (1975): 583–94.

Stump, Elemore. "Aquinas on Justice." *American Catholic Philosophical Quarterly* 71 (1997, Suppl.): 61–78.

———. "Aquinas on the Sufferings of Job." In *The Evidential Argument from Evil,* ed. Daniel Howard-Snyder (Bloomington: Indiana University Press, 1996), 49–68.

Ten, C. L. *Crime, Guilt and Punishment.* Oxford: Oxford University Press, 1987.

Tunick, Mark. "Is Kant a Retributivist?" *History of Political Thought* 17 (1996): 60–78.

Wasserstrom, Richard. *Philosophy and Social Issues.* South Bend, Ind.: University of Notre Dame Press, 1980.

Weinrib, Ernest. "Law as Idea of Reason." In *Essays on Kant's Political Philosophy,* ed. Howard Williams (Cardiff: University of Wales Press, 1992), 15–49.

Index

Thomas Aquinas and the Philosophy of Punishment was designed in Cheltenham with Hiroshige display and typeset by Kachergis Book Design of Pittsboro, North Carolina. It was printed on 55-pound Natures Natural Recycled and bound by Sheridan Books of Ann Arbor, Michigan.